"The structure and the character
story are elevated to such a level
the reader didn't know any better
think these two had been working
comics for 20+ years."

— ALL COMIC

"Sanchez and Echert are master
storytellers who always find a new way of
looking at tired, old genres."

— NEED TO CONSUME

"This comic is cerebral, cunning, and it
strikes when you least expect it."

— GEEKS OF DOOM

"An incredibly smart book that conducts
itself on a grand operatic scale at times
and at other times slows down to sublime
moments of self-reflection."

— BLOODY DISGUSTING

"There isn't a page in this book that's
not brilliantly realized and painstakingly
created."

— CAPELESS CRUSADER

TRANSLUCID

SANCHEZ • ECHERT • BAYLISS

BOOM! STUDIOS

ROSS RICHIE CEO & Founder • MARK SMYLIE Founder of Archaia • MATT GAGNON Editor-in-Chief • FILIP SABLIK President of Publishing & Marketing • STEPHEN CHRISTY President of Development
LANCE KREITER VP of Licensing & Merchandising • PHIL BARBARO VP of Finance • BRYCE CARLSON Managing Editor • MEL CAYLO Marketing Manager • SCOTT NEWMAN Production Design Manager
IRENE BRADISH Operations Manager • CHRISTINE DINH Brand Communications Manager • DAFNA PLEBAN Editor • SHANNON WATTERS Editor • ERIC HARBURN Editor • REBECCA TAYLOR Editor • IAN BRILL Editor
CHRIS ROSA Assistant Editor • ALEX GALER Assistant Editor • WHITNEY LEOPARD Assistant Editor • JASMINE AMIRI Assistant Editor • CAMERON CHITTOCK Assistant Editor • KELSEY DIETERICH Production Designer
JILLIAN CRAB Production Designer • KARA LEOPARD Production Designer • DEVIN FUNCHES E-Commerce & Inventory Coordinator • ANDY LIEGL Event Coordinator • BRIANNA HART Administrative Coordinator
AARON FERRARA Operations Assistant • JOSÉ MEZA Sales Assistant • MICHELLE ANKLEY Sales Assistant • ELIZABETH LOUGHRIDGE Accounting Assistant • STEPHANIE HOCUTT PR Assistant

TRANSLUCID, April 2015. Published by BOOM! Studios, a division of Boom Entertainment, Inc. Translucid is ™ & © 2015 Boom Entertainment, Inc. and Evil
Ink Comics LLC. Originally published in single magazine form as TRANSLUCID No. 1-6. ™ & © 2014 Boom Entertainment, Inc and Evil Ink Comics LLC. All
rights reserved. BOOM! Studios™ and the BOOM! Studios logo are trademarks of Boom Entertainment, Inc., registered in various countries and categories.
All characters, events, and institutions depicted herein are fictional. Any similarity between any of the names, characters, persons, events, and/or institutions
in this publication to actual names, characters, persons, events, and/or institutions, whether living or dead, events, and/or institutions is unintended and purely coincidental. BOOM!
Studios does not read or accept unsolicited submissions of ideas, stories, or artwork.

A catalog record of this book is available from OCLC and from the BOOM! Studios website, www.boom-studios.com, on the Librarians Page.

BOOM! Studios, 5670 Wilshire Boulevard, Suite 450, Los Angeles, CA 90036-5679. Printed in China. First Printing.

WRITTEN AND CREATED BY
CLAUDIO SANCHEZ & CHONDRA ECHERT

ILLUSTRATED BY
DANIEL BAYLISS

COLORED BY
ADAM METCALFE

LETTERED BY
ED DUKESHIRE

COVER BY
JEFF STOKELY

THE NAVIGATOR AND THE HORSE
CHARACTER DESIGNS BY
DAN DUNCAN

DESIGNER
KELSEY DIETERICH

ASSISTANT EDITOR
JASMINE AMIRI

EDITOR
IAN BRILL

SPECIAL THANKS
DAFNA PLEBAN

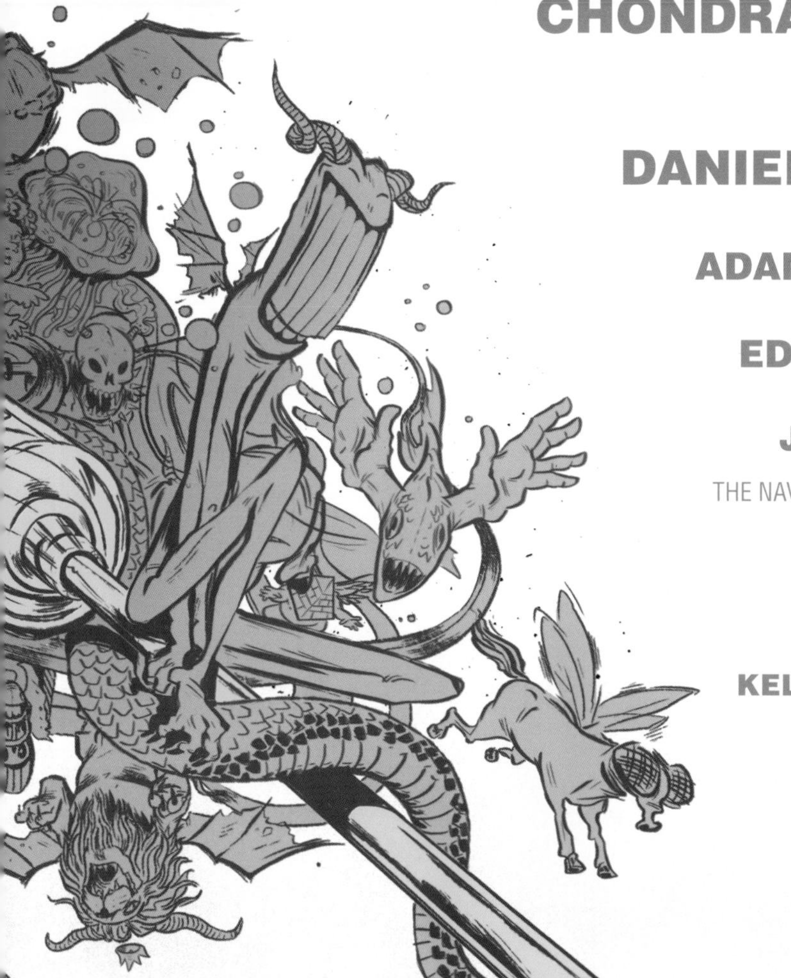

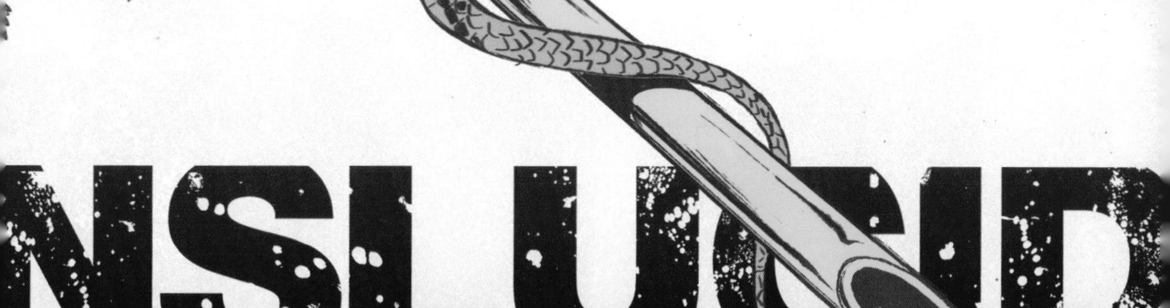

ISSUE ONE COVER BY **JEFF STOKELY**

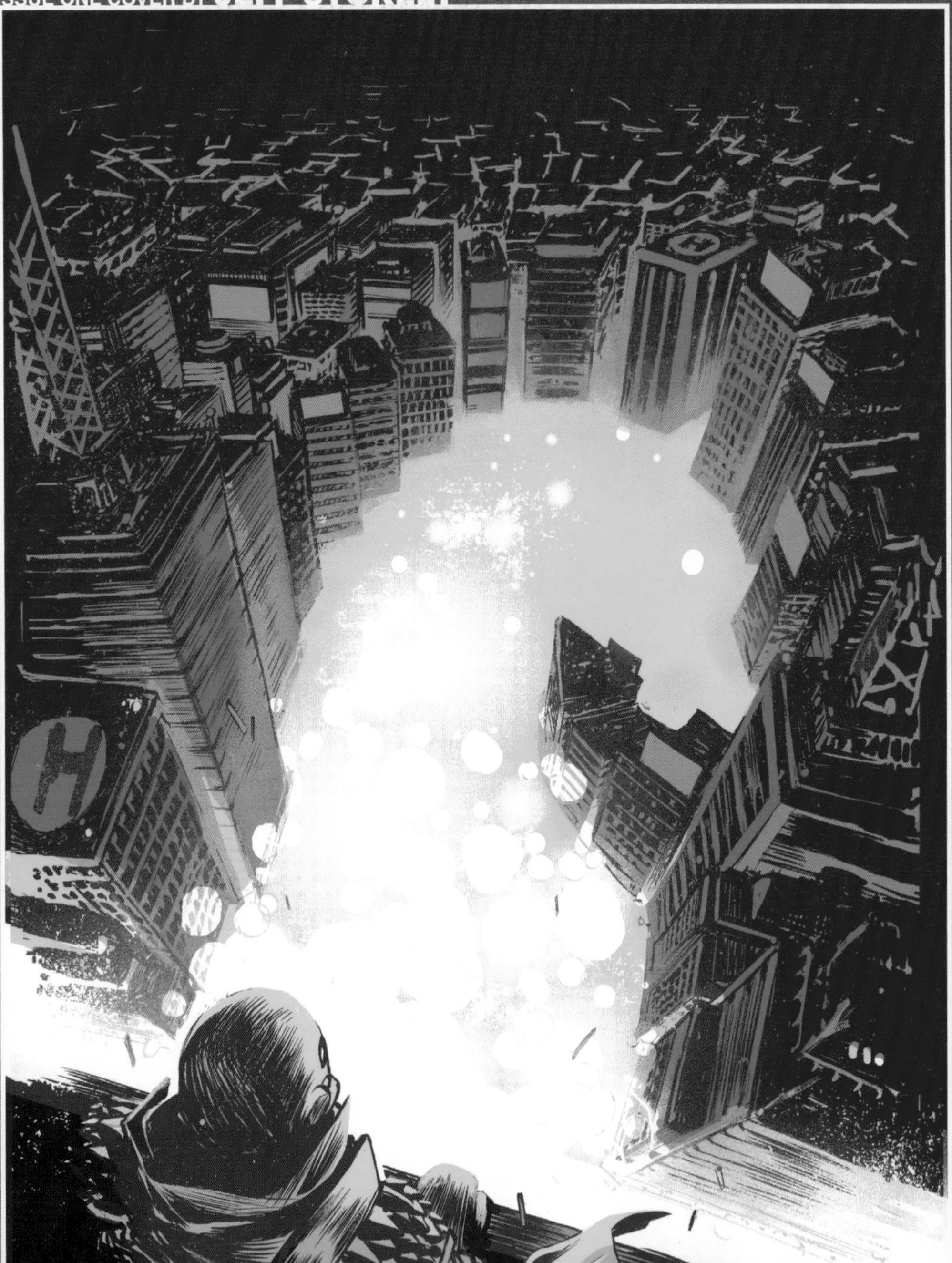

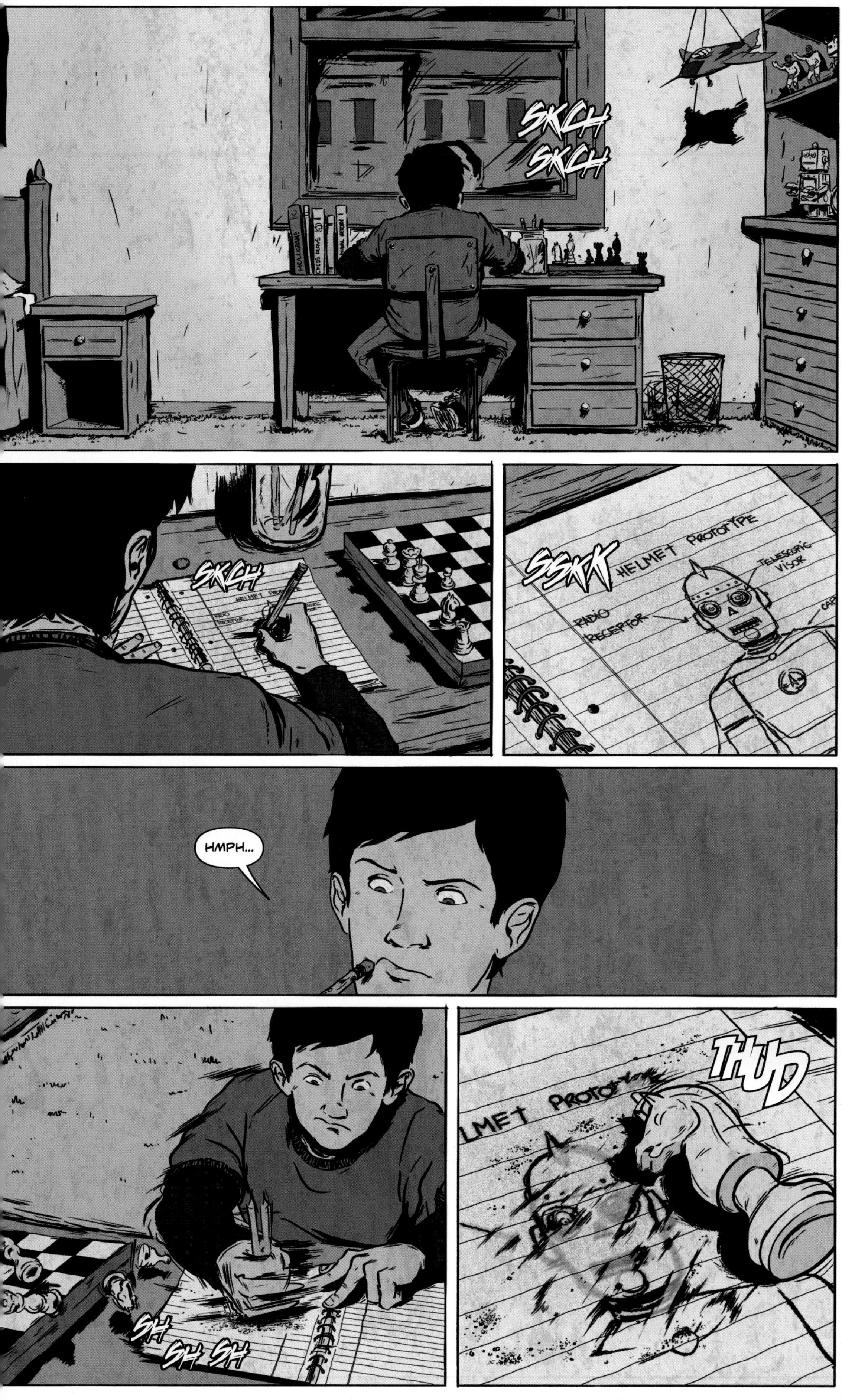
SKCH
SKCH
SKCH
SSKK
HELMET PROTOTYPE
TELESCOPIC VISOR
RADIO RECEPTOR
HMPH...
SH
SH SH
THUD

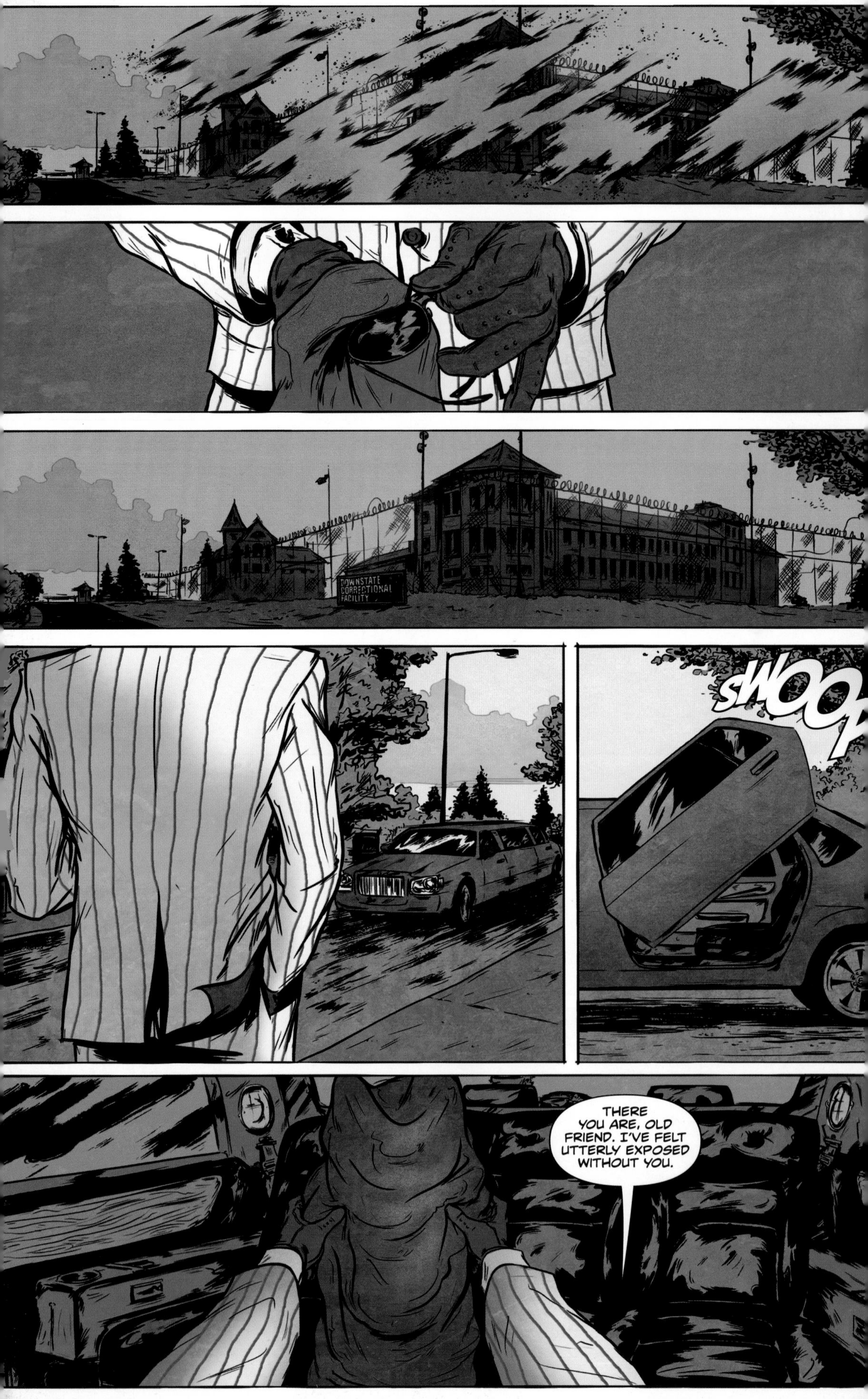
DOWNSTATE CORRECTIONAL FACILITY
SWOO
THERE YOU ARE, OLD FRIEND. I'VE FELT UTTERLY EXPOSED WITHOUT YOU.

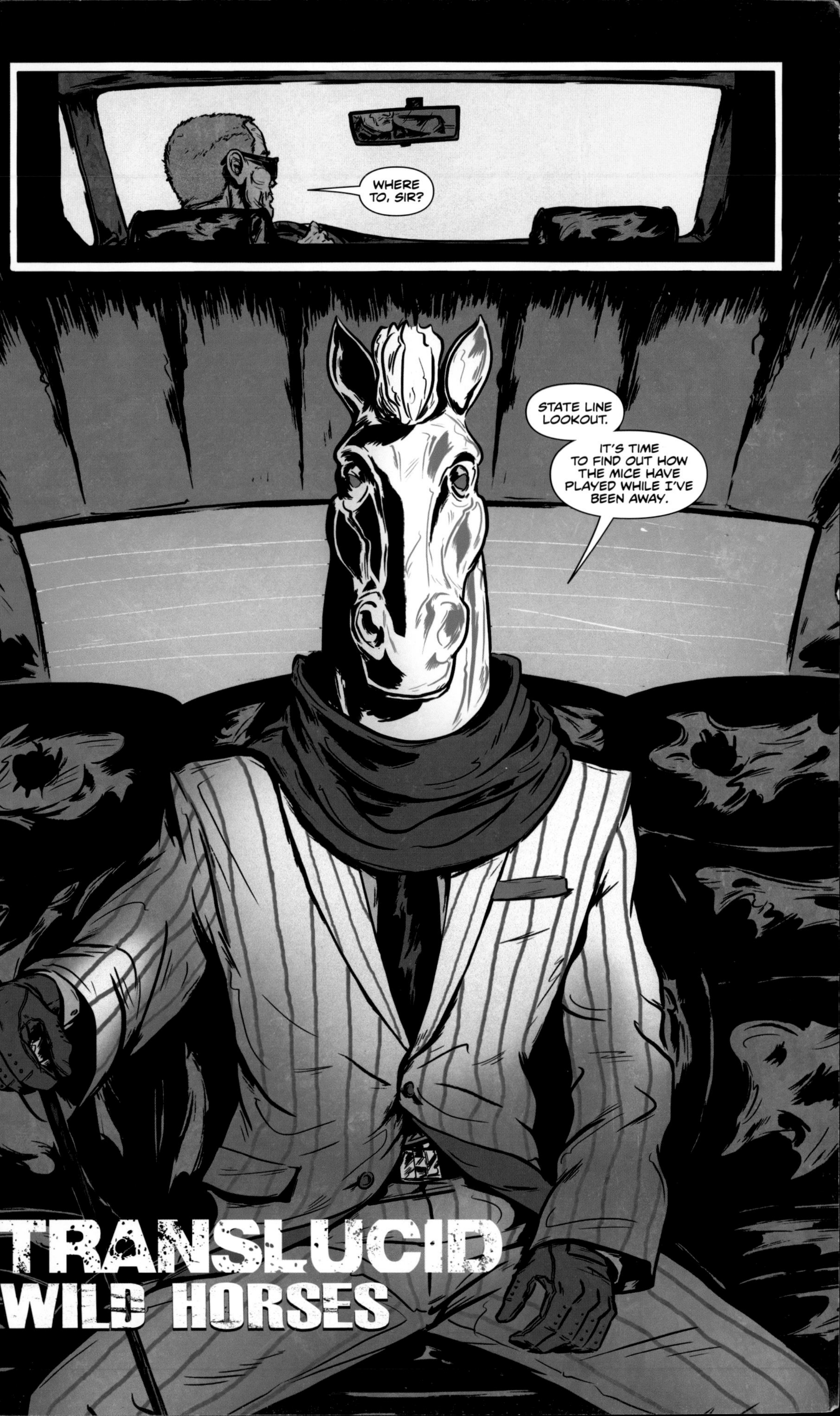
WHERE TO, SIR?
STATE LINE LOOKOUT.
IT'S TIME TO FIND OUT HOW THE MICE HAVE PLAYED WHILE I'VE BEEN AWAY.
TRANSLUCID
WILD HORSES

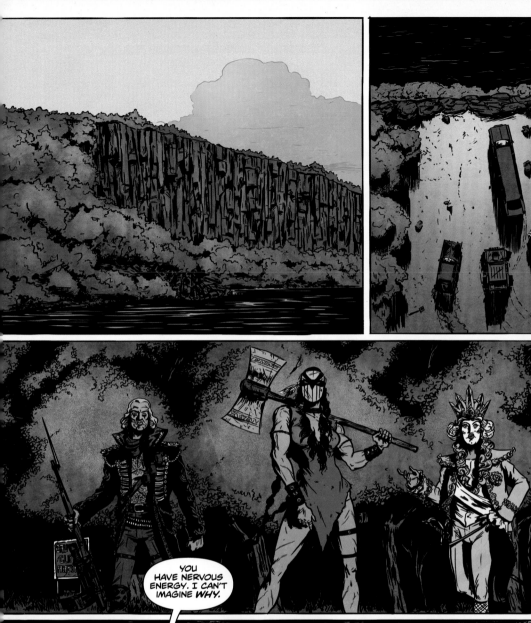

YOU HAVE NERVOUS ENERGY. I CAN'T IMAGINE *WHY.*

A MAN'S NOT FREE TO INVITE HIS CONTEMPORARIES FOR A CATCH-UP AFTER A SHORT STINT IN THE POUND?

WE THOUGHT YOU MIGHT TAKE SOME ISSUE WITH US TRYING TO PICK UP THE SLACK WHILE YOU WERE GONE CONSIDERING WHAT HAPPENED TO THE LEPER--

THAT'S UNFAIR. MY INSISTENCE ON PERFECTION ISN'T FOR MY BENEFIT. I BELIEVED THE *APOCALYPSE 3* UNDERSTOOD THAT EXCELLENCE ISN'T SOMETHING TO *TRY FOR.*

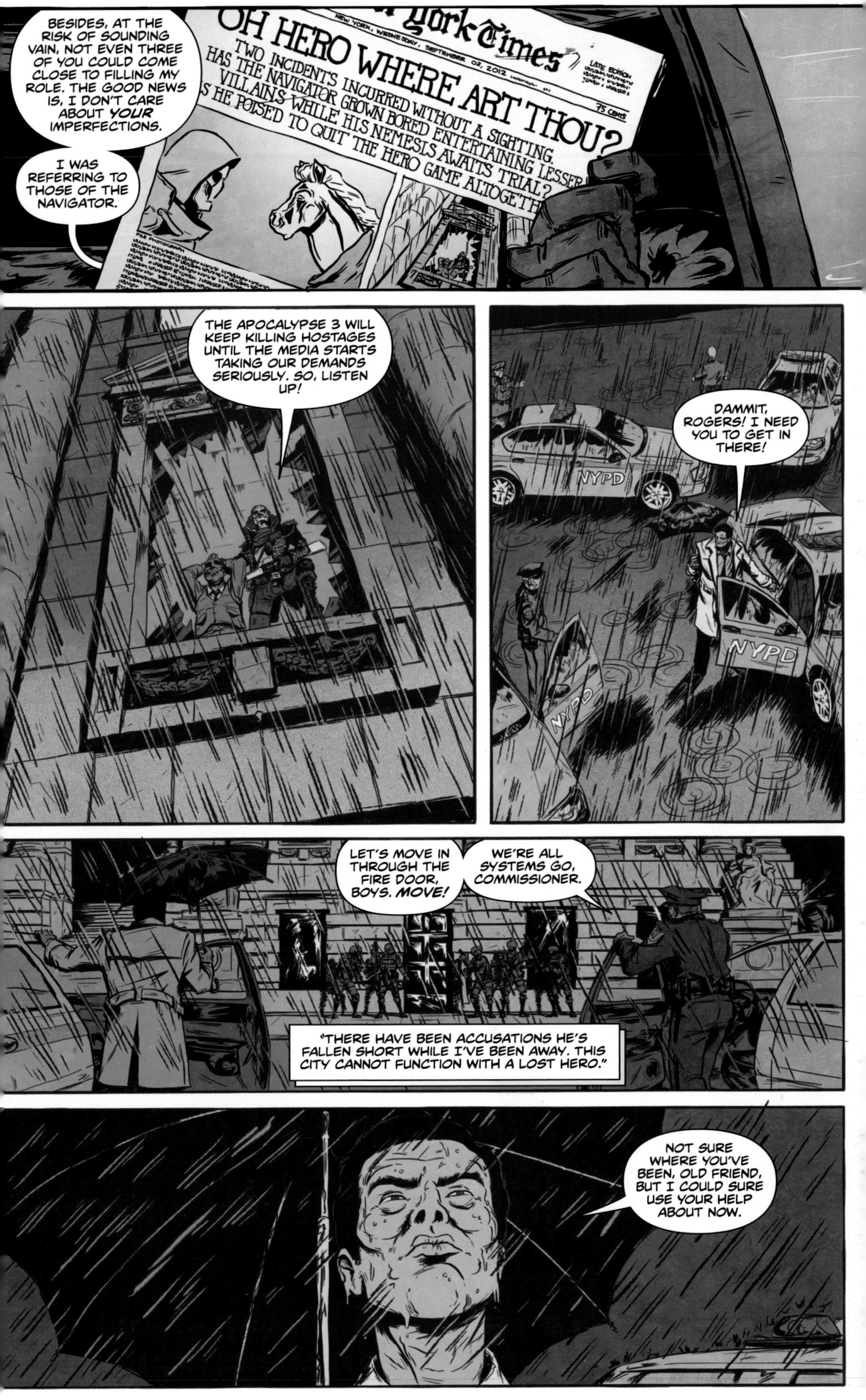
BESIDES, AT THE RISK OF SOUNDING VAIN, NOT EVEN THREE OF YOU COULD COME CLOSE TO FILLING MY ROLE. THE GOOD NEWS IS, I DON'T CARE ABOUT YOUR IMPERFECTIONS.
I WAS REFERRING TO THOSE OF THE NAVIGATOR.
OH HERO WHERE ART THOU?
TWO INCIDENTS INCURRED WITHOUT A SIGHTING.
HAS THE NAVIGATOR GROWN BORED ENTERTAINING LESSER VILLAINS WHILE HIS NEMESIS AWAITS TRIAL?
IS HE POISED TO QUIT THE HERO GAME ALTOGETH
LATE EDITION
75 CENTS
THE APOCALYPSE 3 WILL KEEP KILLING HOSTAGES UNTIL THE MEDIA STARTS TAKING OUR DEMANDS SERIOUSLY. SO, LISTEN UP!
DAMMIT, ROGERS! I NEED YOU TO GET IN THERE!
NYPD
NYPD
NYPD
LET'S MOVE IN THROUGH THE FIRE DOOR, BOYS. MOVE!
WE'RE ALL SYSTEMS GO, COMMISSIONER.
"THERE HAVE BEEN ACCUSATIONS HE'S FALLEN SHORT WHILE I'VE BEEN AWAY. THIS CITY CANNOT FUNCTION WITH A LOST HERO."
NOT SURE WHERE YOU'VE BEEN, OLD FRIEND, BUT I COULD SURE USE YOUR HELP ABOUT NOW.

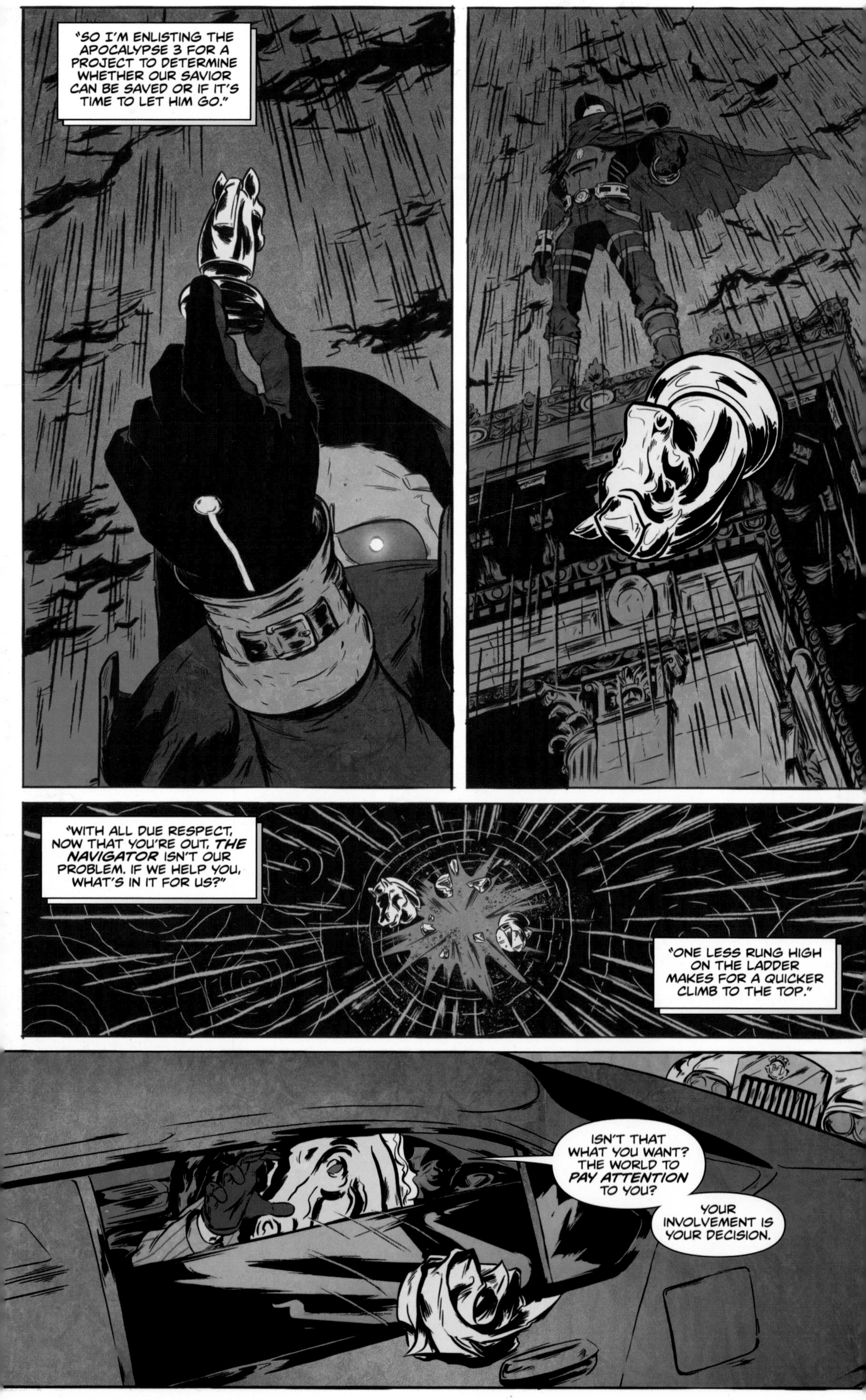
"SO I'M ENLISTING THE APOCALYPSE 3 FOR A PROJECT TO DETERMINE WHETHER OUR SAVIOR CAN BE SAVED OR IF IT'S TIME TO LET HIM GO."
"WITH ALL DUE RESPECT, NOW THAT YOU'RE OUT, *THE NAVIGATOR* ISN'T OUR PROBLEM. IF WE HELP YOU, WHAT'S IN IT FOR US?"
"ONE LESS RUNG HIGH ON THE LADDER MAKES FOR A QUICKER CLIMB TO THE TOP."
ISN'T THAT WHAT YOU WANT? THE WORLD TO *PAY ATTENTION* TO YOU?
YOUR INVOLVEMENT IS YOUR DECISION.

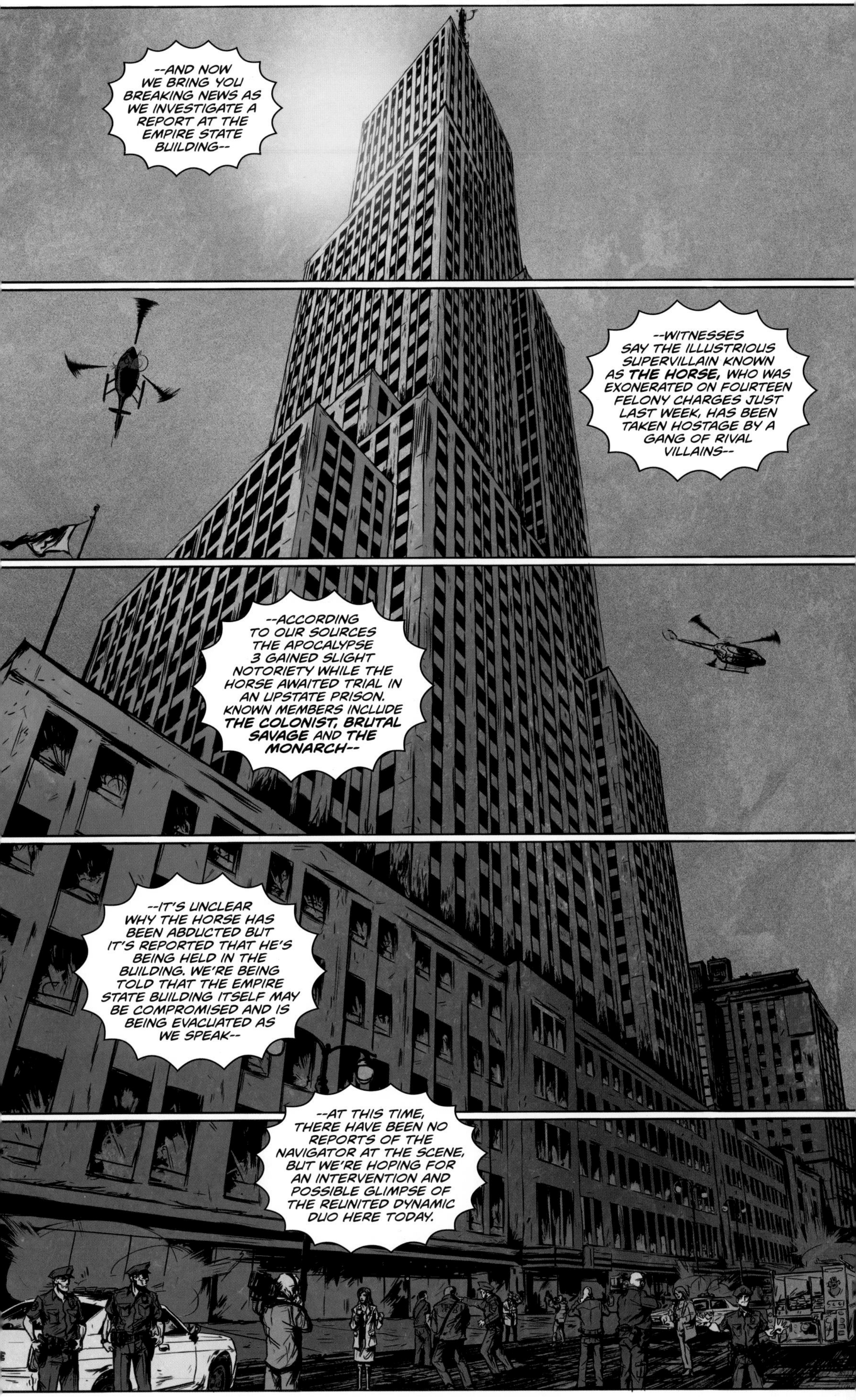
--AND NOW WE BRING YOU BREAKING NEWS AS WE INVESTIGATE A REPORT AT THE EMPIRE STATE BUILDING--
--WITNESSES SAY THE ILLUSTRIOUS SUPERVILLAIN KNOWN AS THE HORSE, WHO WAS EXONERATED ON FOURTEEN FELONY CHARGES JUST LAST WEEK, HAS BEEN TAKEN HOSTAGE BY A GANG OF RIVAL VILLAINS--
--ACCORDING TO OUR SOURCES THE APOCALYPSE 3 GAINED SLIGHT NOTORIETY WHILE THE HORSE AWAITED TRIAL IN AN UPSTATE PRISON. KNOWN MEMBERS INCLUDE THE COLONIST, BRUTAL SAVAGE AND THE MONARCH--
--IT'S UNCLEAR WHY THE HORSE HAS BEEN ABDUCTED BUT IT'S REPORTED THAT HE'S BEING HELD IN THE BUILDING. WE'RE BEING TOLD THAT THE EMPIRE STATE BUILDING ITSELF MAY BE COMPROMISED AND IS BEING EVACUATED AS WE SPEAK--
--AT THIS TIME, THERE HAVE BEEN NO REPORTS OF THE NAVIGATOR AT THE SCENE, BUT WE'RE HOPING FOR AN INTERVENTION AND POSSIBLE GLIMPSE OF THE REUNITED DYNAMIC DUO HERE TODAY.

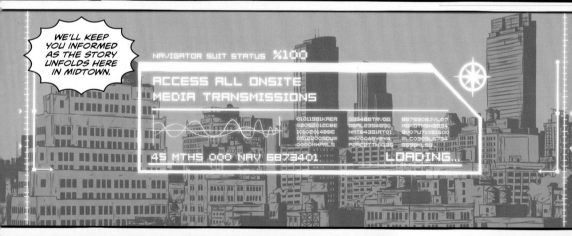

WE'LL KEEP YOU INFORMED AS THE STORY UNFOLDS HERE IN MIDTOWN.

NAVIGATOR SUIT STATUS X100

ACCESS ALL ONSITE MEDIA TRANSMISSIONS

01011981KAER   02548BTRVGG   8679309JVLO7
02052012DBE   8GAL2354890   MGKOTMSNSB34
1010201488E   NMT84391RTQ1   3VX07U71051500
051220090UW   WHY0045V2X4   WLC0909L6734
0000MHPRLS   P2AC21THX135   9B98KL90

45 MTHS 000 NAV 6B73401   LOADING...

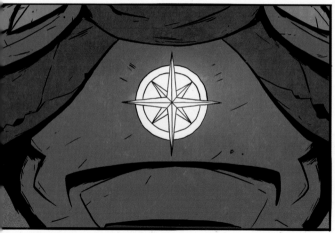

SHOW ME GRIPS.

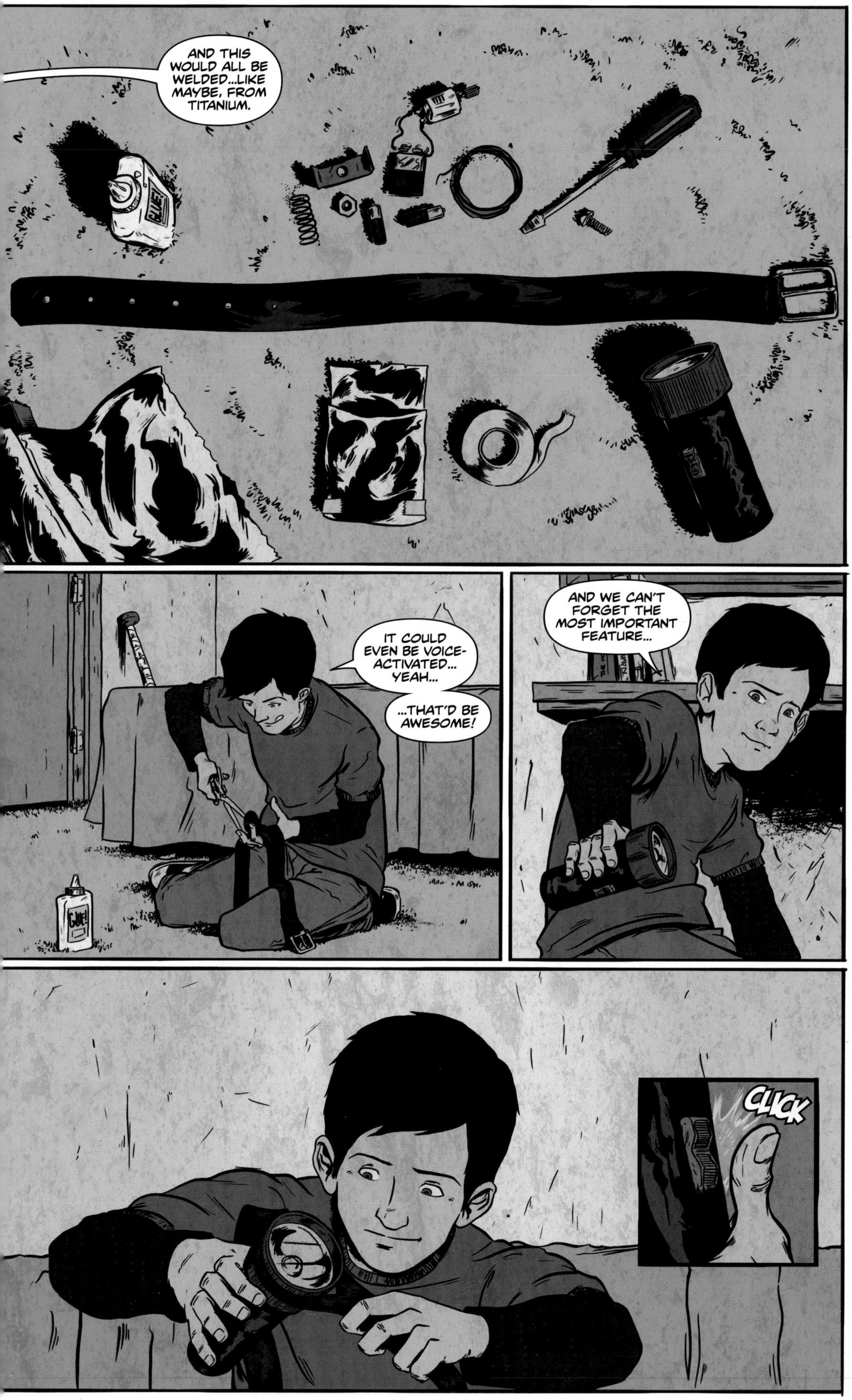
AND THIS WOULD ALL BE WELDED...LIKE MAYBE, FROM TITANIUM.
GLUE!
IT COULD EVEN BE VOICE-ACTIVATED... YEAH...
...THAT'D BE AWESOME!
GLUE!
AND WE CAN'T FORGET THE MOST IMPORTANT FEATURE...
CLICK

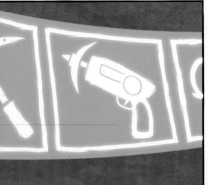
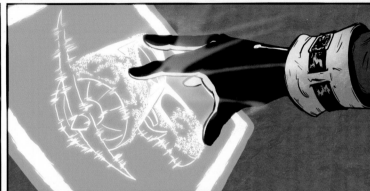

GIVE ME A SCOPE.

THOOCK

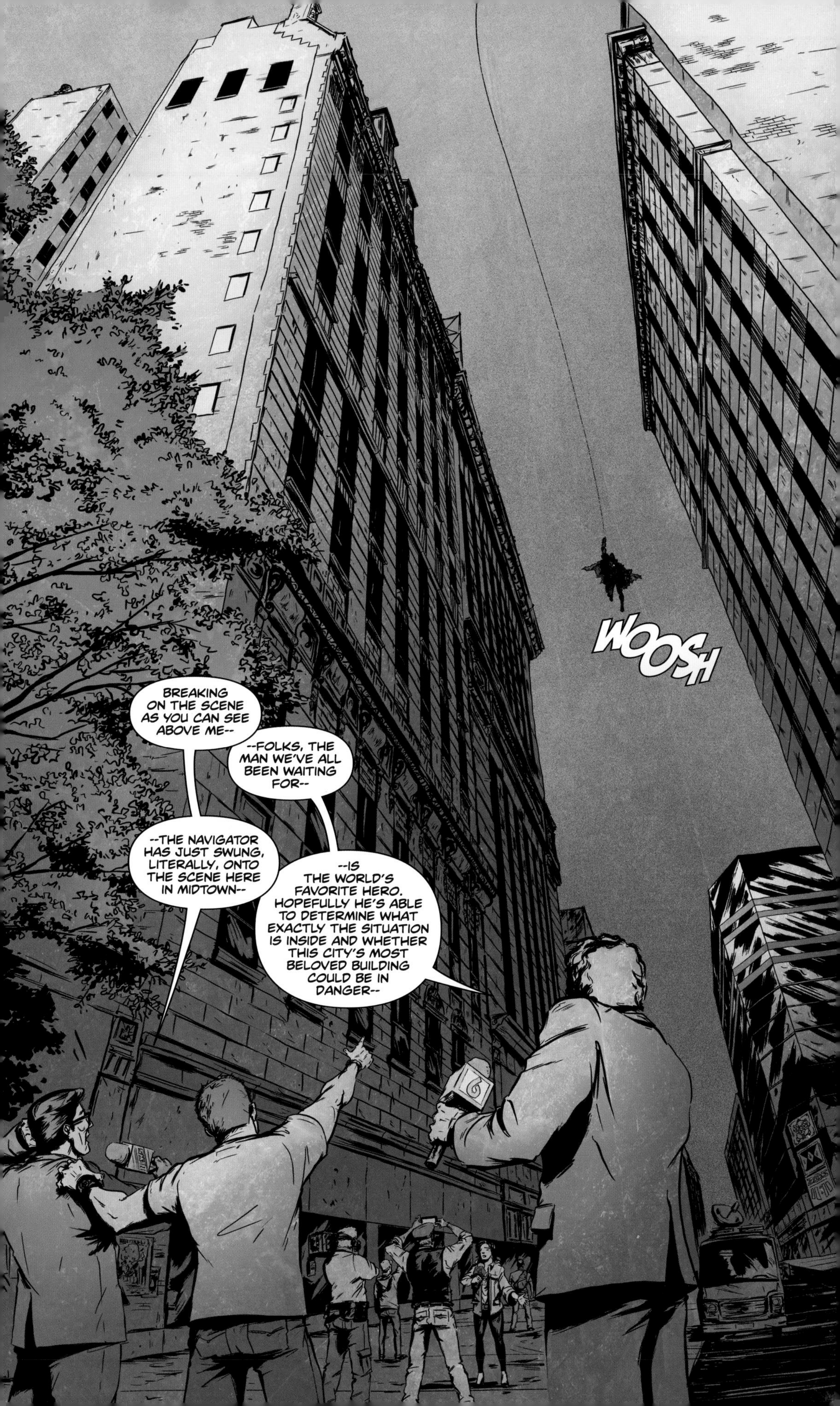
WOOSH
BREAKING ON THE SCENE AS YOU CAN SEE ABOVE ME--
--FOLKS, THE MAN WE'VE ALL BEEN WAITING FOR--
--THE NAVIGATOR HAS JUST SWUNG, LITERALLY, ONTO THE SCENE HERE IN MIDTOWN--
--IS THE WORLD'S FAVORITE HERO. HOPEFULLY HE'S ABLE TO DETERMINE WHAT EXACTLY THE SITUATION IS INSIDE AND WHETHER THIS CITY'S MOST BELOVED BUILDING COULD BE IN DANGER--

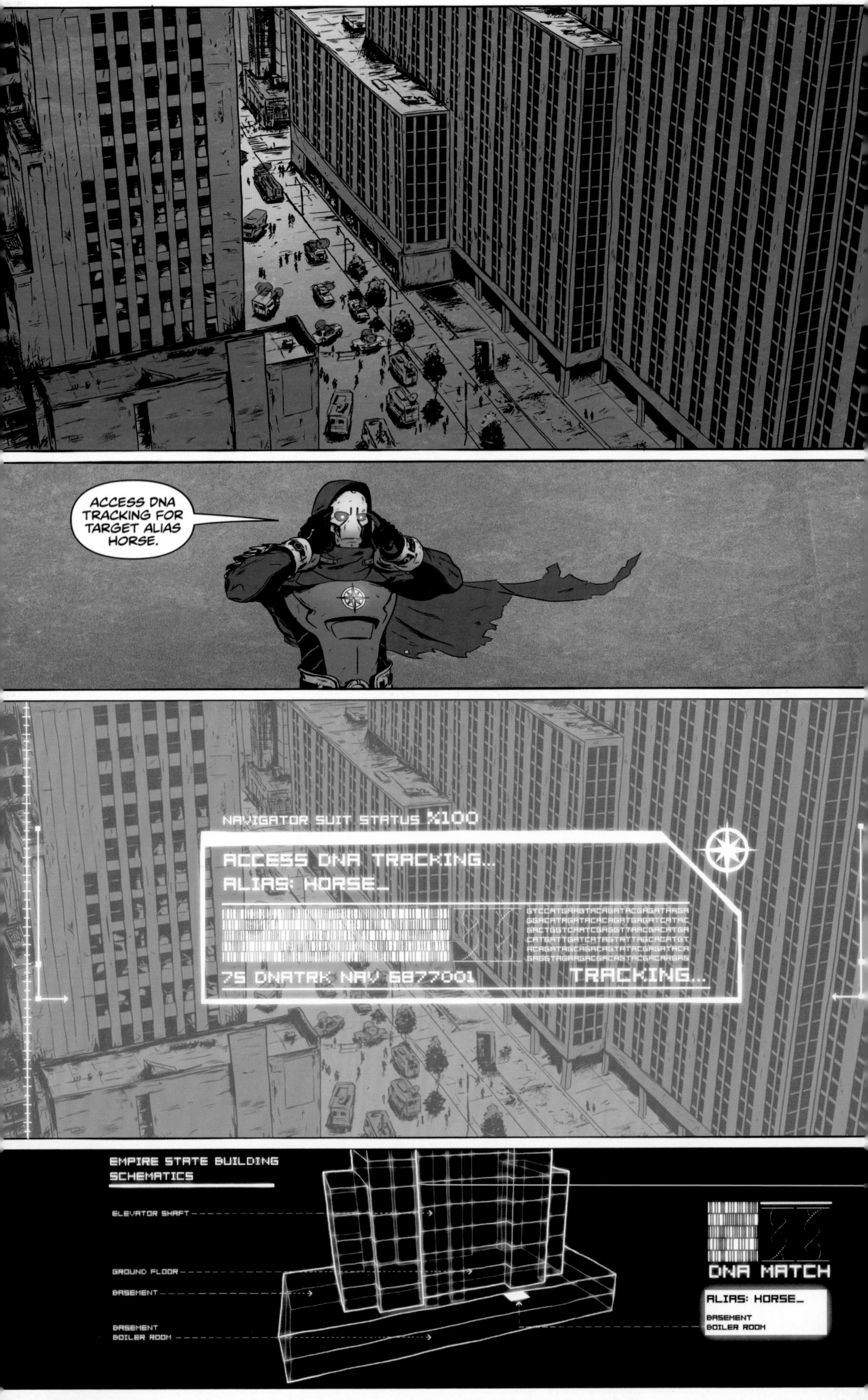
ACCESS DNA TRACKING FOR TARGET ALIAS HORSE.
NAVIGATOR SUIT STATUS %100
ACCESS DNA TRACKING...
ALIAS: HORSE_
GTCCATGAAGTACAGATACGAGATAAGA
GGACATAGATACACAGATGAGATCATAC
GACTGGTCAATCGAGGTTAACGACATGA
CATGATTGATCATAGTATTAGCACATGT
ACAGATAGCAGACAGTATACGAGATACA
GAGGTAGAAGACGACAGTACGACAAGAG
75 DNATRK NAV 6877001
TRACKING...
EMPIRE STATE BUILDING SCHEMATICS
ELEVATOR SHAFT
GROUND FLOOR
BASEMENT
BASEMENT BOILER ROOM
DNA MATCH
ALIAS: HORSE_
BASEMENT BOILER ROOM

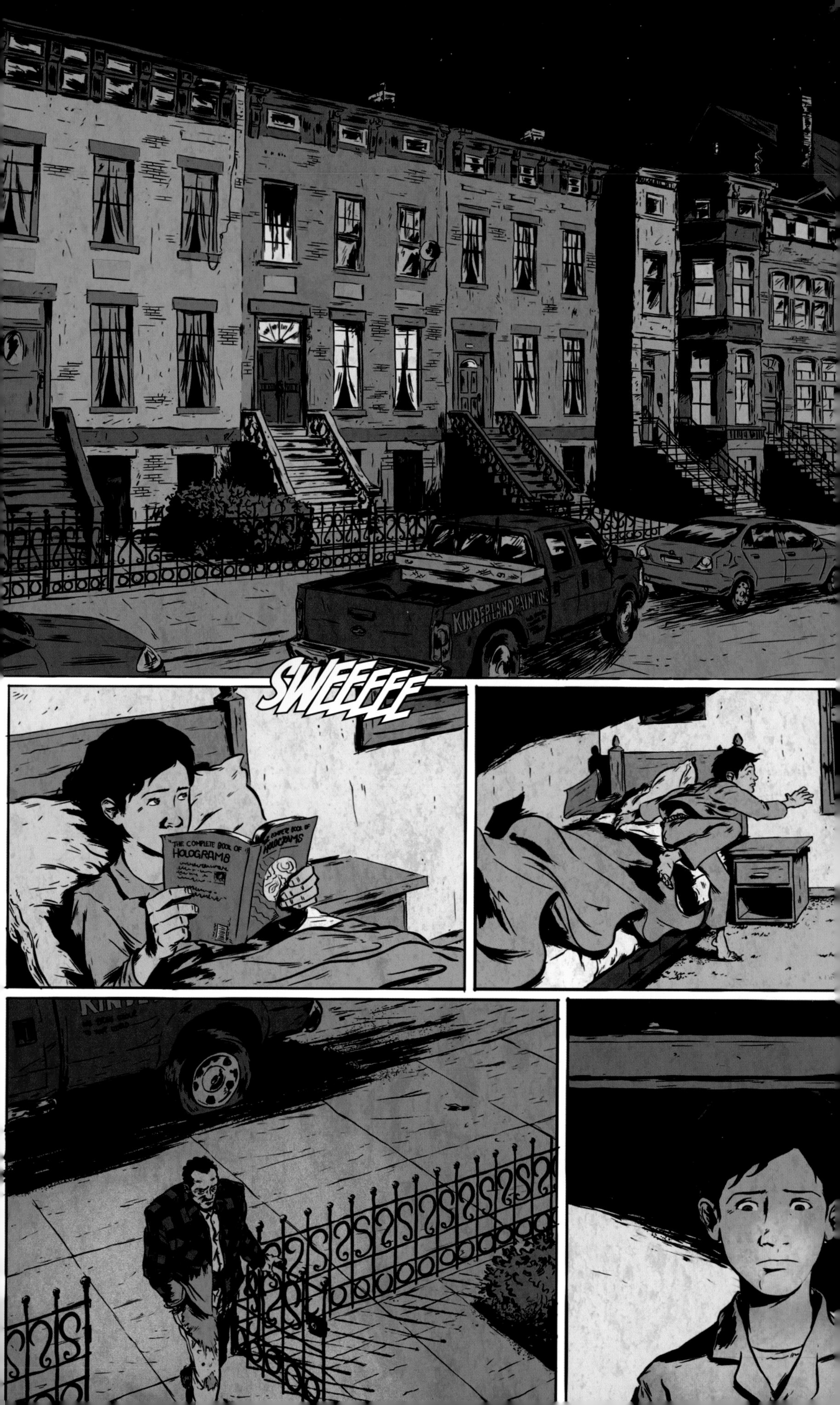
KINDERLAND PAINT INC.
SWEEEEE
THE COMPLETE BOOK OF HOLOGRAMS

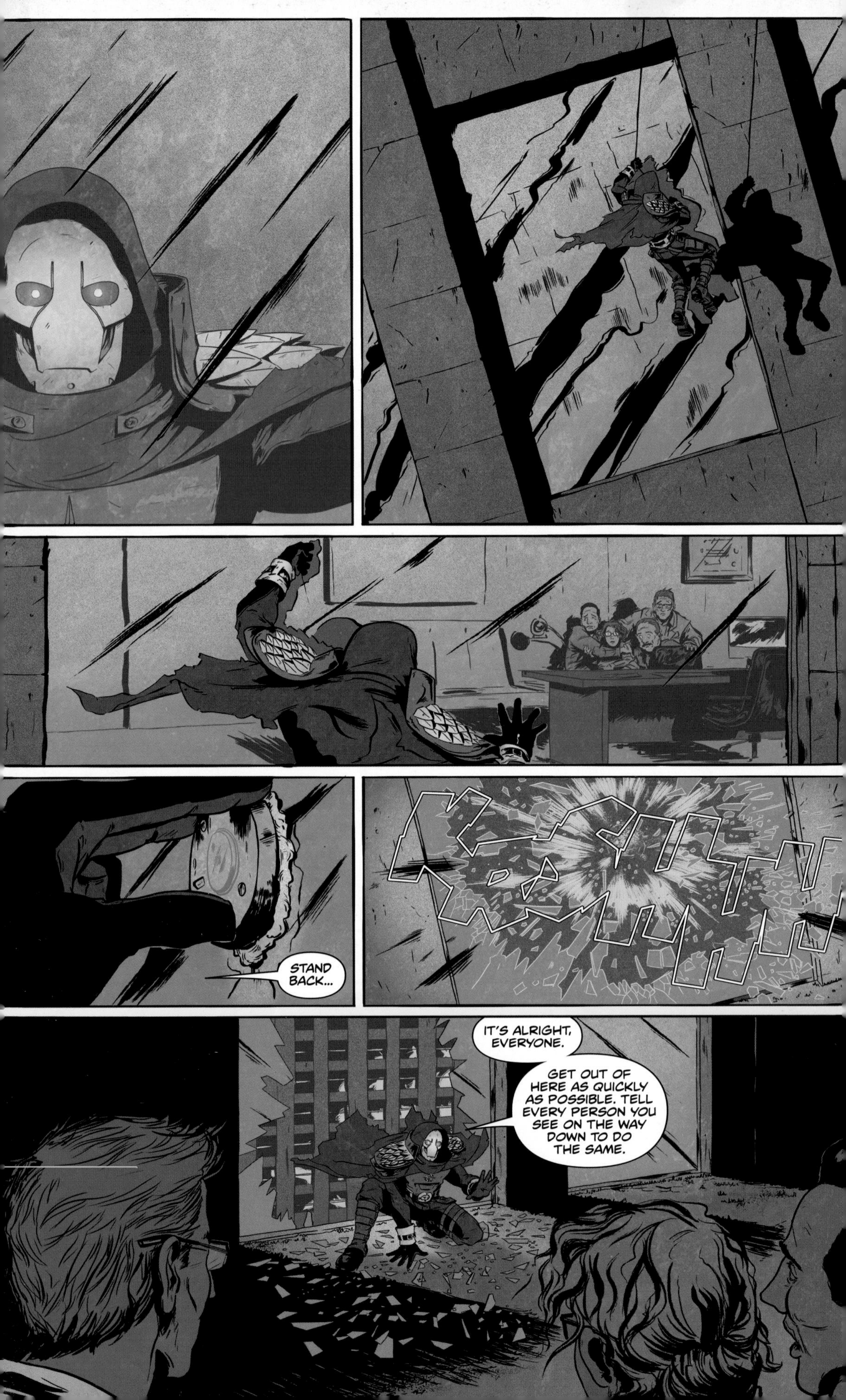
STAND BACK...
IT'S ALRIGHT, EVERYONE.
GET OUT OF HERE AS QUICKLY AS POSSIBLE. TELL EVERY PERSON YOU SEE ON THE WAY DOWN TO DO THE SAME.

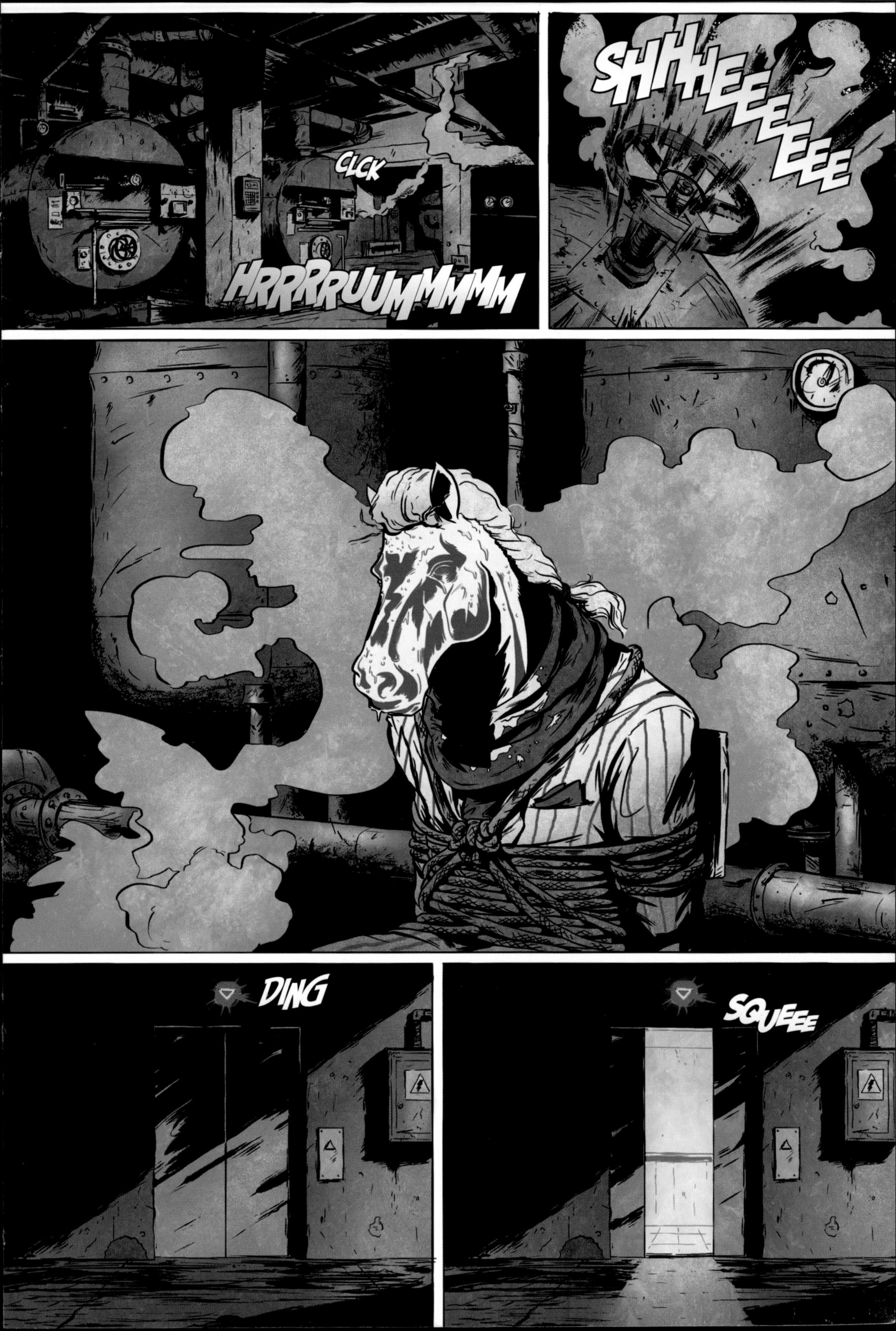
CLCK
HRRRRUUMMMMM
SHHHEEEEEEEE
DING
SQUEEE

I SHOULD HAVE KNOWN...YOU'D MAKE...AN ENTRANCE.

IS IT TRUE? DID THE 3 DO THIS TO YOU?

THE 10 O'CLOCK NEWS...NEVER... GETS IT WRONG.

BUT HOW? YOU'RE SO MUCH *BETTER* THAN THEM.

AND WHERE ARE THEY? I'M UNABLE TO TRACE THEIR WHEREABOUTS IN THE BUILDING.

OH, THEY'VE GONE.

TECHNOLOGY THESE DAYS IS A MARVEL...YOU JUST WIRE A MAN'S DNA TO THE TAIL END OF A BOMB IN ONE OF THE MOST BELOVED BUILDINGS ON EARTH...AND *VOILÀ!* NOT EVEN GANDHI... WOULD LEND HIM... A HAND.

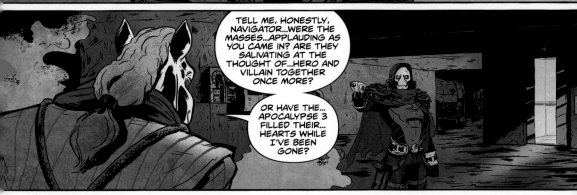

TELL ME, HONESTLY, NAVIGATOR...WERE THE MASSES...APPLAUDING AS YOU CAME IN? ARE THEY SALIVATING AT THE THOUGHT OF...HERO AND VILLAIN TOGETHER ONCE MORE?

OR HAVE THE... APOCALYPSE 3 FILLED THEIR... HEARTS WHILE I'VE BEEN GONE?

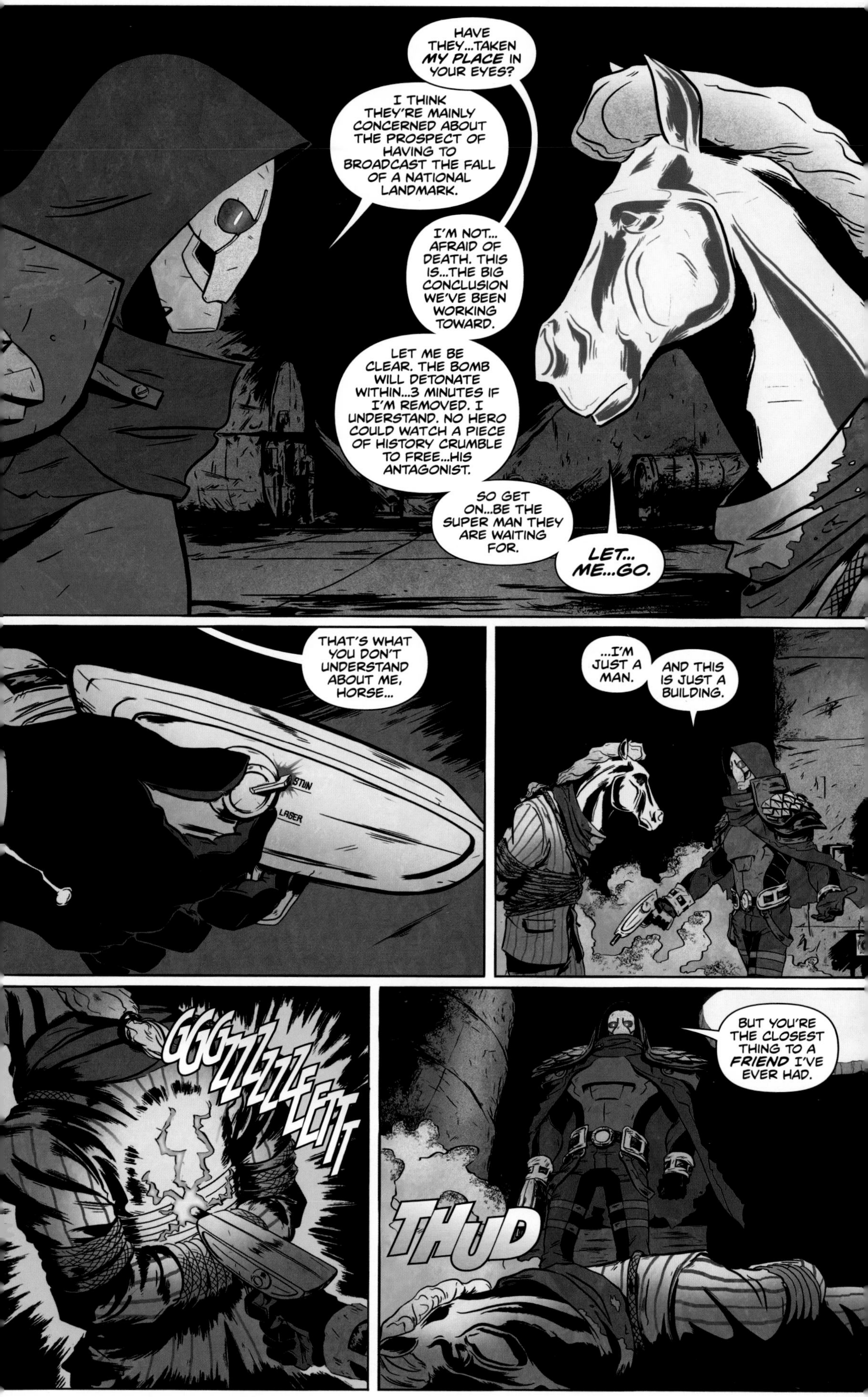

HAVE THEY...TAKEN MY PLACE IN YOUR EYES?
I THINK THEY'RE MAINLY CONCERNED ABOUT THE PROSPECT OF HAVING TO BROADCAST THE FALL OF A NATIONAL LANDMARK.
I'M NOT... AFRAID OF DEATH. THIS IS...THE BIG CONCLUSION WE'VE BEEN WORKING TOWARD.
LET ME BE CLEAR. THE BOMB WILL DETONATE WITHIN...3 MINUTES IF I'M REMOVED. I UNDERSTAND. NO HERO COULD WATCH A PIECE OF HISTORY CRUMBLE TO FREE...HIS ANTAGONIST.
SO GET ON...BE THE SUPER MAN THEY ARE WAITING FOR.
LET... ME...GO.
THAT'S WHAT YOU DON'T UNDERSTAND ABOUT ME, HORSE...
STUN
LASER
...I'M JUST A MAN.
AND THIS IS JUST A BUILDING.
GGGZZZZZZZZEEETTT
THUD
BUT YOU'RE THE CLOSEST THING TO A FRIEND I'VE EVER HAD.

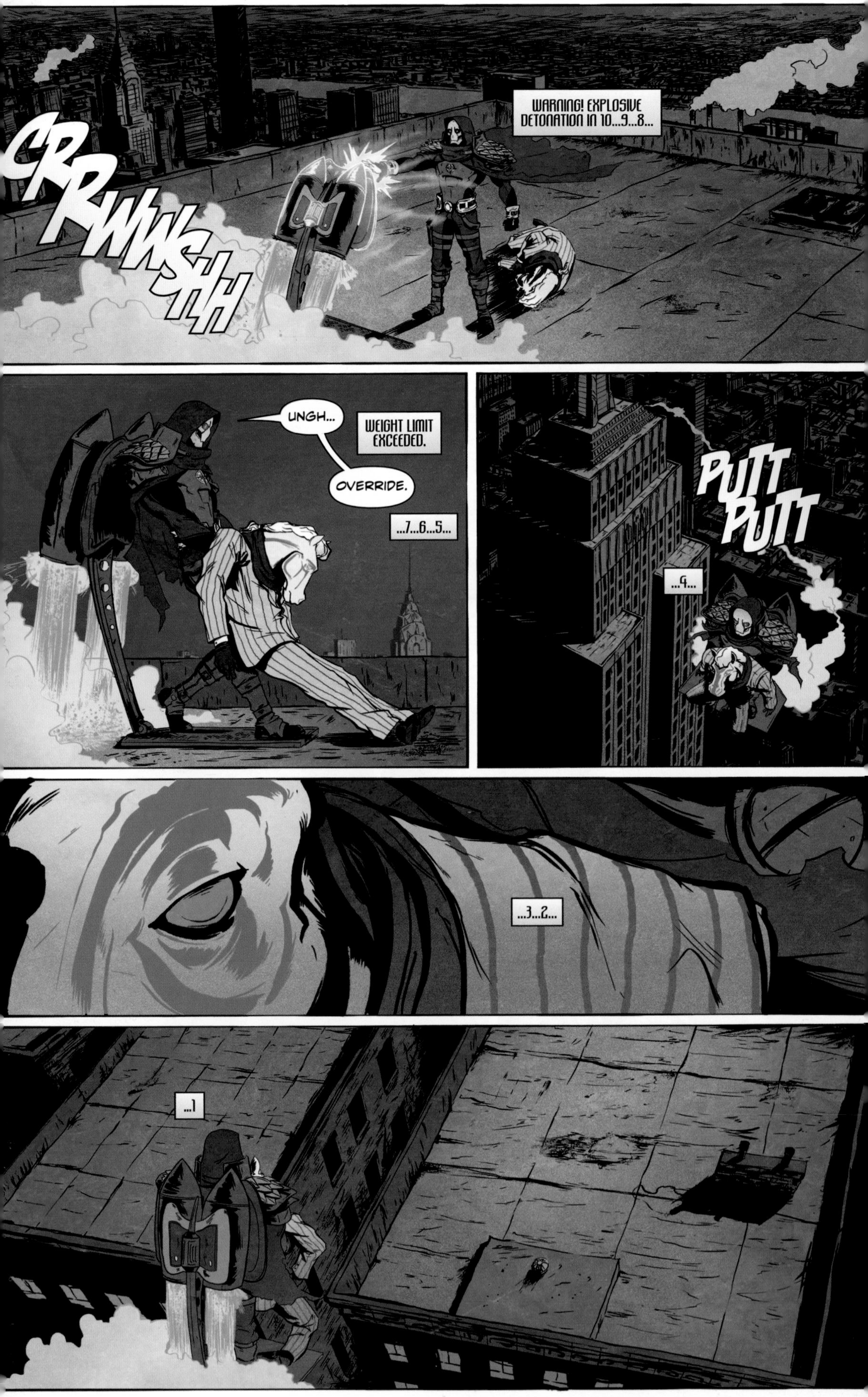

CRRWWSHH
WARNING! EXPLOSIVE DETONATION IN 10...9...8...
UNGH...
WEIGHT LIMIT EXCEEDED.
OVERRIDE.
...7...6...5...
PUTT PUTT
...4...
...3...2...
...1

DELAYED DETONATION?

UNGG!

SPUT SPUT SPRUU

HALLUCINOGENS. THEY'LL TURN YOUR WORLD UPSIDE DOWN!

CRAAAANGG

LIFE IS A SERIES OF PRISONS, DEAR FRIEND. THE ONLY WAY TO SURVIVE IS TO BREAK YOURSELF OUT. I MUST SAY MY PRIDE IS HURT... AS IF I'D EVER ALLOW MYSELF TO BE CAPTURED AND HARD-WIRED TO A BUILDING BY THAT TRIO OF DUNCES!

I WANT TO TELL YOU A STORY.

YOU'LL PROBABLY THINK YOU'VE HEARD IT BEFORE, BUT THIS STORY IS NOT JUST ANOTHER PARABLE OF GOOD AND EVIL.

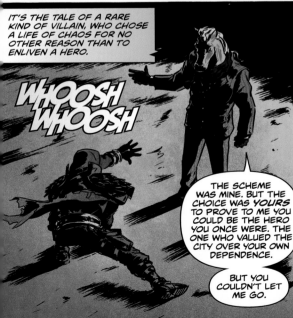

IT'S THE TALE OF A RARE KIND OF VILLAIN, WHO CHOSE A LIFE OF CHAOS FOR NO OTHER REASON THAN TO ENLIVEN A HERO.

WHOOSH WHOOSH

THE SCHEME WAS MINE. BUT THE CHOICE WAS YOURS TO PROVE TO ME YOU COULD BE THE HERO YOU ONCE WERE. THE ONE WHO VALUED THE CITY OVER YOUR OWN DEPENDENCE.

BUT YOU COULDN'T LET ME GO.

SO YOU DESERVE TO WITNESS THE EXPLOSIVE REPERCUSSIONS OF THAT DECISION.

AND IT BEGINS DECADES AFTER THEIR FIRST MEETING, AFTER YEARS OF WEIGHTS BEING QUIETLY STACKED UPON THEM, UNTIL THEIR CO-DEPENDENCY HAD REACHED A TIPPING POINT.

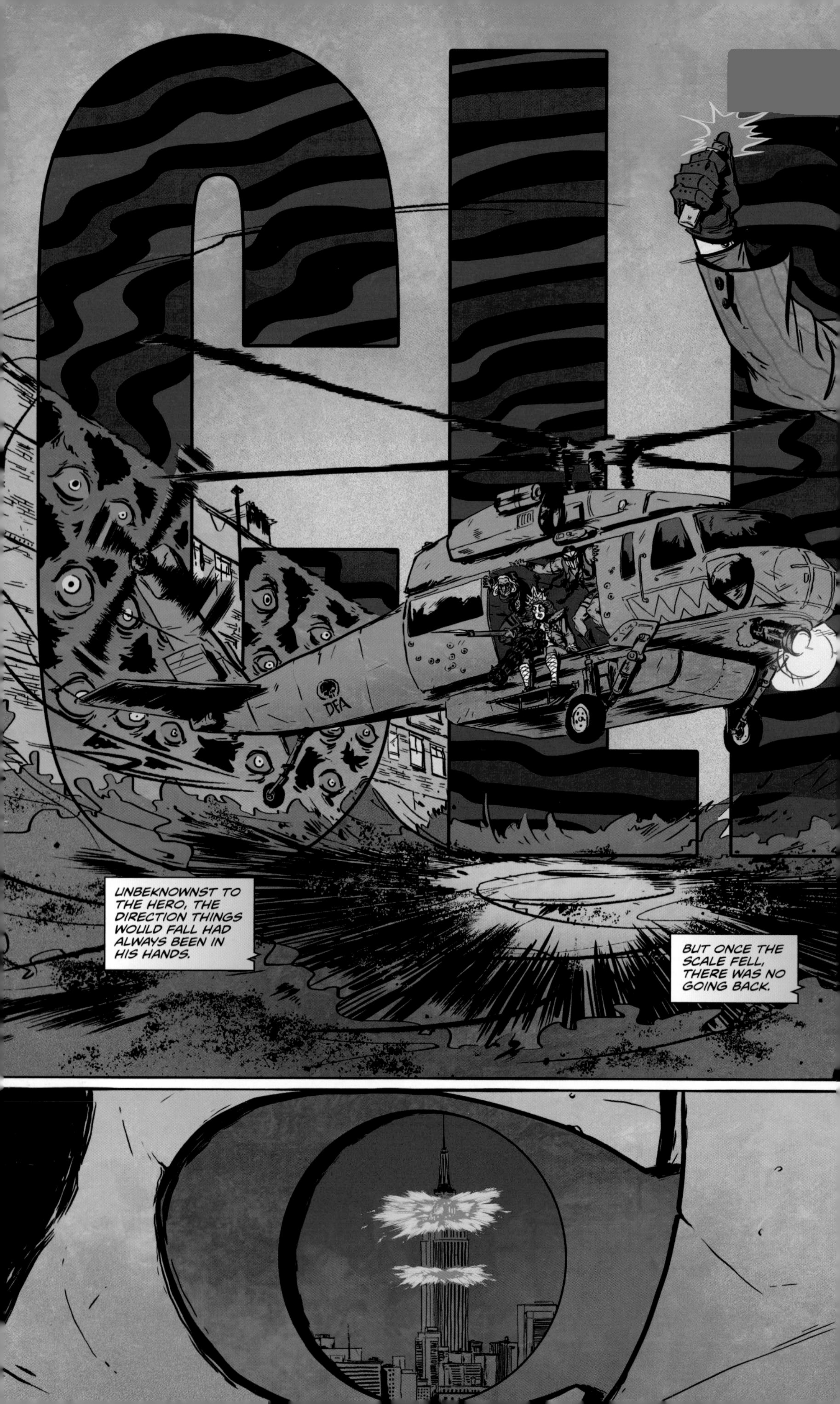
UNBEKNOWNST TO THE HERO, THE DIRECTION THINGS WOULD FALL HAD ALWAYS BEEN IN HIS HANDS.
BUT ONCE THE SCALE FELL, THERE WAS NO GOING BACK.

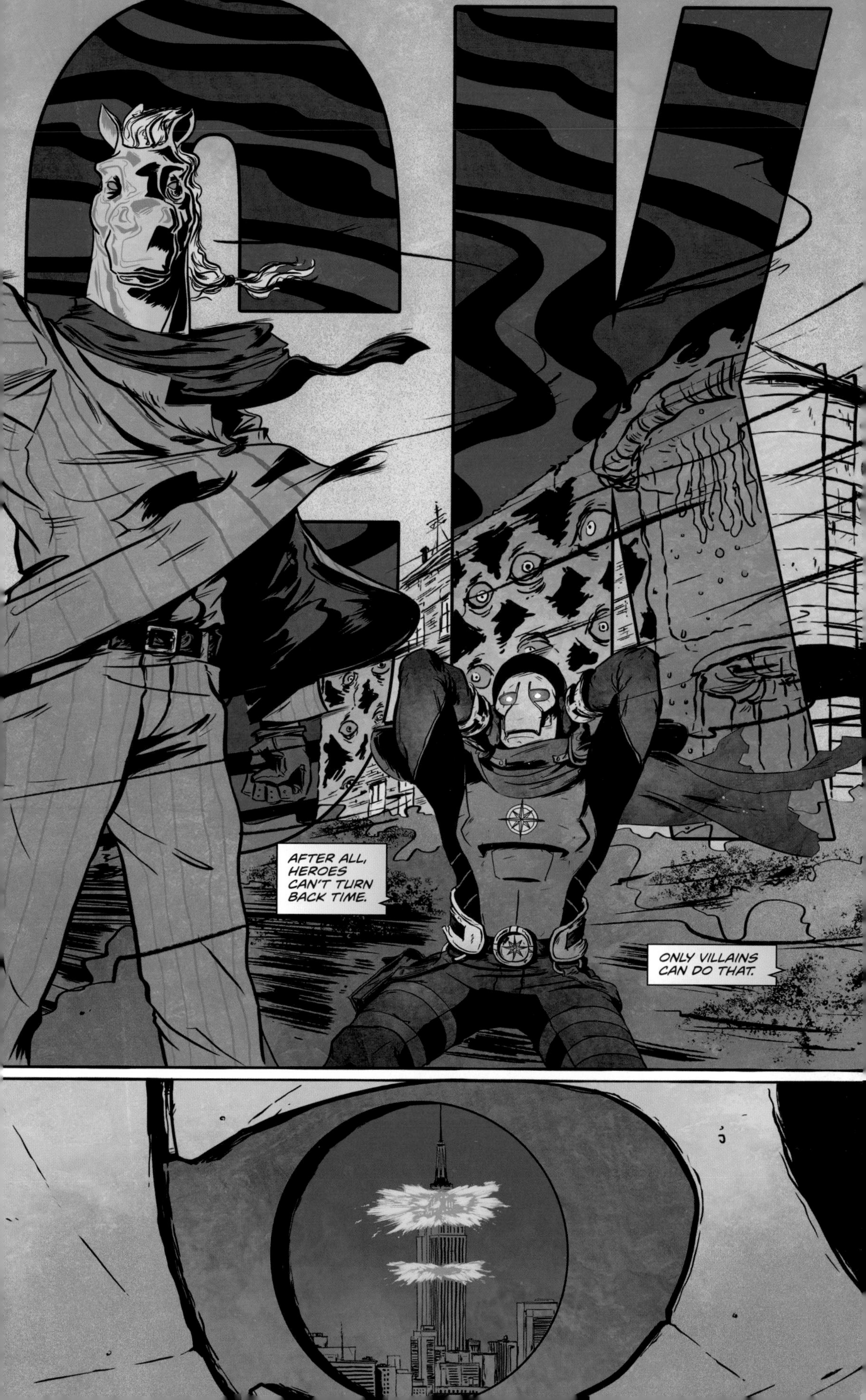
AFTER ALL, HEROES CAN'T TURN BACK TIME.
ONLY VILLAINS CAN DO THAT.

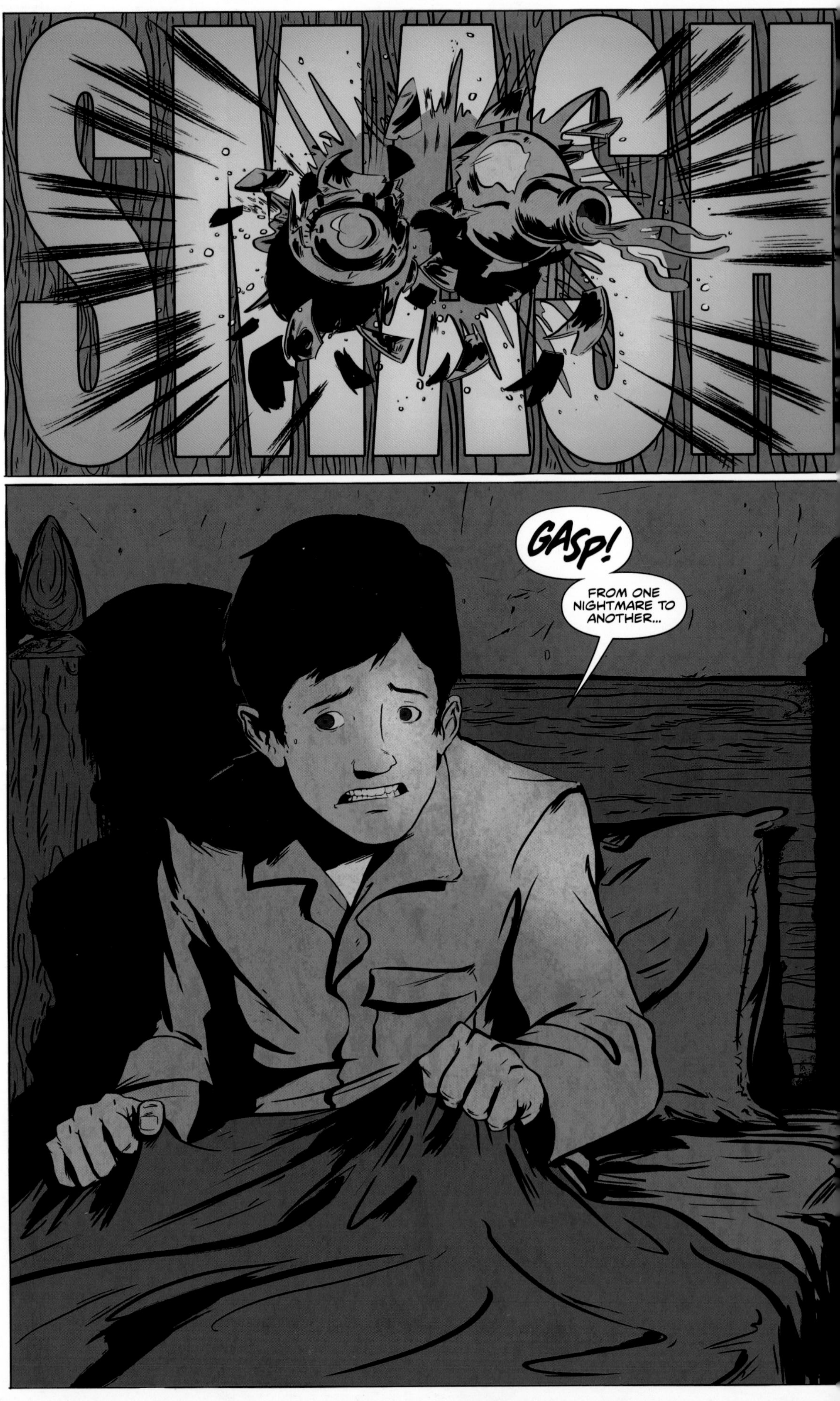
SMASH
GASP!
FROM ONE NIGHTMARE TO ANOTHER...

ISSUE ONE BOOM! STUDIOS EXCLUSIVE COVER BY **FELIPE SMITH**

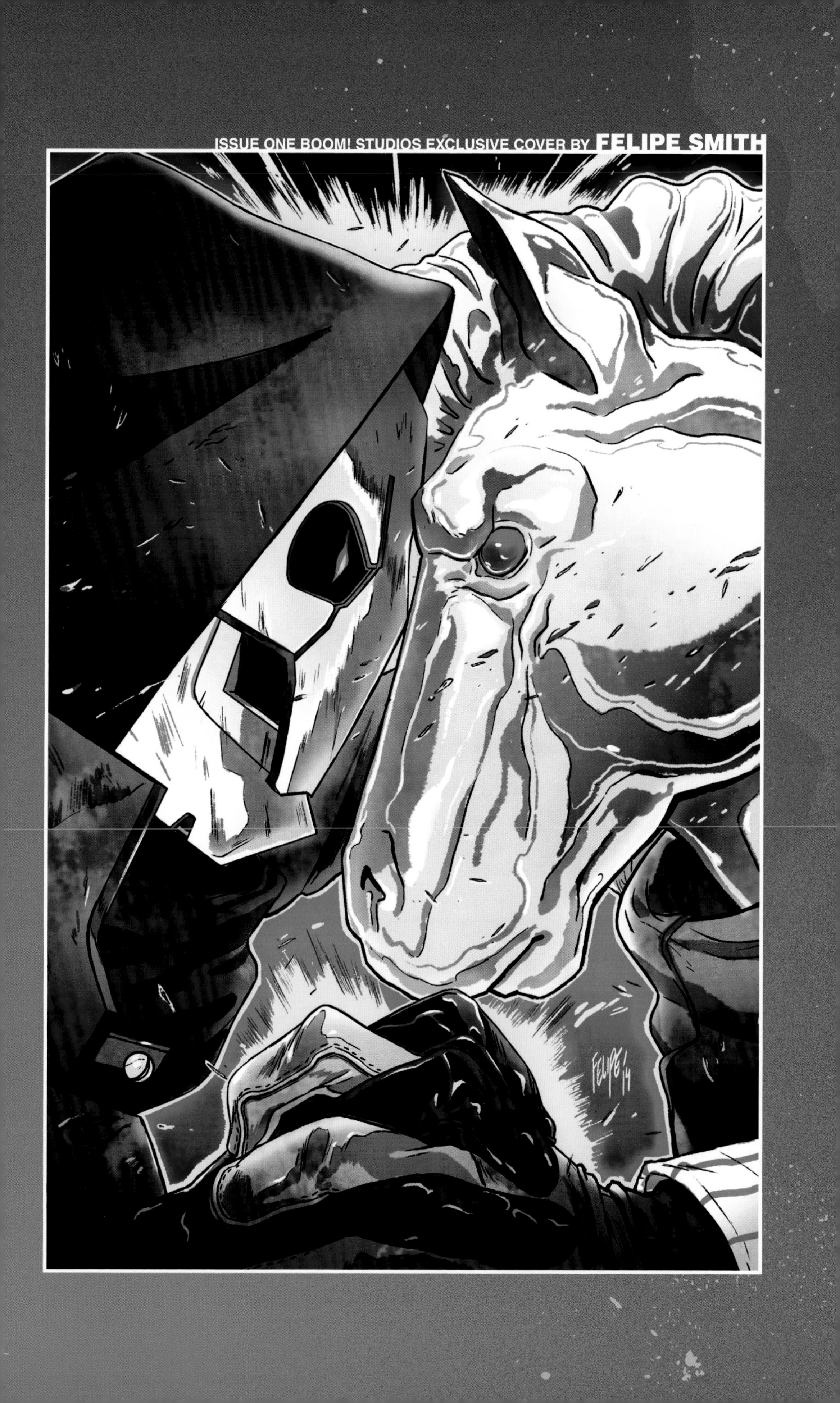

FELIPE '14

ISSUE TWO COVER BY **JEFF STOKELY**

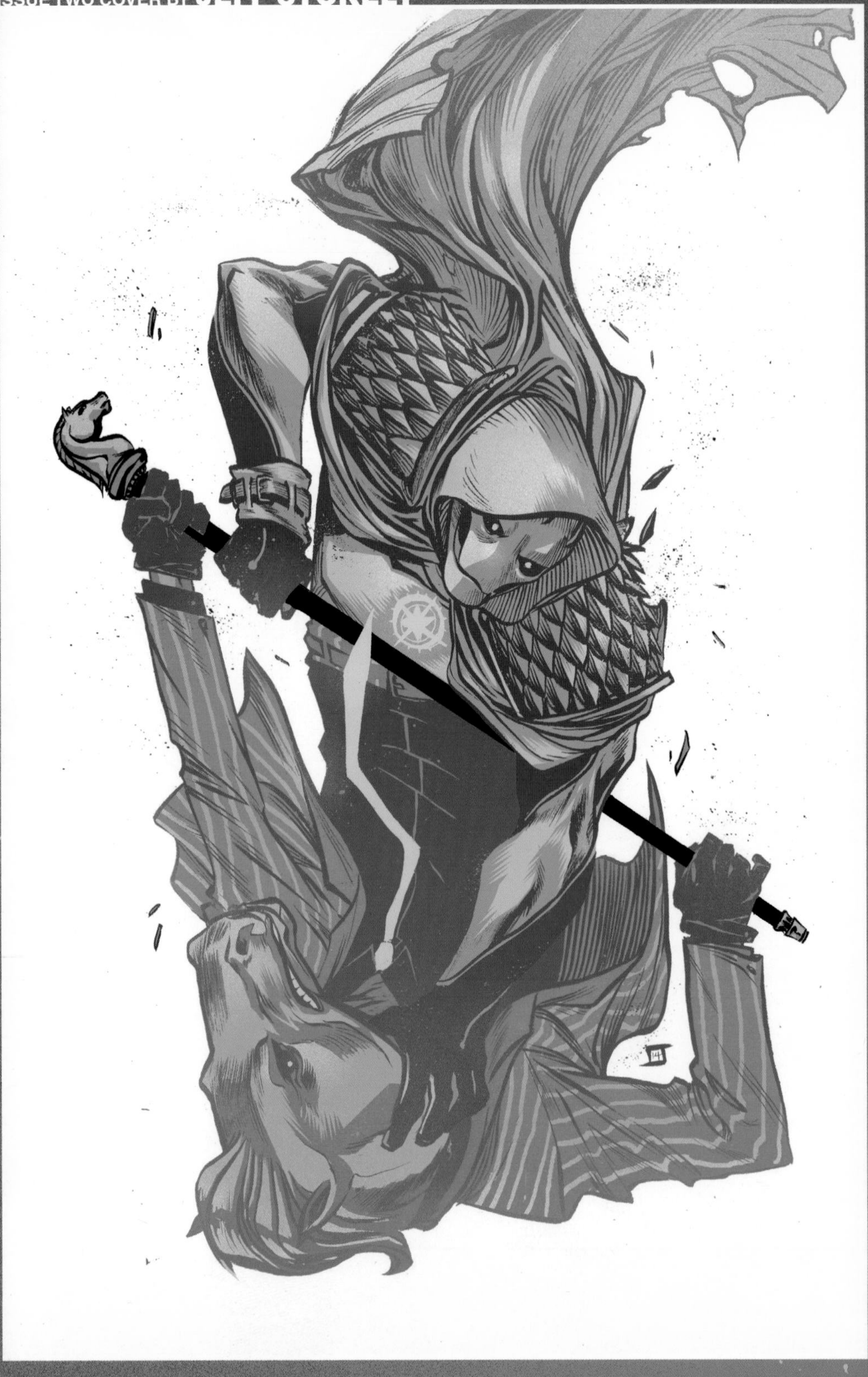

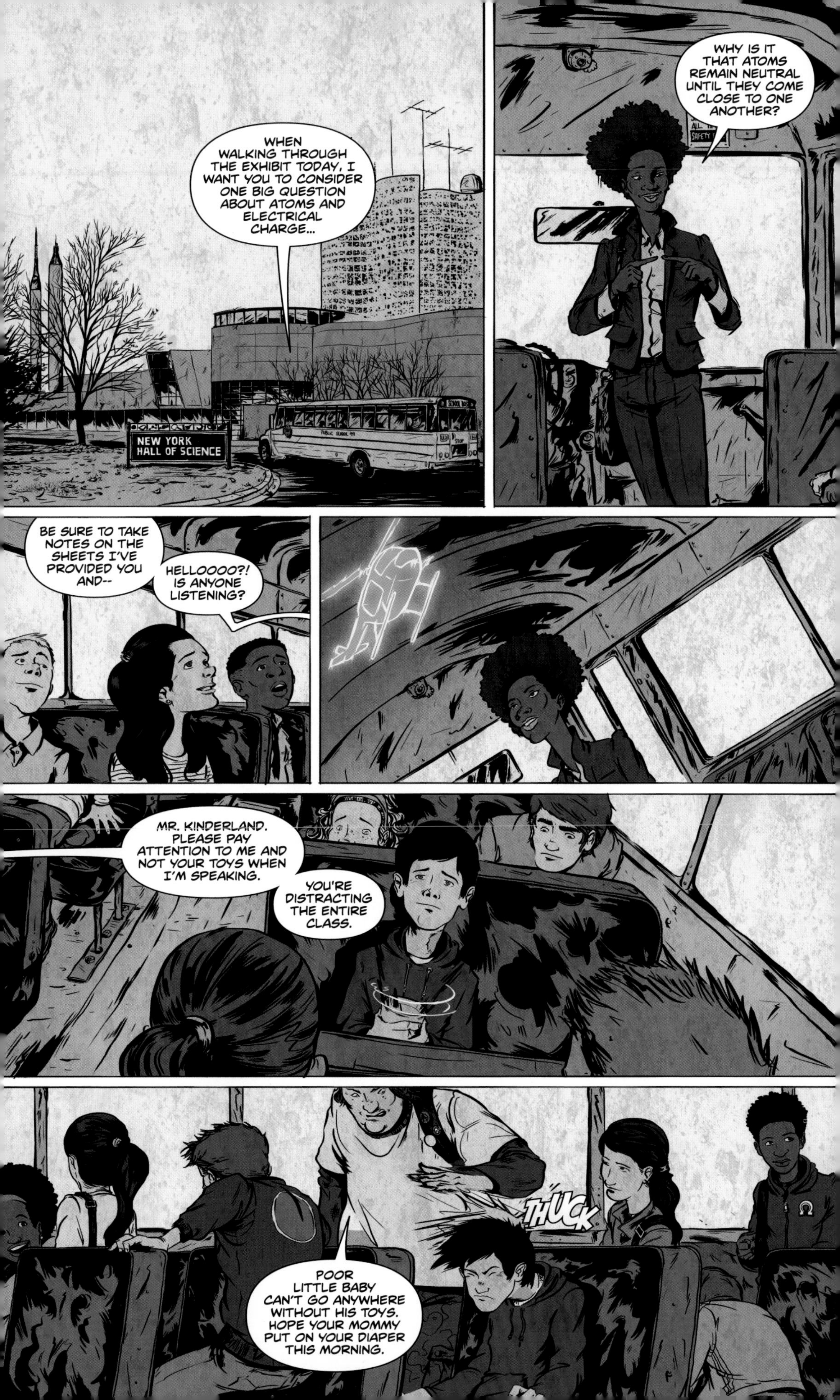

WHEN WALKING THROUGH THE EXHIBIT TODAY, I WANT YOU TO CONSIDER ONE BIG QUESTION ABOUT ATOMS AND ELECTRICAL CHARGE...
NEW YORK HALL OF SCIENCE
WHY IS IT THAT ATOMS REMAIN NEUTRAL UNTIL THEY COME CLOSE TO ONE ANOTHER?
BE SURE TO TAKE NOTES ON THE SHEETS I'VE PROVIDED YOU AND--
HELLOOOO?! IS ANYONE LISTENING?
MR. KINDERLAND. PLEASE PAY ATTENTION TO ME AND NOT YOUR TOYS WHEN I'M SPEAKING.
YOU'RE DISTRACTING THE ENTIRE CLASS.
THUCK
POOR LITTLE BABY CAN'T GO ANYWHERE WITHOUT HIS TOYS. HOPE YOUR MOMMY PUT ON YOUR DIAPER THIS MORNING.

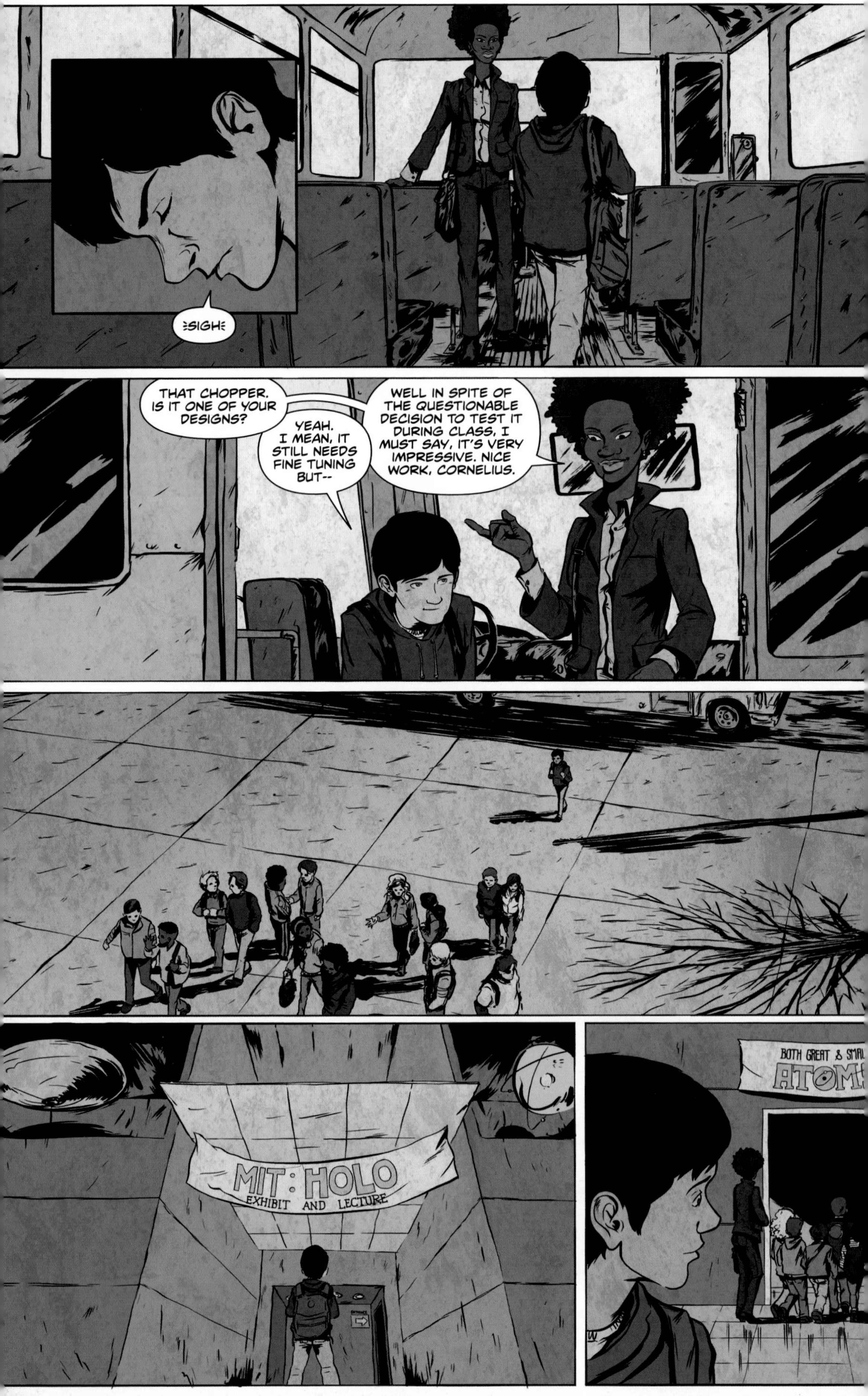
SIGH
THAT CHOPPER. IS IT ONE OF YOUR DESIGNS?
YEAH. I MEAN, IT STILL NEEDS FINE TUNING BUT--
WELL IN SPITE OF THE QUESTIONABLE DECISION TO TEST IT DURING CLASS, I MUST SAY, IT'S VERY IMPRESSIVE. NICE WORK, CORNELIUS.
MIT : HOLO
EXHIBIT AND LECTURE
BOTH GREAT & SMAL
ATOM

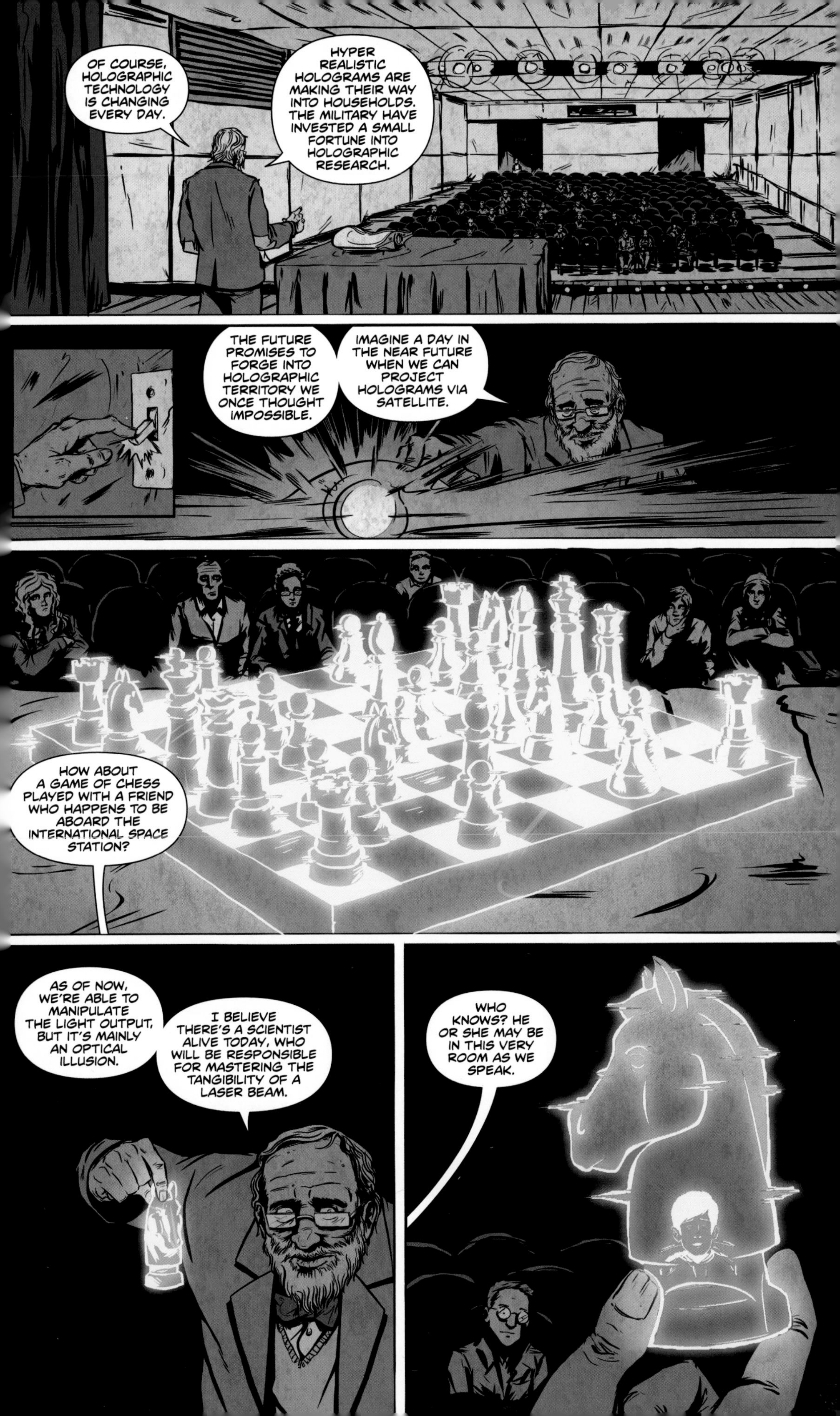
OF COURSE, HOLOGRAPHIC TECHNOLOGY IS CHANGING EVERY DAY.
HYPER REALISTIC HOLOGRAMS ARE MAKING THEIR WAY INTO HOUSEHOLDS. THE MILITARY HAVE INVESTED A SMALL FORTUNE INTO HOLOGRAPHIC RESEARCH.
THE FUTURE PROMISES TO FORGE INTO HOLOGRAPHIC TERRITORY WE ONCE THOUGHT IMPOSSIBLE.
IMAGINE A DAY IN THE NEAR FUTURE WHEN WE CAN PROJECT HOLOGRAMS VIA SATELLITE.
HOW ABOUT A GAME OF CHESS PLAYED WITH A FRIEND WHO HAPPENS TO BE ABOARD THE INTERNATIONAL SPACE STATION?
AS OF NOW, WE'RE ABLE TO MANIPULATE THE LIGHT OUTPUT, BUT IT'S MAINLY AN OPTICAL ILLUSION.
I BELIEVE THERE'S A SCIENTIST ALIVE TODAY, WHO WILL BE RESPONSIBLE FOR MASTERING THE TANGIBILITY OF A LASER BEAM.
WHO KNOWS? HE OR SHE MAY BE IN THIS VERY ROOM AS WE SPEAK.

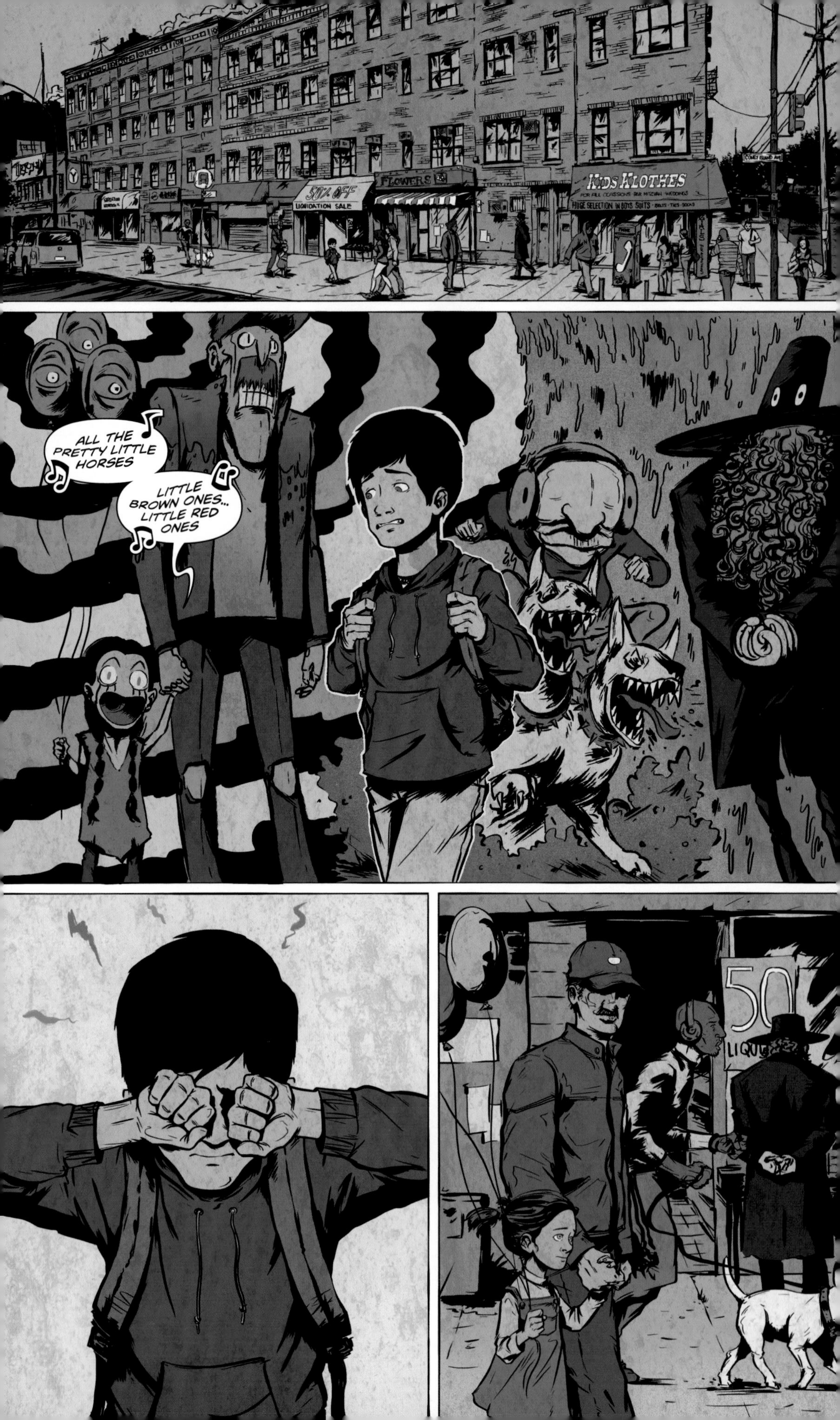
50% OFF
LIQUIDATION SALE
FLOWERS
KIDS KLOTHES
HUGE SELECTION IN BOYS SUITS
ALL THE PRETTY LITTLE HORSES
LITTLE BROWN ONES... LITTLE RED ONES

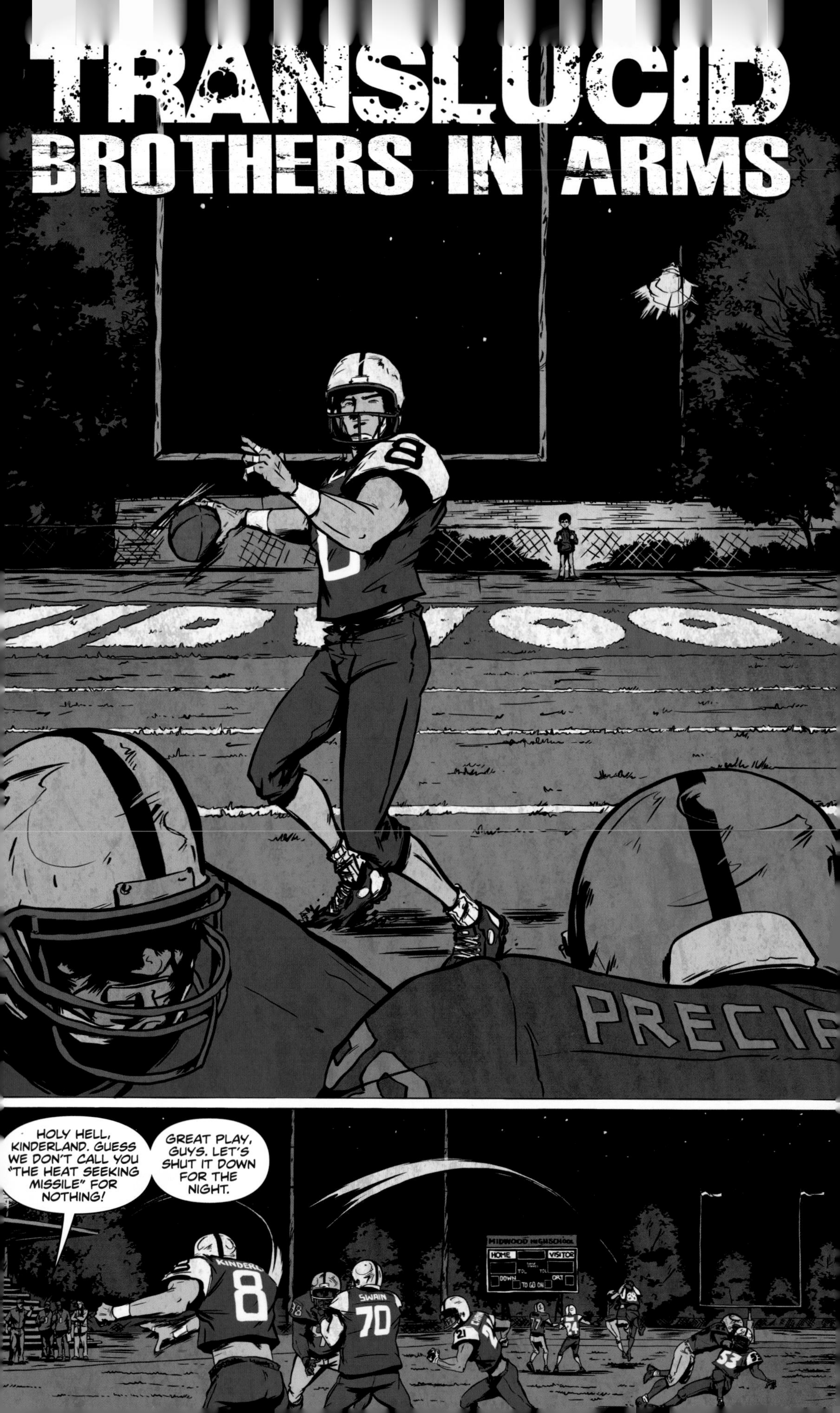
TRANSLUCID
BROTHERS IN ARMS
HOLY HELL, KINDERLAND. GUESS WE DON'T CALL YOU "THE HEAT SEEKING MISSILE" FOR NOTHING!
GREAT PLAY, GUYS. LET'S SHUT IT DOWN FOR THE NIGHT.
MIDWOOD HIGHSCHOOL
HOME
VISITOR
DOWN
TO GO ON
8
SWAIN
70

HEY, YOU! YOU SEE ALL THE RECRUITERS HERE TONIGHT?

HOW COULD I MISS THEM?! IT MUST BE EXCITING TO HAVE SO MANY PEOPLE HERE JUST TO WATCH YOU.

EXCITING...AND EQUAL PARTS TERRIFYING.

HEY LISTEN, CORNELIUS, SORRY YOU GOT PUT IN THE MIDDLE OF OUR PARENTS' CRAP LAST NIGHT.

IT'S OK--

NO. IT'S NOT. I SHOULD HAVE BEEN THERE TO PROTECT YOU. IF I CAN JUST SCORE A FULL RIDE SOMEWHERE OUT OF STATE... WE WON'T HAVE TO RELY ON *THEM* ANYMORE.

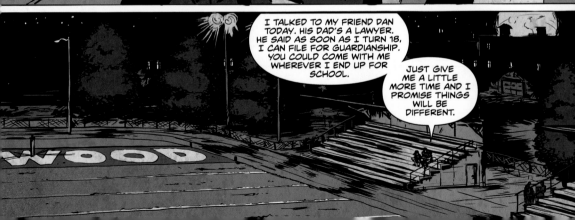

I TALKED TO MY FRIEND DAN TODAY. HIS DAD'S A LAWYER. HE SAID AS SOON AS I TURN 18, I CAN FILE FOR GUARDIANSHIP. YOU COULD COME WITH ME WHEREVER I END UP FOR SCHOOL.

JUST GIVE ME A LITTLE MORE TIME AND I PROMISE THINGS WILL BE DIFFERENT.

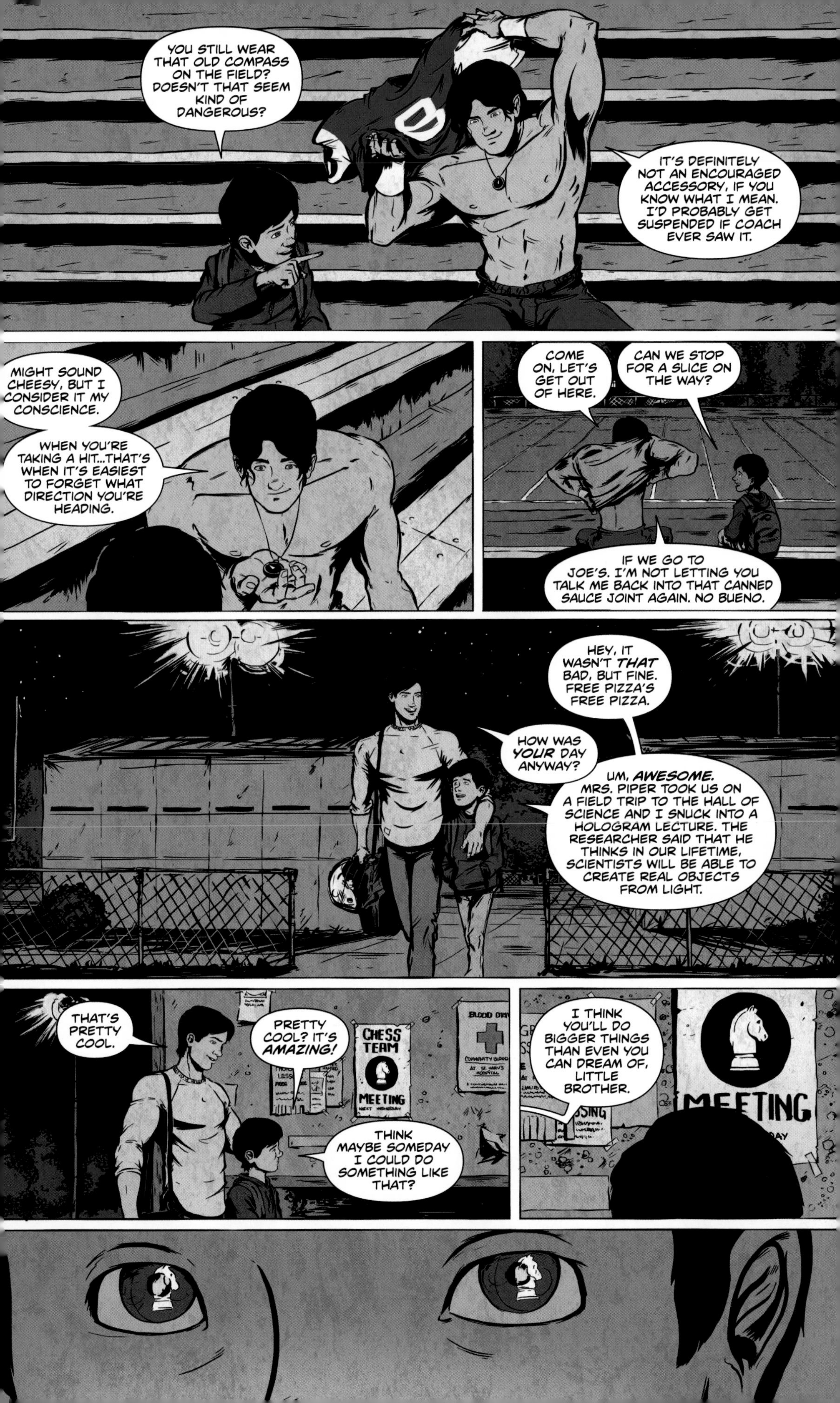
YOU STILL WEAR THAT OLD COMPASS ON THE FIELD? DOESN'T THAT SEEM KIND OF DANGEROUS?
IT'S DEFINITELY NOT AN ENCOURAGED ACCESSORY, IF YOU KNOW WHAT I MEAN. I'D PROBABLY GET SUSPENDED IF COACH EVER SAW IT.
MIGHT SOUND CHEESY, BUT I CONSIDER IT MY CONSCIENCE.
WHEN YOU'RE TAKING A HIT...THAT'S WHEN IT'S EASIEST TO FORGET WHAT DIRECTION YOU'RE HEADING.
COME ON, LET'S GET OUT OF HERE.
CAN WE STOP FOR A SLICE ON THE WAY?
IF WE GO TO JOE'S. I'M NOT LETTING YOU TALK ME BACK INTO THAT CANNED SAUCE JOINT AGAIN. NO BUENO.
HEY, IT WASN'T *THAT* BAD, BUT FINE. FREE PIZZA'S FREE PIZZA.
HOW WAS *YOUR* DAY ANYWAY?
UM, ***AWESOME.*** MRS. PIPER TOOK US ON A FIELD TRIP TO THE HALL OF SCIENCE AND I SNUCK INTO A HOLOGRAM LECTURE. THE RESEARCHER SAID THAT HE THINKS IN OUR LIFETIME, SCIENTISTS WILL BE ABLE TO CREATE REAL OBJECTS FROM LIGHT.
THAT'S PRETTY COOL.
PRETTY COOL? IT'S *AMAZING!*
CHESS TEAM
MEETING
BLOOD DRIVE
THINK MAYBE SOMEDAY I COULD DO SOMETHING LIKE THAT?
I THINK YOU'LL DO BIGGER THINGS THAN EVEN YOU CAN DREAM OF, LITTLE BROTHER.
MEETING

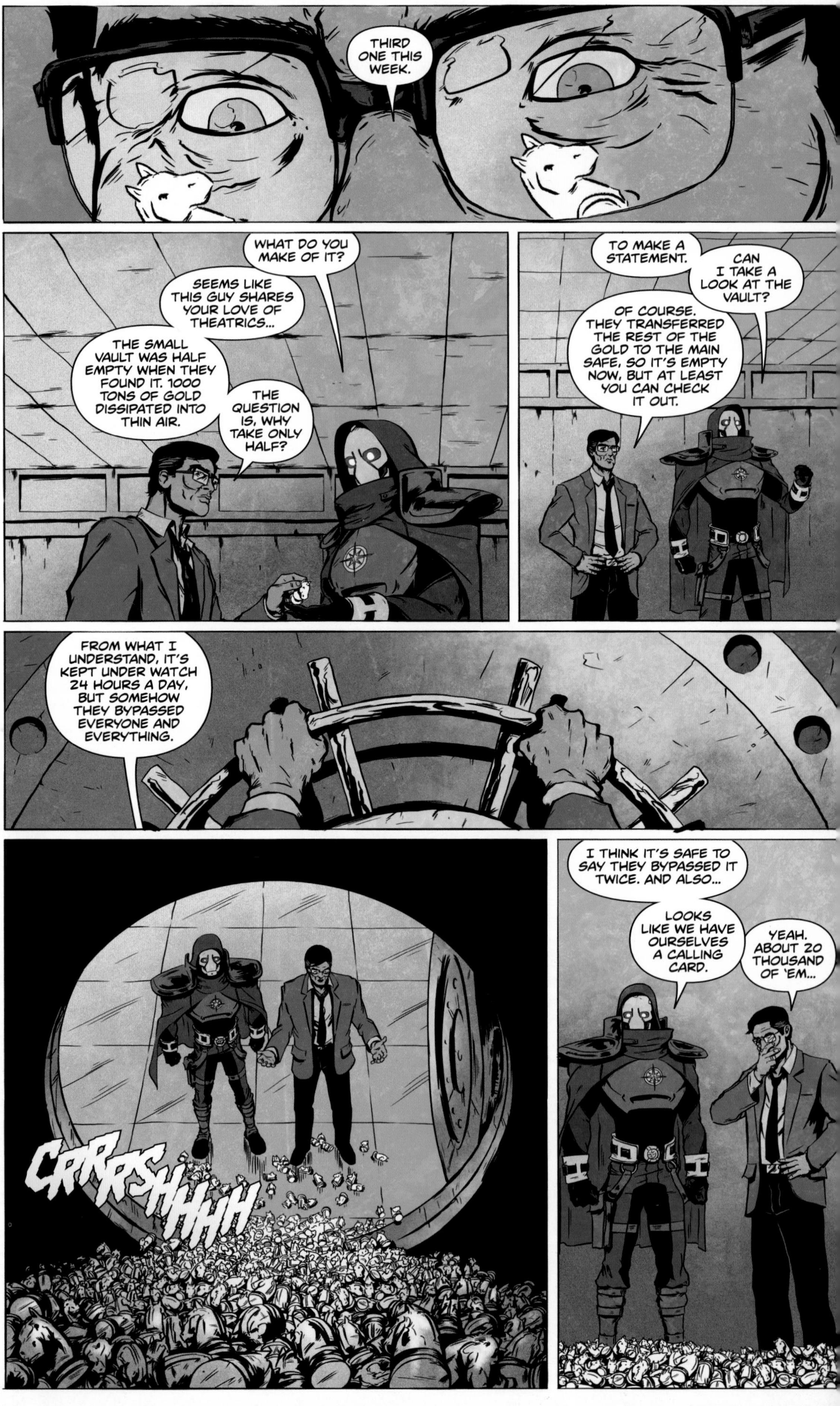
THIRD ONE THIS WEEK.
WHAT DO YOU MAKE OF IT?
SEEMS LIKE THIS GUY SHARES YOUR LOVE OF THEATRICS...
THE SMALL VAULT WAS HALF EMPTY WHEN THEY FOUND IT. 1000 TONS OF GOLD DISSIPATED INTO THIN AIR.
THE QUESTION IS, WHY TAKE ONLY HALF?
TO MAKE A STATEMENT.
CAN I TAKE A LOOK AT THE VAULT?
OF COURSE. THEY TRANSFERRED THE REST OF THE GOLD TO THE MAIN SAFE, SO IT'S EMPTY NOW, BUT AT LEAST YOU CAN CHECK IT OUT.
FROM WHAT I UNDERSTAND, IT'S KEPT UNDER WATCH 24 HOURS A DAY, BUT SOMEHOW THEY BYPASSED EVERYONE AND EVERYTHING.
CRRRSHHHHH
I THINK IT'S SAFE TO SAY THEY BYPASSED IT TWICE. AND ALSO...
LOOKS LIKE WE HAVE OURSELVES A CALLING CARD.
YEAH. ABOUT 20 THOUSAND OF 'EM...

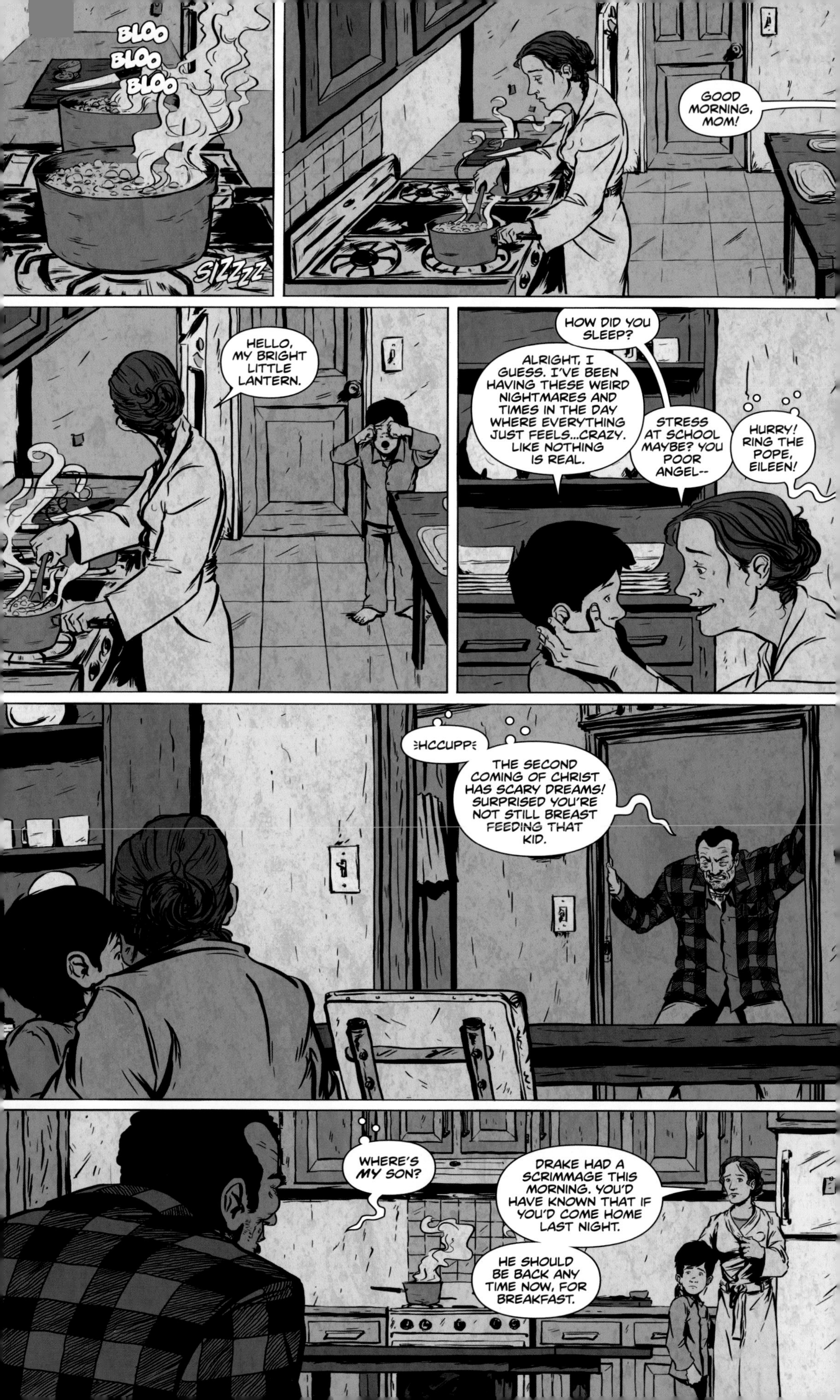

BLOO
BLOO
BLOO
SIZZZZ
GOOD MORNING, MOM!
HELLO, MY BRIGHT LITTLE LANTERN.
HOW DID YOU SLEEP?
ALRIGHT, I GUESS. I'VE BEEN HAVING THESE WEIRD NIGHTMARES AND TIMES IN THE DAY WHERE EVERYTHING JUST FEELS...CRAZY. LIKE NOTHING IS REAL.
STRESS AT SCHOOL MAYBE? YOU POOR ANGEL--
HURRY! RING THE POPE, EILEEN!
HCCUPP
THE SECOND COMING OF CHRIST HAS SCARY DREAMS! SURPRISED YOU'RE NOT STILL BREAST FEEDING THAT KID.
WHERE'S *MY* SON?
DRAKE HAD A SCRIMMAGE THIS MORNING. YOU'D HAVE KNOWN THAT IF YOU'D COME HOME LAST NIGHT.
HE SHOULD BE BACK ANY TIME NOW, FOR BREAKFAST.

WHY DON'T YOU SIT DOWN AND I'LL MAKE YOU A PLATE.

WHAT IS THIS?

I'VE TOLD YOU MORE THAN ONCE NOT TO SERVE ME PEASANT FOOD. LIKE WE'RE A BUNCH OF ANIMALS--

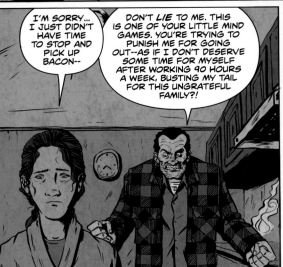

I'M SORRY... I JUST DIDN'T HAVE TIME TO STOP AND PICK UP BACON--

DON'T LIE TO ME. THIS IS ONE OF YOUR LITTLE MIND GAMES. YOU'RE TRYING TO PUNISH ME FOR GOING OUT--AS IF I DON'T DESERVE SOME TIME FOR MYSELF AFTER WORKING 90 HOURS A WEEK, BUSTING MY TAIL FOR THIS UNGRATEFUL FAMILY?!

MAYBE IF YOU SPENT LESS OF YOUR DAY FOCUSING ON THE LITTLE PRINCESS, I WOULDN'T HAVE TO GET SO ANGRY.

NOW I'VE LOST MY APPETITE!

MOM!

ONE SHOULD NEVER DOUBT THE IMPACT OF BEING DESENSITIZED TO UNCONDITIONAL FEAR AT AN EARLY AGE.

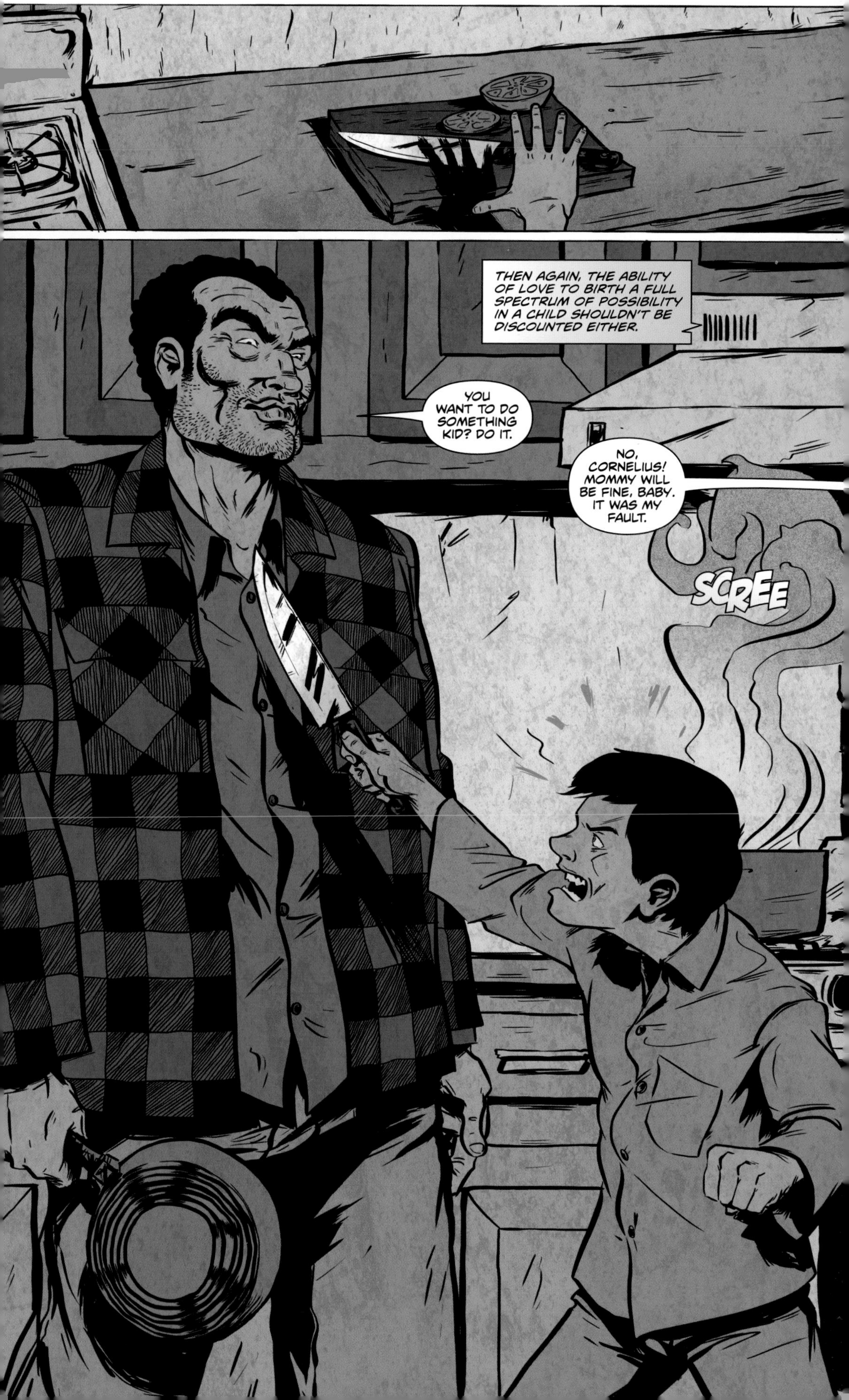
THEN AGAIN, THE ABILITY OF LOVE TO BIRTH A FULL SPECTRUM OF POSSIBILITY IN A CHILD SHOULDN'T BE DISCOUNTED EITHER.
YOU WANT TO DO SOMETHING KID? DO IT.
NO, CORNELIUS! MOMMY WILL BE FINE, BABY. IT WAS MY FAULT.
SCREE

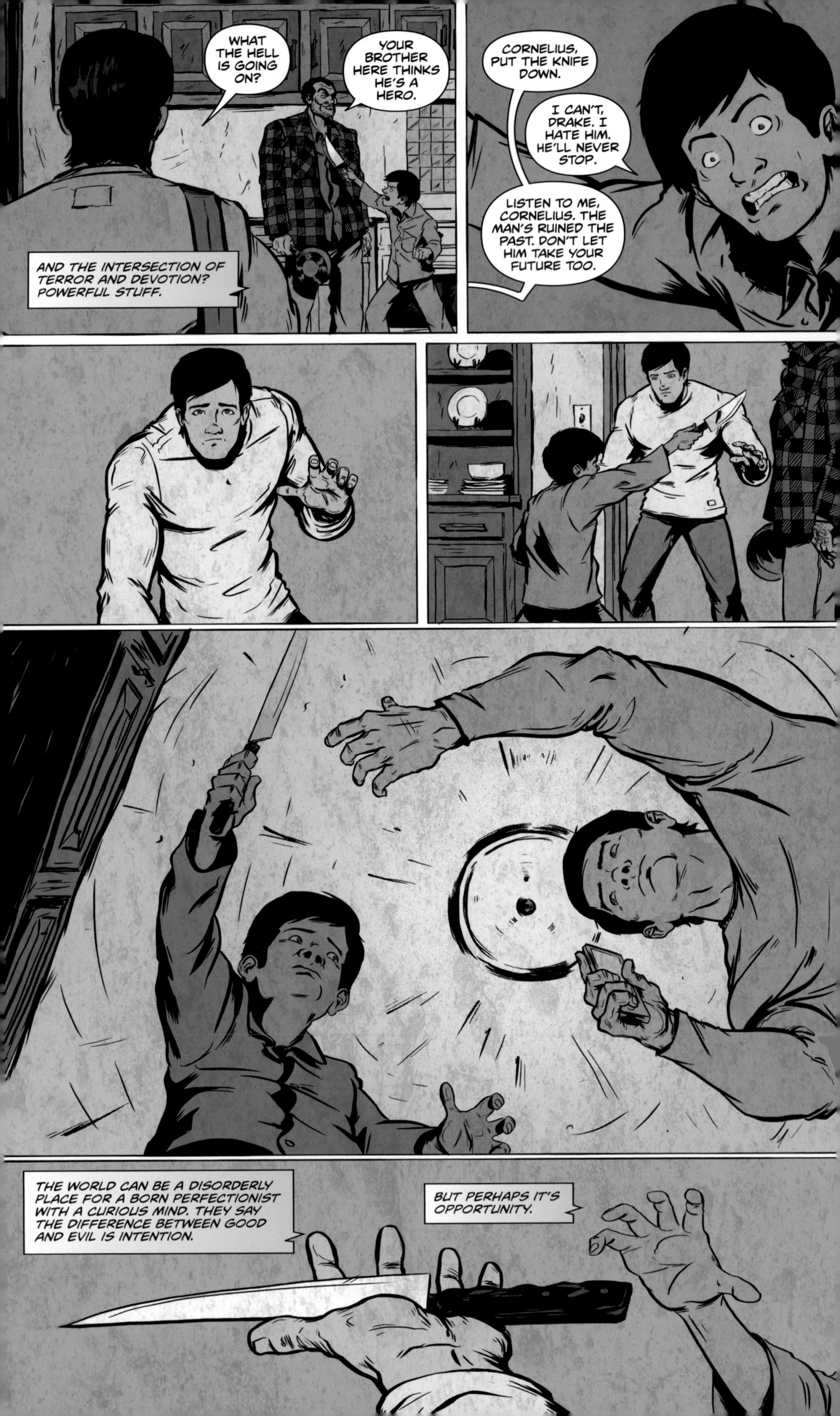

WHAT THE HELL IS GOING ON?
YOUR BROTHER HERE THINKS HE'S A HERO.
AND THE INTERSECTION OF TERROR AND DEVOTION? POWERFUL STUFF.
CORNELIUS, PUT THE KNIFE DOWN.
I CAN'T, DRAKE. I HATE HIM. HE'LL NEVER STOP.
LISTEN TO ME, CORNELIUS. THE MAN'S RUINED THE PAST. DON'T LET HIM TAKE YOUR FUTURE TOO.
THE WORLD CAN BE A DISORDERLY PLACE FOR A BORN PERFECTIONIST WITH A CURIOUS MIND. THEY SAY THE DIFFERENCE BETWEEN GOOD AND EVIL IS INTENTION.
BUT PERHAPS IT'S OPPORTUNITY.

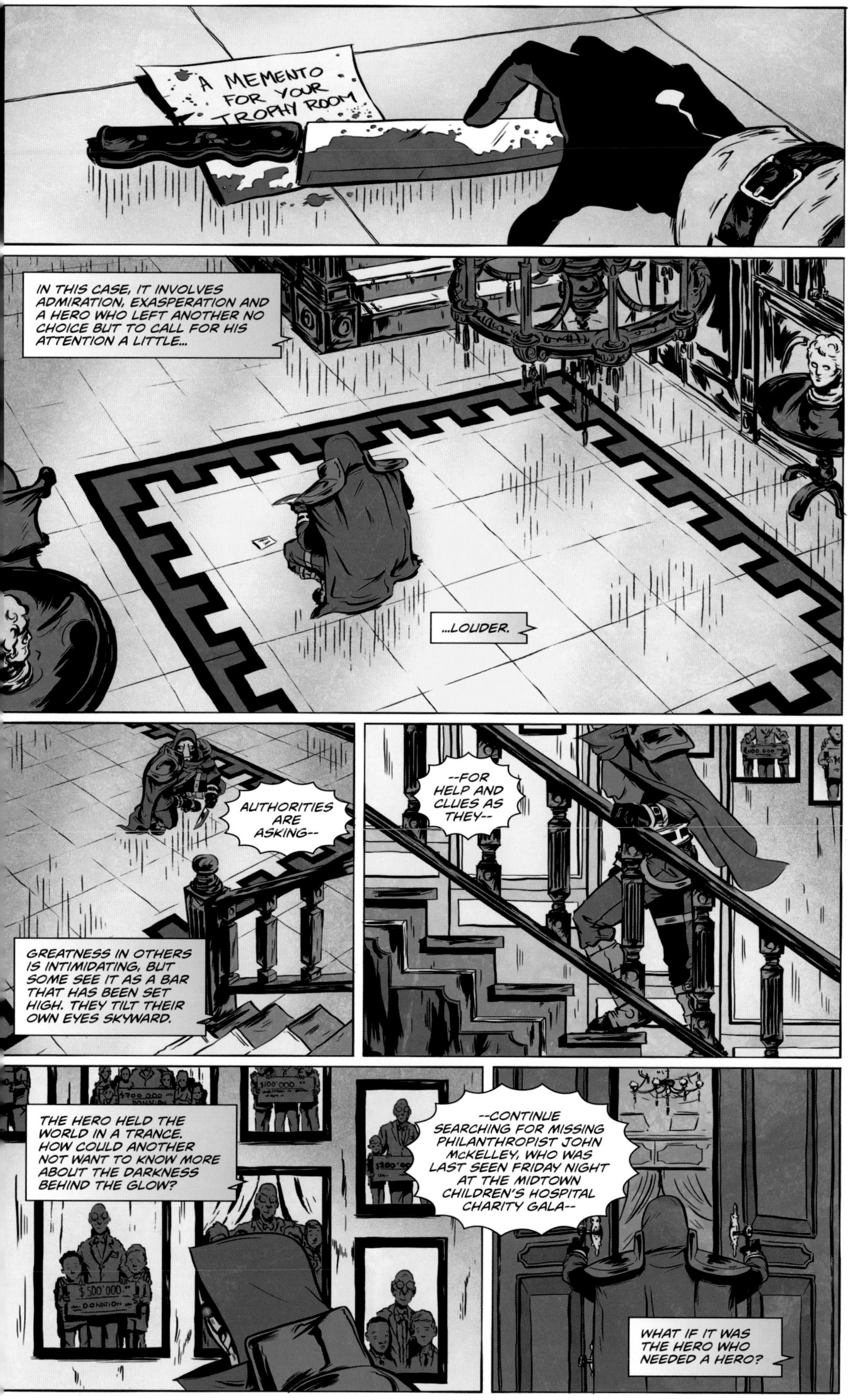
A MEMENTO FOR YOUR TROPHY ROOM
IN THIS CASE, IT INVOLVES ADMIRATION, EXASPERATION AND A HERO WHO LEFT ANOTHER NO CHOICE BUT TO CALL FOR HIS ATTENTION A LITTLE...
...LOUDER.
AUTHORITIES ARE ASKING--
GREATNESS IN OTHERS IS INTIMIDATING, BUT SOME SEE IT AS A BAR THAT HAS BEEN SET HIGH. THEY TILT THEIR OWN EYES SKYWARD.
--FOR HELP AND CLUES AS THEY--
THE HERO HELD THE WORLD IN A TRANCE. HOW COULD ANOTHER NOT WANT TO KNOW MORE ABOUT THE DARKNESS BEHIND THE GLOW?
--CONTINUE SEARCHING FOR MISSING PHILANTHROPIST JOHN McKELLEY, WHO WAS LAST SEEN FRIDAY NIGHT AT THE MIDTOWN CHILDREN'S HOSPITAL CHARITY GALA--
WHAT IF IT WAS THE HERO WHO NEEDED A HERO?

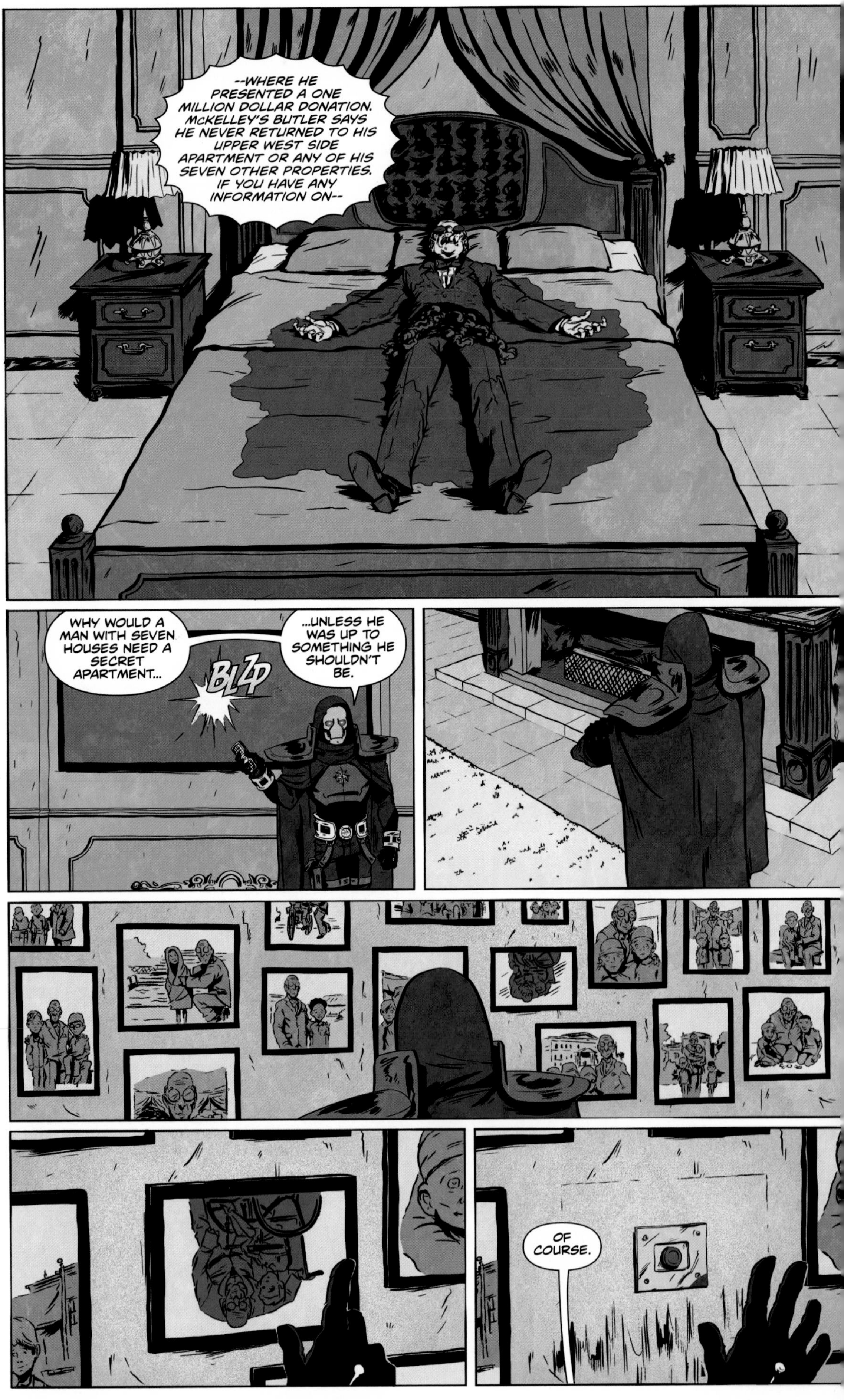
--WHERE HE PRESENTED A ONE MILLION DOLLAR DONATION. McKELLEY'S BUTLER SAYS HE NEVER RETURNED TO HIS UPPER WEST SIDE APARTMENT OR ANY OF HIS SEVEN OTHER PROPERTIES. IF YOU HAVE ANY INFORMATION ON--
WHY WOULD A MAN WITH SEVEN HOUSES NEED A SECRET APARTMENT...
BLZP
...UNLESS HE WAS UP TO SOMETHING HE SHOULDN'T BE.
OF COURSE.

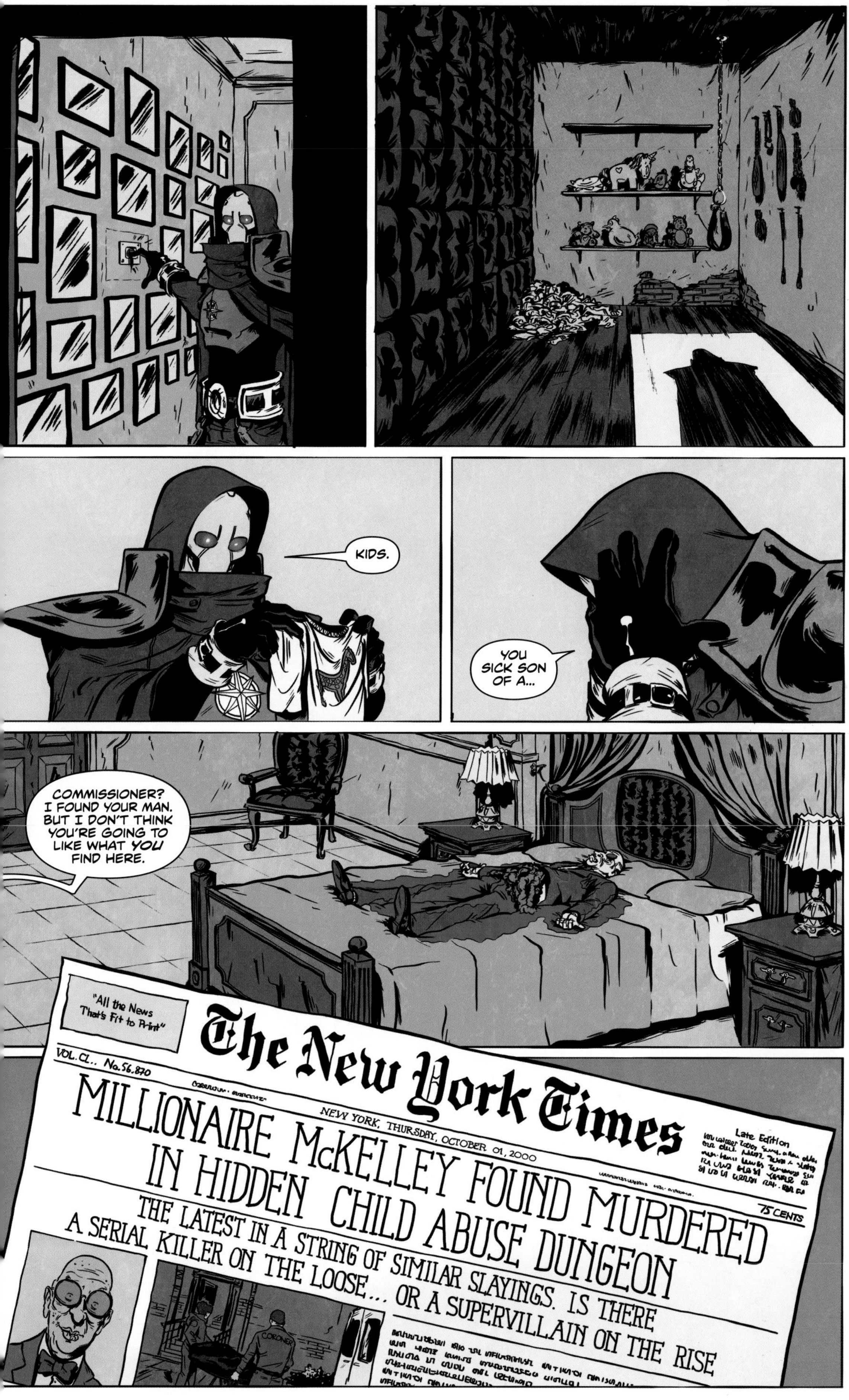
KIDS.
YOU SICK SON OF A...
COMMISSIONER? I FOUND YOUR MAN. BUT I DON'T THINK YOU'RE GOING TO LIKE WHAT YOU FIND HERE.
"All the News That's Fit to Print"
The New York Times
VOL. CL.. No. 56.870
NEW YORK, THURSDAY, OCTOBER 01, 2000
Late Edition
75 CENTS
MILLIONAIRE McKELLEY FOUND MURDERED IN HIDDEN CHILD ABUSE DUNGEON
THE LATEST IN A STRING OF SIMILAR SLAYINGS. IS THERE A SERIAL KILLER ON THE LOOSE... OR A SUPERVILLAIN ON THE RISE
CORONER

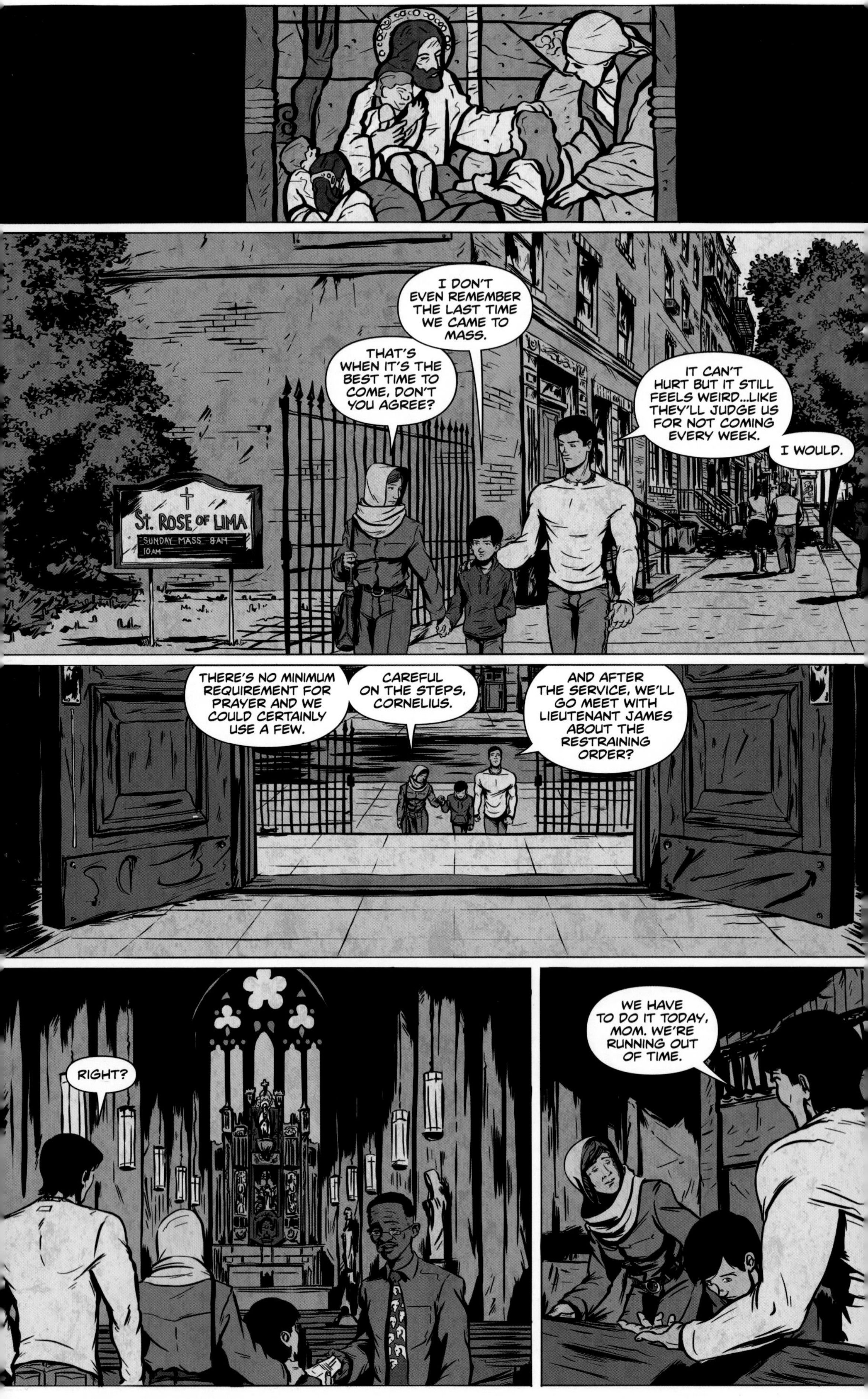
I DON'T EVEN REMEMBER THE LAST TIME WE CAME TO MASS.
THAT'S WHEN IT'S THE BEST TIME TO COME, DON'T YOU AGREE?
IT CAN'T HURT BUT IT STILL FEELS WEIRD...LIKE THEY'LL JUDGE US FOR NOT COMING EVERY WEEK.
I WOULD.
St. ROSE OF LIMA
SUNDAY MASS 8AM 10AM
THERE'S NO MINIMUM REQUIREMENT FOR PRAYER AND WE COULD CERTAINLY USE A FEW.
CAREFUL ON THE STEPS, CORNELIUS.
AND AFTER THE SERVICE, WE'LL GO MEET WITH LIEUTENANT JAMES ABOUT THE RESTRAINING ORDER?
RIGHT?
WE HAVE TO DO IT TODAY, MOM. WE'RE RUNNING OUT OF TIME.

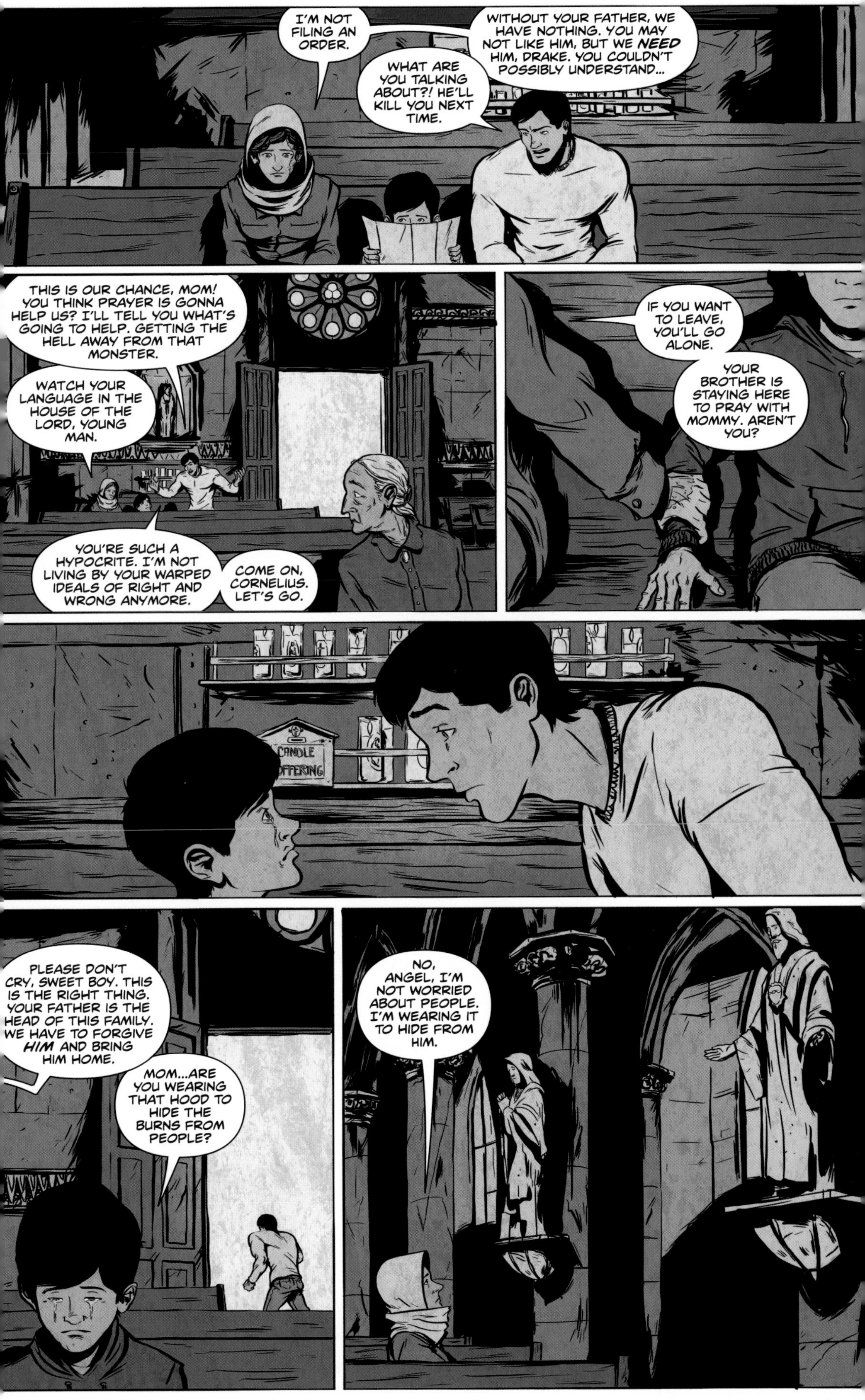

I'M NOT FILING AN ORDER.
WITHOUT YOUR FATHER, WE HAVE NOTHING. YOU MAY NOT LIKE HIM, BUT WE NEED HIM, DRAKE. YOU COULDN'T POSSIBLY UNDERSTAND...
WHAT ARE YOU TALKING ABOUT?! HE'LL KILL YOU NEXT TIME.
THIS IS OUR CHANCE, MOM! YOU THINK PRAYER IS GONNA HELP US? I'LL TELL YOU WHAT'S GOING TO HELP. GETTING THE HELL AWAY FROM THAT MONSTER.
WATCH YOUR LANGUAGE IN THE HOUSE OF THE LORD, YOUNG MAN.
YOU'RE SUCH A HYPOCRITE. I'M NOT LIVING BY YOUR WARPED IDEALS OF RIGHT AND WRONG ANYMORE.
COME ON, CORNELIUS. LET'S GO.
IF YOU WANT TO LEAVE, YOU'LL GO ALONE.
YOUR BROTHER IS STAYING HERE TO PRAY WITH MOMMY. AREN'T YOU?
CANDLE OFFERING
PLEASE DON'T CRY, SWEET BOY. THIS IS THE RIGHT THING. YOUR FATHER IS THE HEAD OF THIS FAMILY. WE HAVE TO FORGIVE HIM AND BRING HIM HOME.
MOM...ARE YOU WEARING THAT HOOD TO HIDE THE BURNS FROM PEOPLE?
NO, ANGEL, I'M NOT WORRIED ABOUT PEOPLE. I'M WEARING IT TO HIDE FROM HIM.

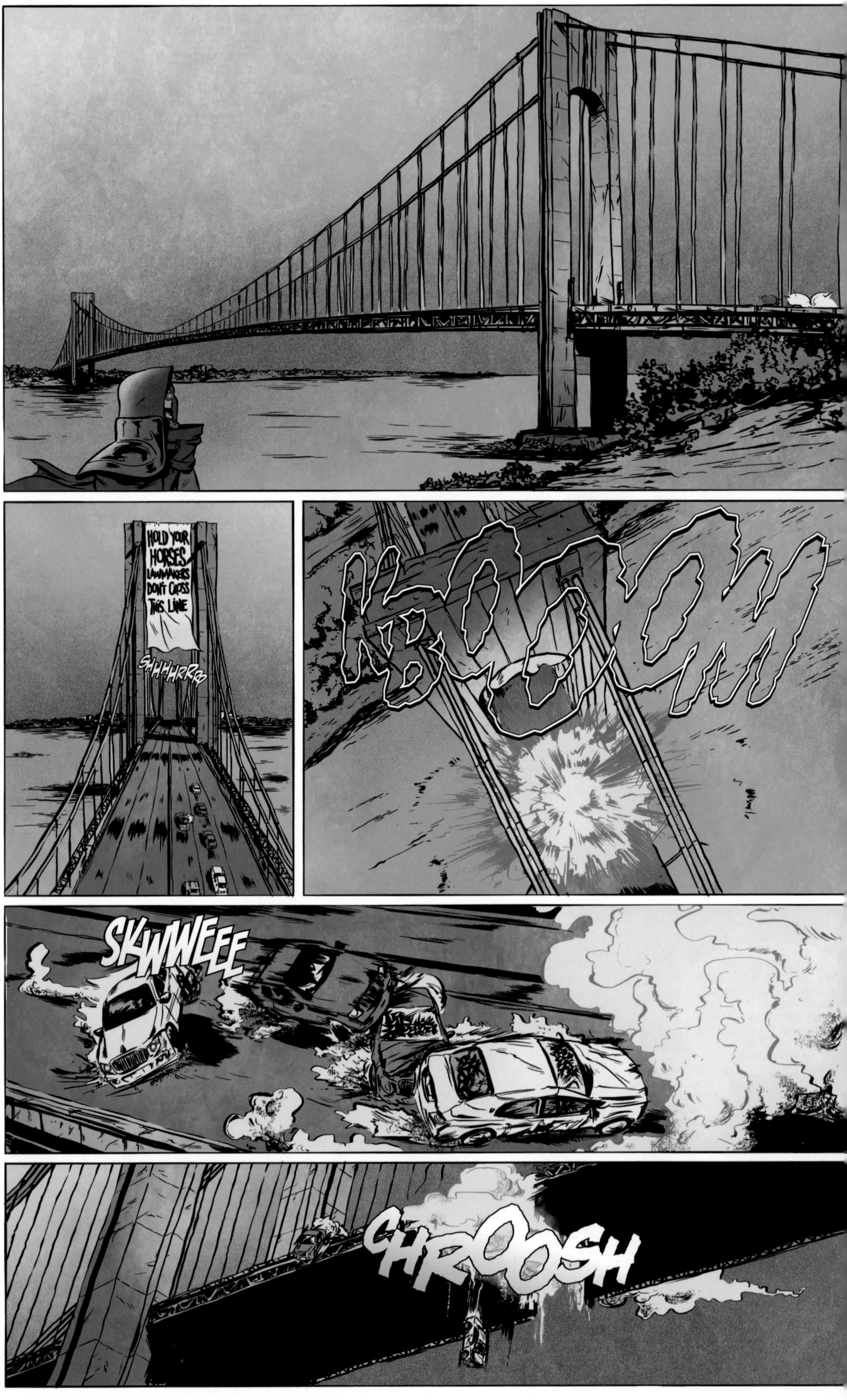
HOLD YOUR HORSES LAWMAKERS DON'T CROSS THIS LINE
SHHHHRRRB
KABOOOM
SKWWEEE
CHROOSH

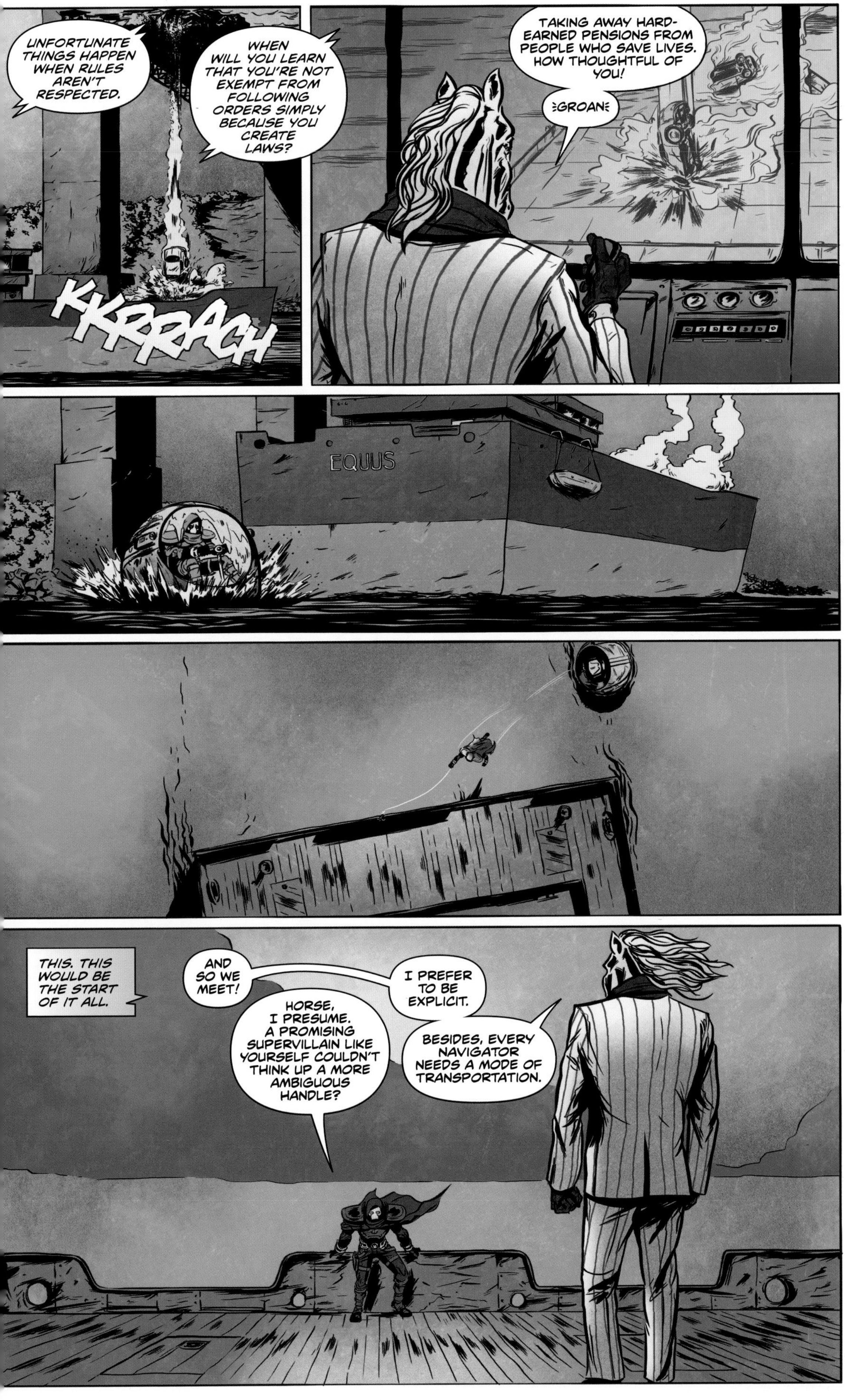
UNFORTUNATE THINGS HAPPEN WHEN RULES AREN'T RESPECTED.
WHEN WILL YOU LEARN THAT YOU'RE NOT EXEMPT FROM FOLLOWING ORDERS SIMPLY BECAUSE YOU CREATE LAWS?
KKRRACH
TAKING AWAY HARD-EARNED PENSIONS FROM PEOPLE WHO SAVE LIVES. HOW THOUGHTFUL OF YOU!
GROAN
EQUUS
THIS. THIS WOULD BE THE START OF IT ALL.
AND SO WE MEET!
HORSE, I PRESUME. A PROMISING SUPERVILLAIN LIKE YOURSELF COULDN'T THINK UP A MORE AMBIGUOUS HANDLE?
I PREFER TO BE EXPLICIT.
BESIDES, EVERY NAVIGATOR NEEDS A MODE OF TRANSPORTATION.

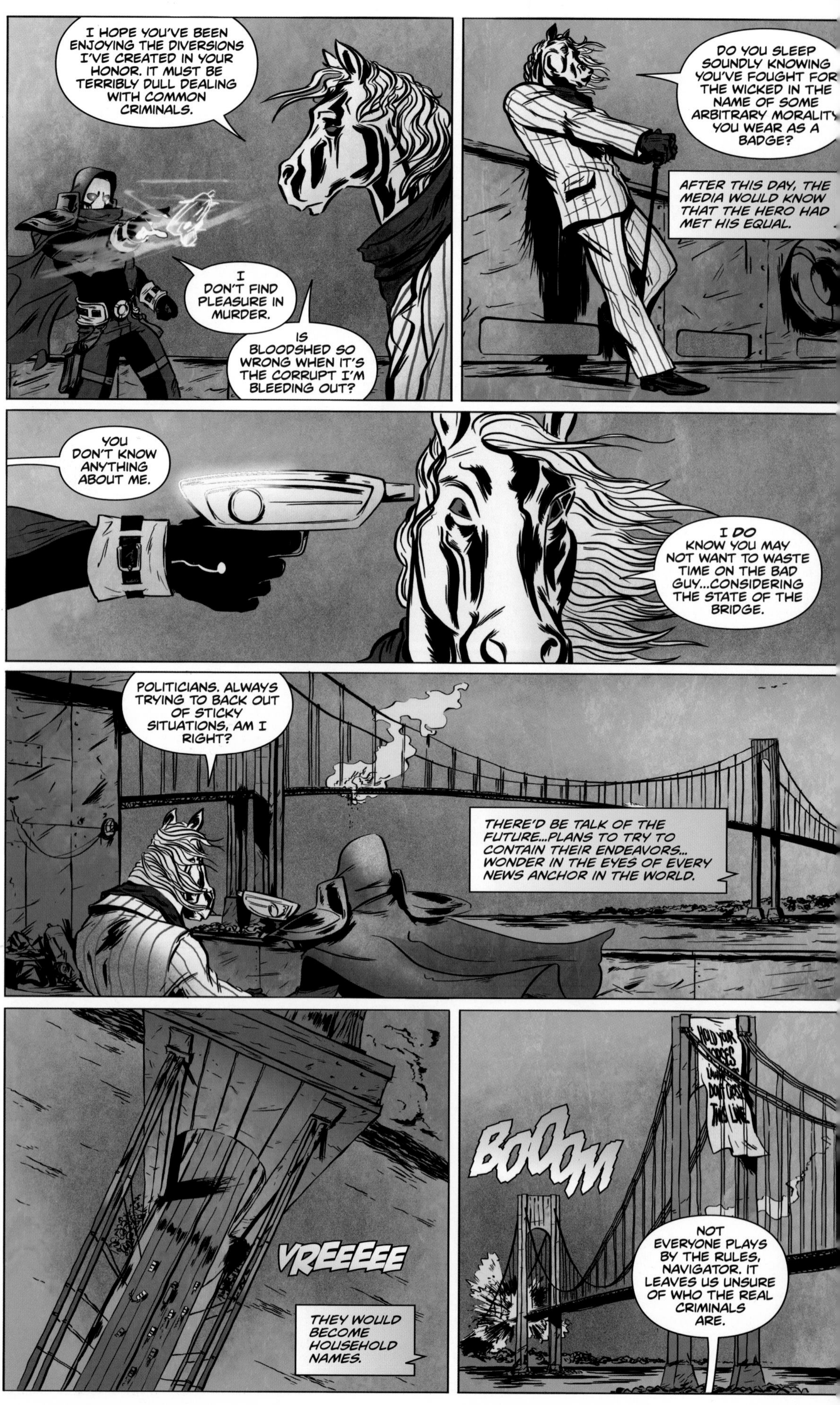
I HOPE YOU'VE BEEN ENJOYING THE DIVERSIONS I'VE CREATED IN YOUR HONOR. IT MUST BE TERRIBLY DULL DEALING WITH COMMON CRIMINALS.
I DON'T FIND PLEASURE IN MURDER.
IS BLOODSHED SO WRONG WHEN IT'S THE CORRUPT I'M BLEEDING OUT?
DO YOU SLEEP SOUNDLY KNOWING YOU'VE FOUGHT FOR THE WICKED IN THE NAME OF SOME ARBITRARY MORALITY YOU WEAR AS A BADGE?
AFTER THIS DAY, THE MEDIA WOULD KNOW THAT THE HERO HAD MET HIS EQUAL.
YOU DON'T KNOW ANYTHING ABOUT ME.
I DO KNOW YOU MAY NOT WANT TO WASTE TIME ON THE BAD GUY...CONSIDERING THE STATE OF THE BRIDGE.
POLITICIANS. ALWAYS TRYING TO BACK OUT OF STICKY SITUATIONS, AM I RIGHT?
THERE'D BE TALK OF THE FUTURE...PLANS TO TRY TO CONTAIN THEIR ENDEAVORS... WONDER IN THE EYES OF EVERY NEWS ANCHOR IN THE WORLD.
VREEEEEE
THEY WOULD BECOME HOUSEHOLD NAMES.
BOOOM
HOLD YOUR HORSES
NOT EVERYONE PLAYS BY THE RULES, NAVIGATOR. IT LEAVES US UNSURE OF WHO THE REAL CRIMINALS ARE.

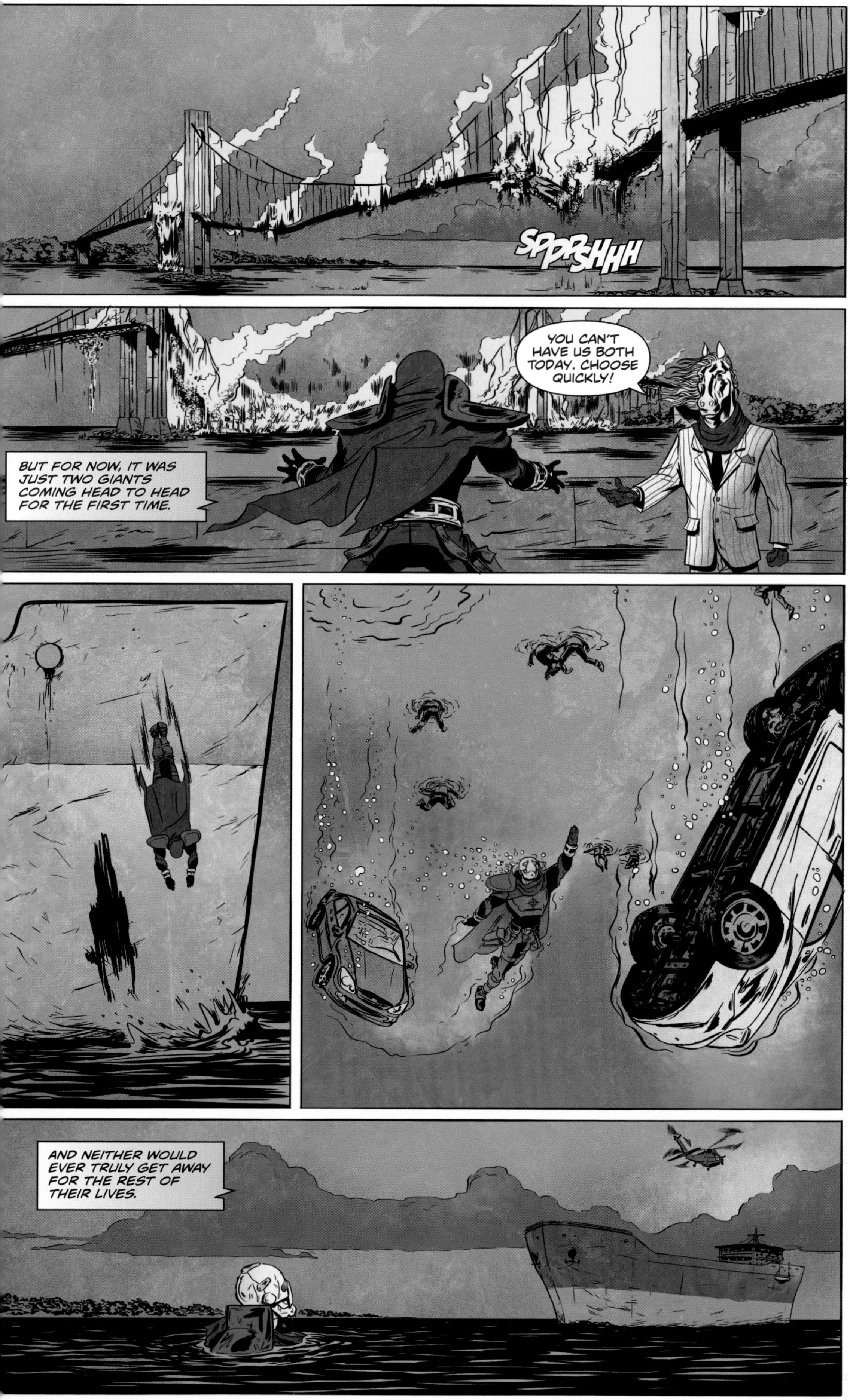
SPPPSHHH
YOU CAN'T HAVE US BOTH TODAY. CHOOSE QUICKLY!
BUT FOR NOW, IT WAS JUST TWO GIANTS COMING HEAD TO HEAD FOR THE FIRST TIME.
AND NEITHER WOULD EVER TRULY GET AWAY FOR THE REST OF THEIR LIVES.

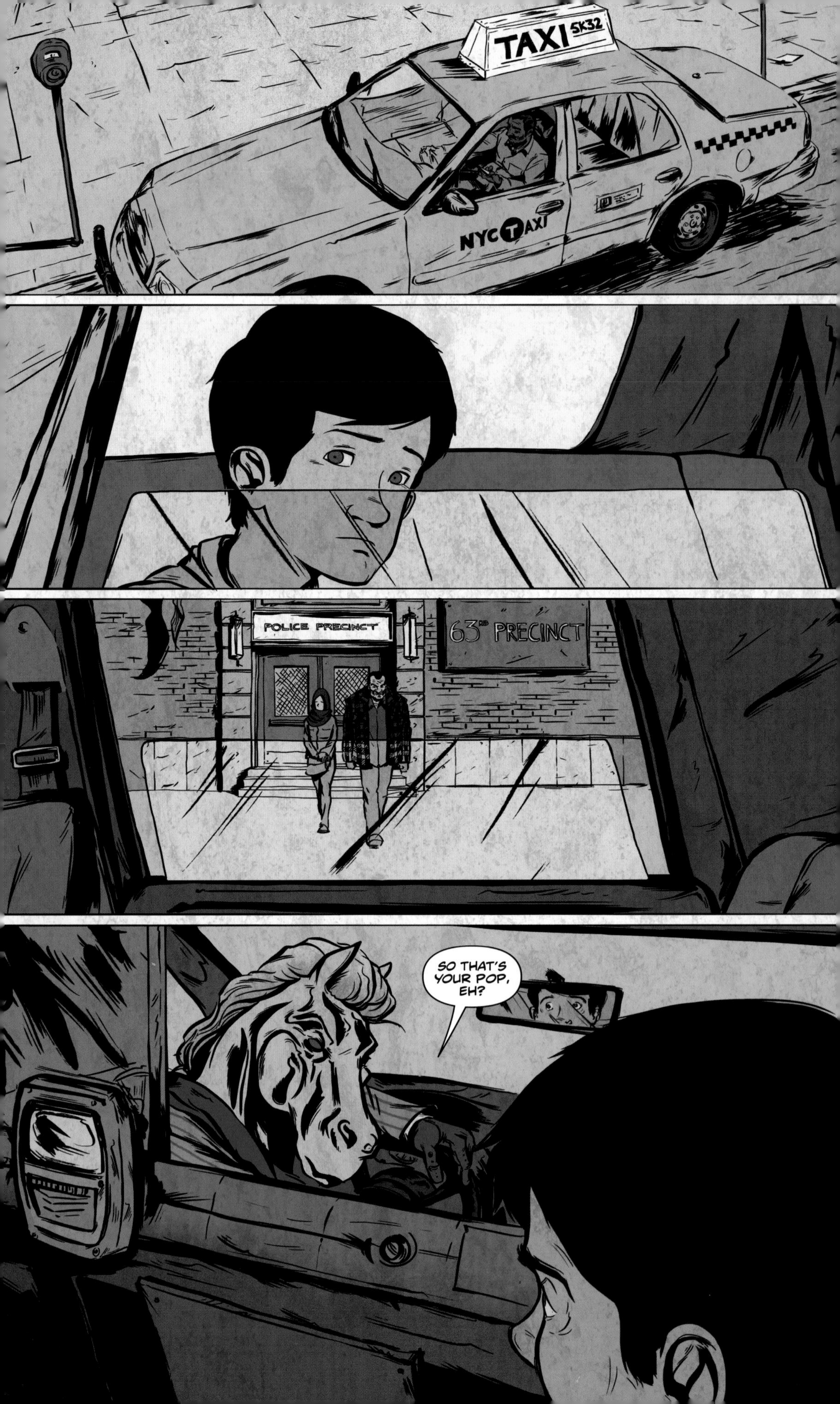

TAXI 5K32
NYC TAXI
POLICE PRECINCT
63RD PRECINCT
SO THAT'S YOUR POP, EH?

ISSUE TWO BOOM! STUDIOS EXCLUSIVE COVER BY **FELIPE SMITH**

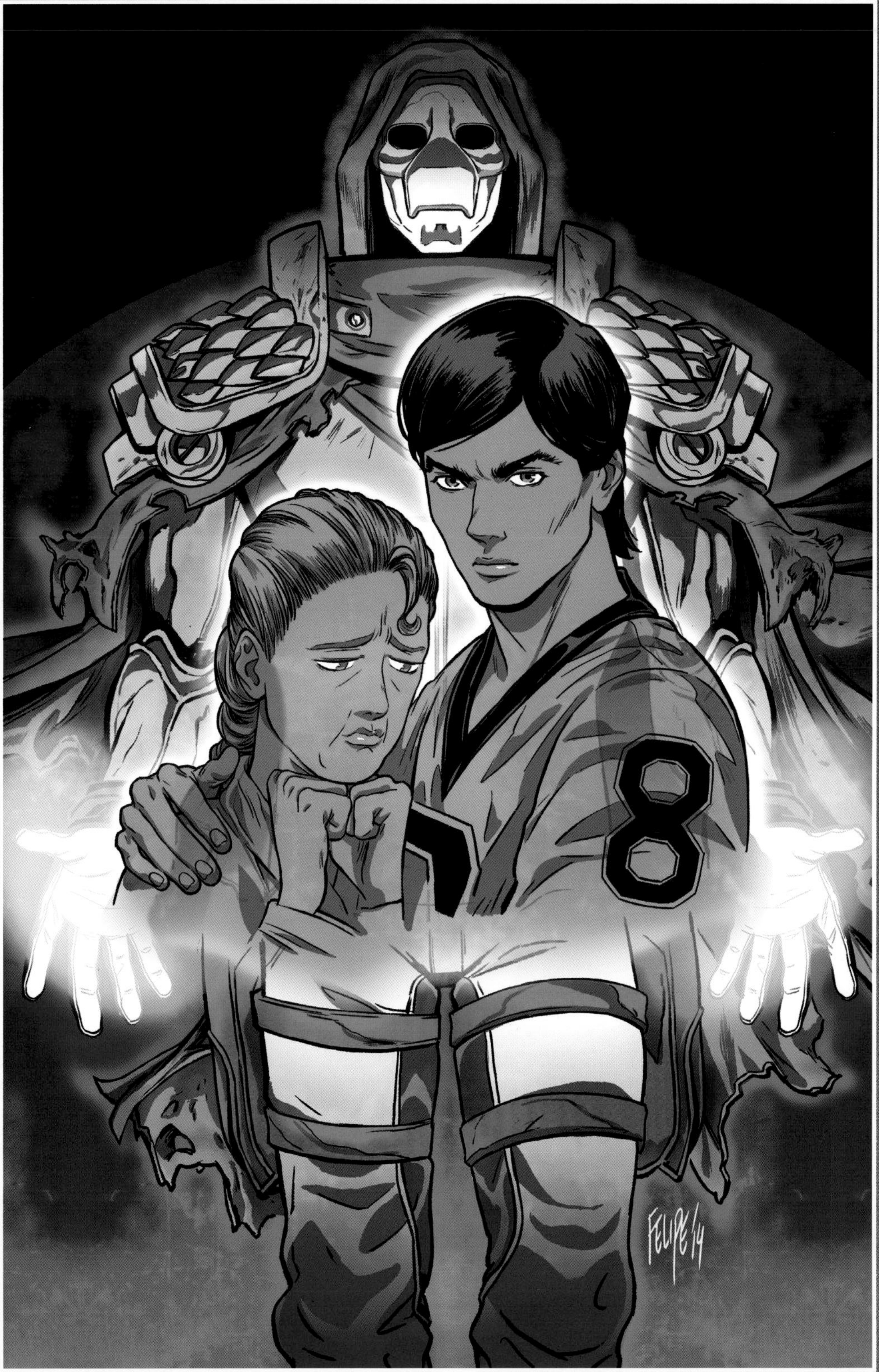

FELIPE '14

ISSUE THREE COVER BY **JEFF STOKELY**

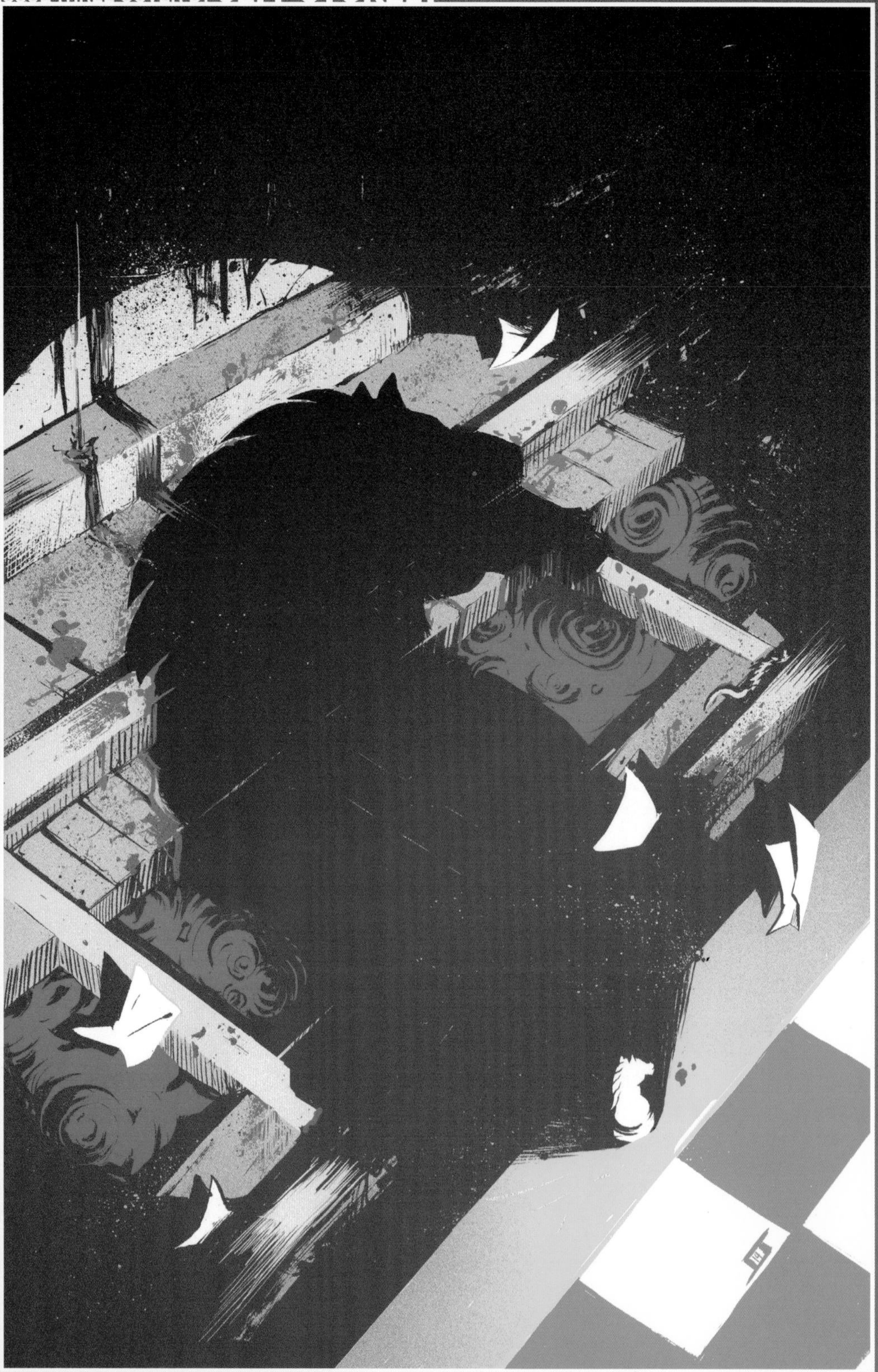

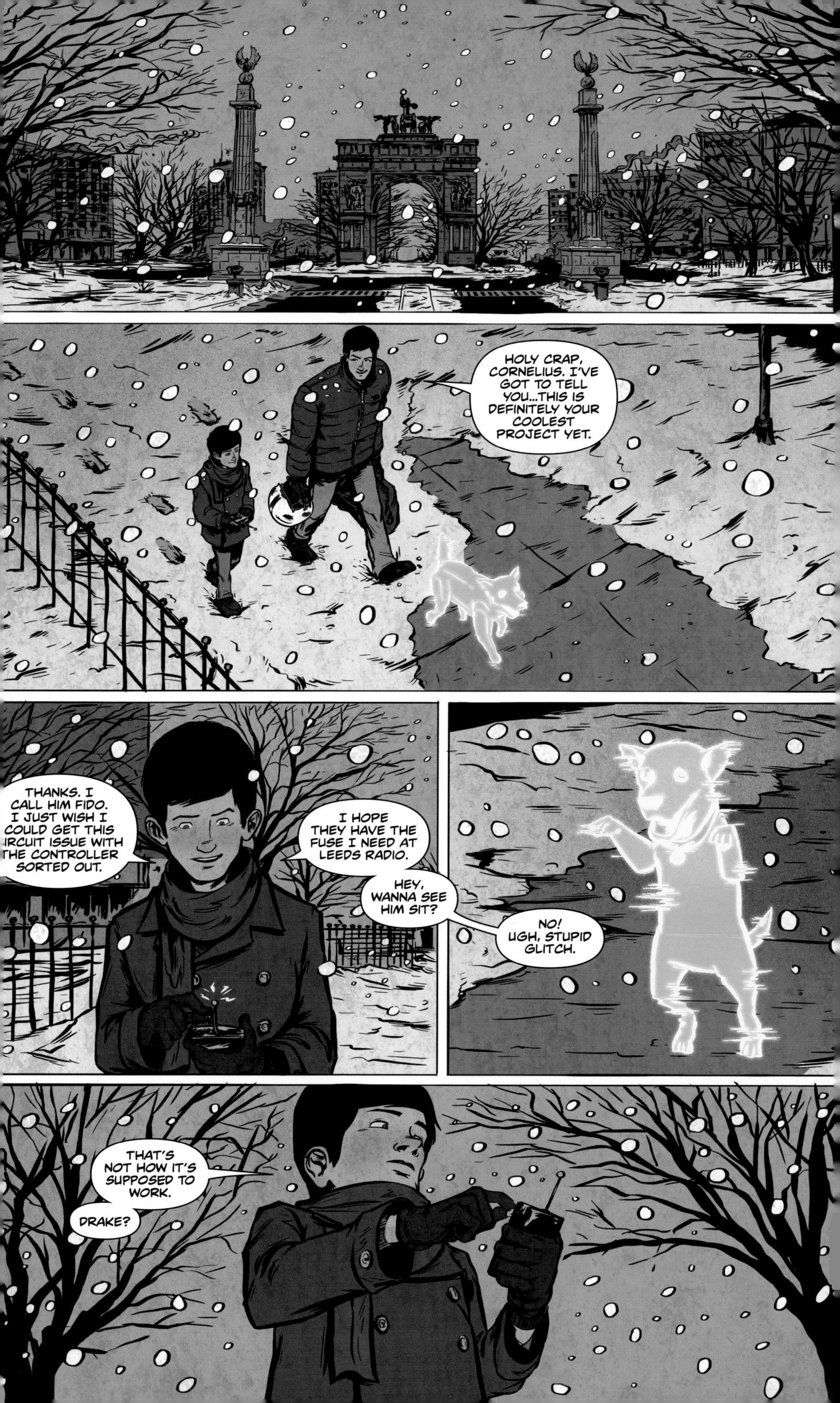
HOLY CRAP, CORNELIUS. I'VE GOT TO TELL YOU...THIS IS DEFINITELY YOUR COOLEST PROJECT YET.
THANKS. I CALL HIM FIDO. I JUST WISH I COULD GET THIS CIRCUIT ISSUE WITH THE CONTROLLER SORTED OUT.
I HOPE THEY HAVE THE FUSE I NEED AT LEEDS RADIO.
HEY, WANNA SEE HIM SIT?
NO! UGH, STUPID GLITCH.
THAT'S NOT HOW IT'S SUPPOSED TO WORK.
DRAKE?

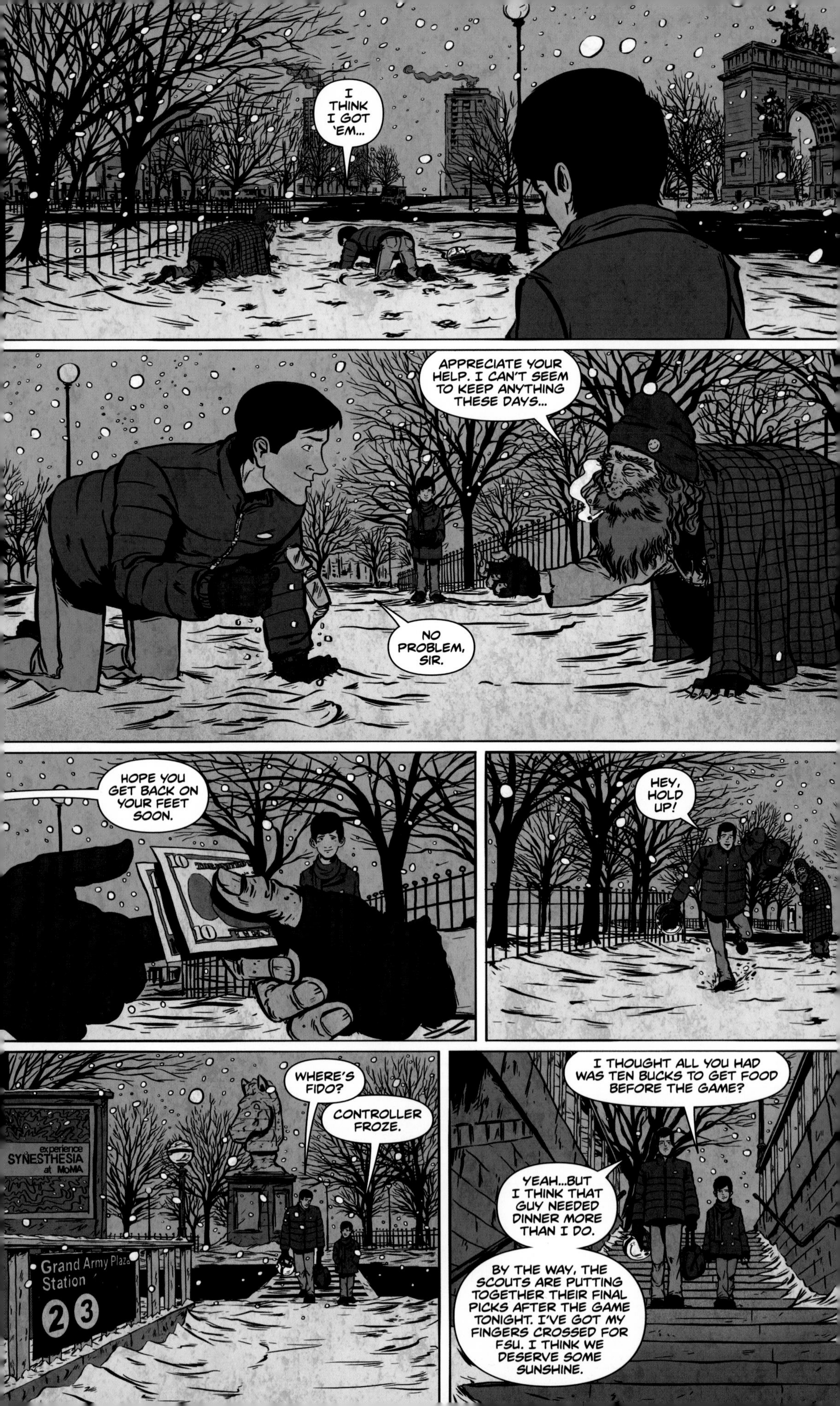
I THINK I GOT 'EM...
APPRECIATE YOUR HELP. I CAN'T SEEM TO KEEP ANYTHING THESE DAYS...
NO PROBLEM, SIR.
HOPE YOU GET BACK ON YOUR FEET SOON.
HEY, HOLD UP!
experience SYNESTHESIA at MoMA
Grand Army Plaza Station
2 3
WHERE'S FIDO?
CONTROLLER FROZE.
I THOUGHT ALL YOU HAD WAS TEN BUCKS TO GET FOOD BEFORE THE GAME?
YEAH...BUT I THINK THAT GUY NEEDED DINNER MORE THAN I DO.
BY THE WAY, THE SCOUTS ARE PUTTING TOGETHER THEIR FINAL PICKS AFTER THE GAME TONIGHT. I'VE GOT MY FINGERS CROSSED FOR FSU. I THINK WE DESERVE SOME SUNSHINE.

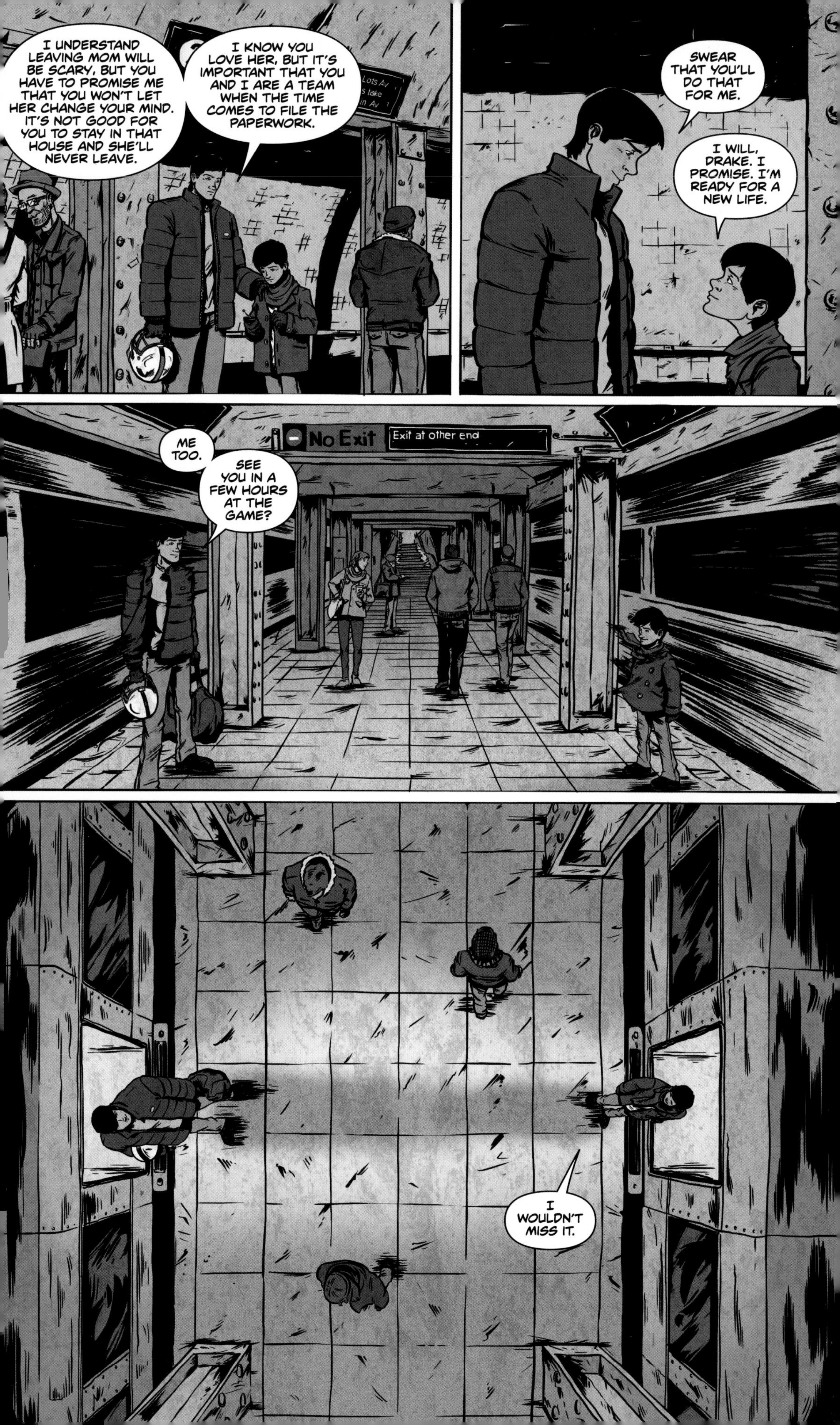
I UNDERSTAND LEAVING MOM WILL BE SCARY, BUT YOU HAVE TO PROMISE ME THAT YOU WON'T LET HER CHANGE YOUR MIND. IT'S NOT GOOD FOR YOU TO STAY IN THAT HOUSE AND SHE'LL NEVER LEAVE.
I KNOW YOU LOVE HER, BUT IT'S IMPORTANT THAT YOU AND I ARE A TEAM WHEN THE TIME COMES TO FILE THE PAPERWORK.
SWEAR THAT YOU'LL DO THAT FOR ME.
I WILL, DRAKE. I PROMISE. I'M READY FOR A NEW LIFE.
No Exit
Exit at other end
ME TOO.
SEE YOU IN A FEW HOURS AT THE GAME?
I WOULDN'T MISS IT.

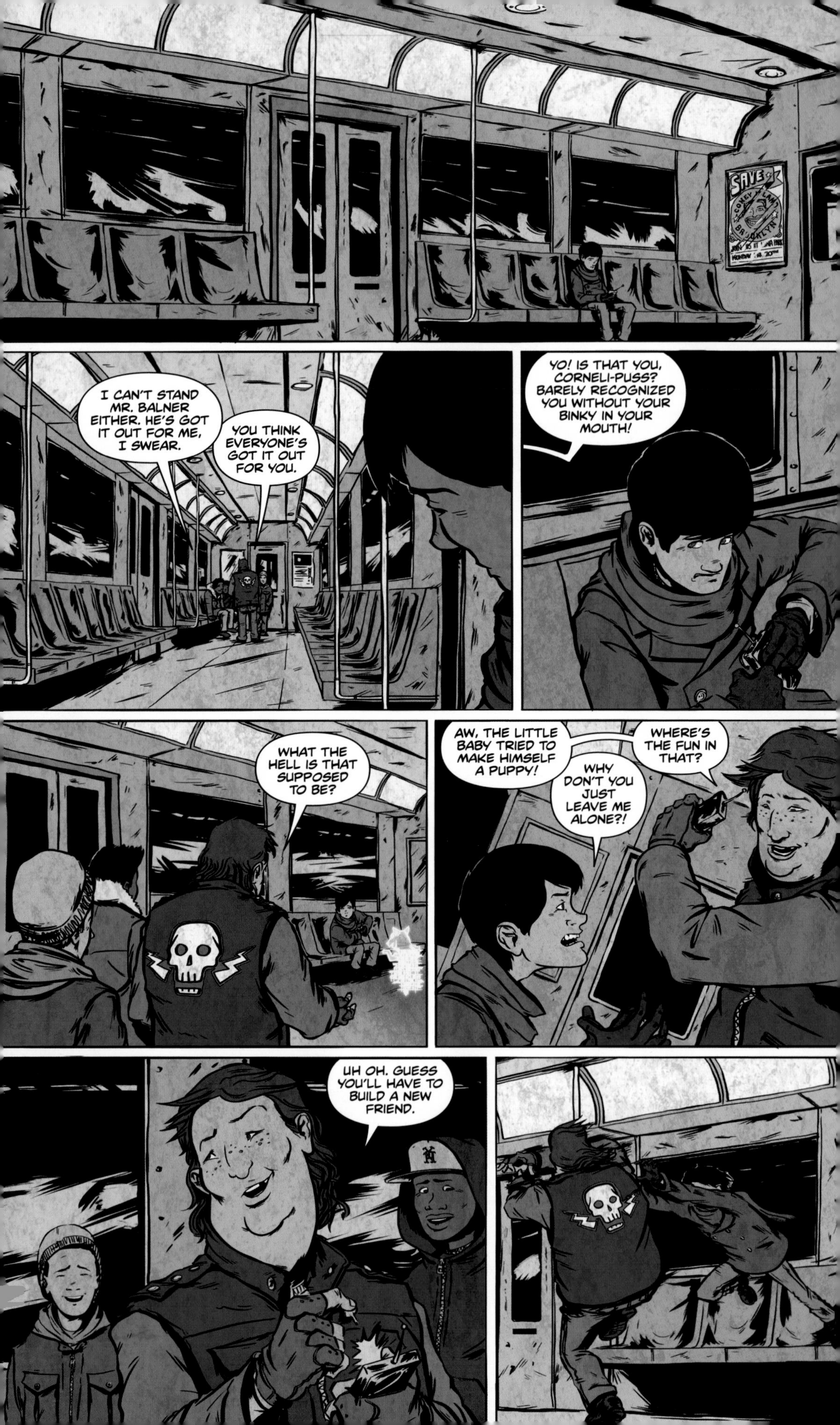
SAVE
I CAN'T STAND MR. BALNER EITHER. HE'S GOT IT OUT FOR ME, I SWEAR.
YOU THINK EVERYONE'S GOT IT OUT FOR YOU.
YO! IS THAT YOU, CORNELI-PUSS? BARELY RECOGNIZED YOU WITHOUT YOUR BINKY IN YOUR MOUTH!
WHAT THE HELL IS THAT SUPPOSED TO BE?
AW, THE LITTLE BABY TRIED TO MAKE HIMSELF A PUPPY!
WHY DON'T YOU JUST LEAVE ME ALONE?!
WHERE'S THE FUN IN THAT?
UH OH. GUESS YOU'LL HAVE TO BUILD A NEW FRIEND.

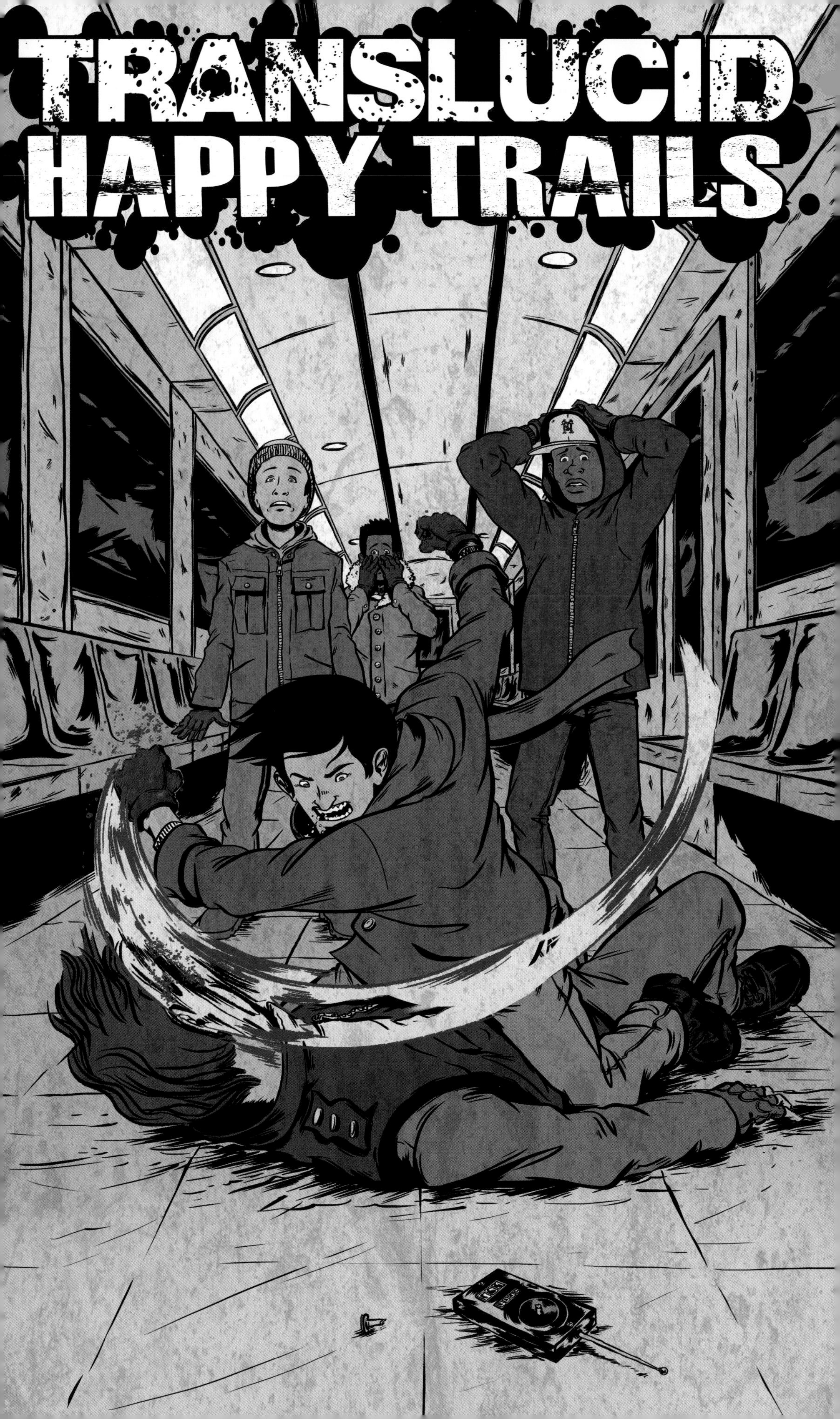
TRANSLUCID
HAPPY TRAILS

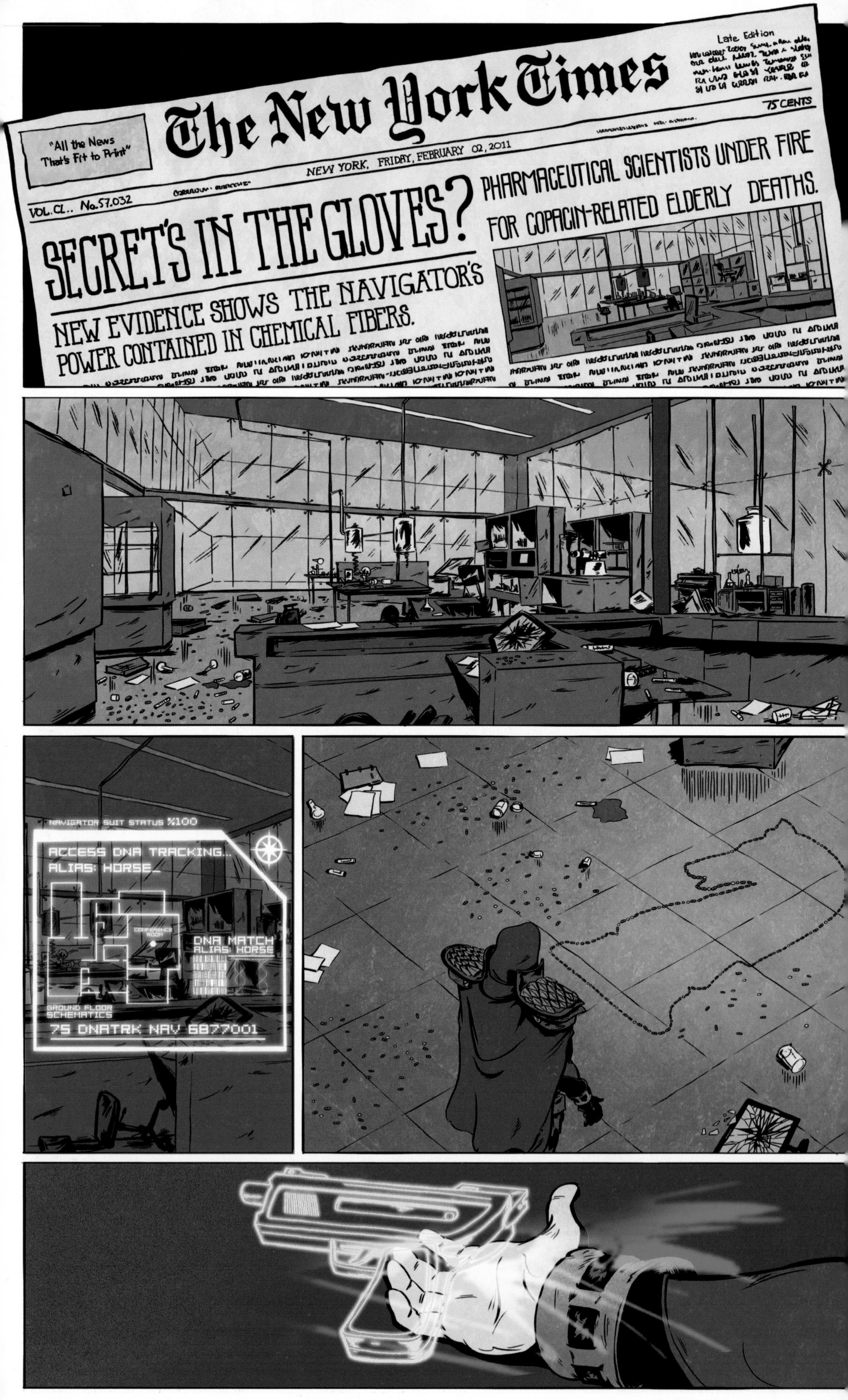
Late Edition
"All the News That's Fit to Print"
The New York Times
75 CENTS
VOL. CL.. No. 57,032
NEW YORK, FRIDAY, FEBRUARY 02, 2011
SECRET'S IN THE GLOVES?
NEW EVIDENCE SHOWS THE NAVIGATOR'S POWER CONTAINED IN CHEMICAL FIBERS.
PHARMACEUTICAL SCIENTISTS UNDER FIRE FOR COPACIN-RELATED ELDERLY DEATHS.
NAVIGATOR SUIT STATUS %100
ACCESS DNA TRACKING...
ALIAS: HORSE_
CONFERENCE ROOM
DNA MATCH
ALIAS: HORSE
GROUND FLOOR SCHEMATICS
75 DNATRK NAV 6877001

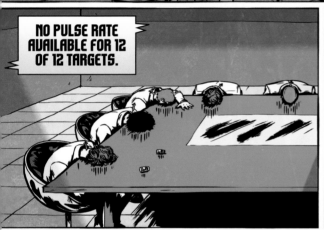

NO PULSE RATE AVAILABLE FOR 12 OF 12 TARGETS.

THOSE SCIENTISTS DESERVED A LITTLE MORE THAN A *TASTE* OF THEIR OWN MEDICINE.

MURDERING THE ELDERLY VIA A DRUG MEANT TO HELP ARTHRITIS IS A PUNISHABLE CRIME, DON'T YOU AGREE?

NOT BY LETHAL INJECTION WITHOUT TRIAL.

AH, NEVER MIND. I'D ALMOST FORGOTTEN THAT YOU STILL BELIEVE JUSTICE COMES AT THE HANDS OF LAWMAKERS.

BUT YOU SEE, I BELIEVE *WE'RE* THE LAW.

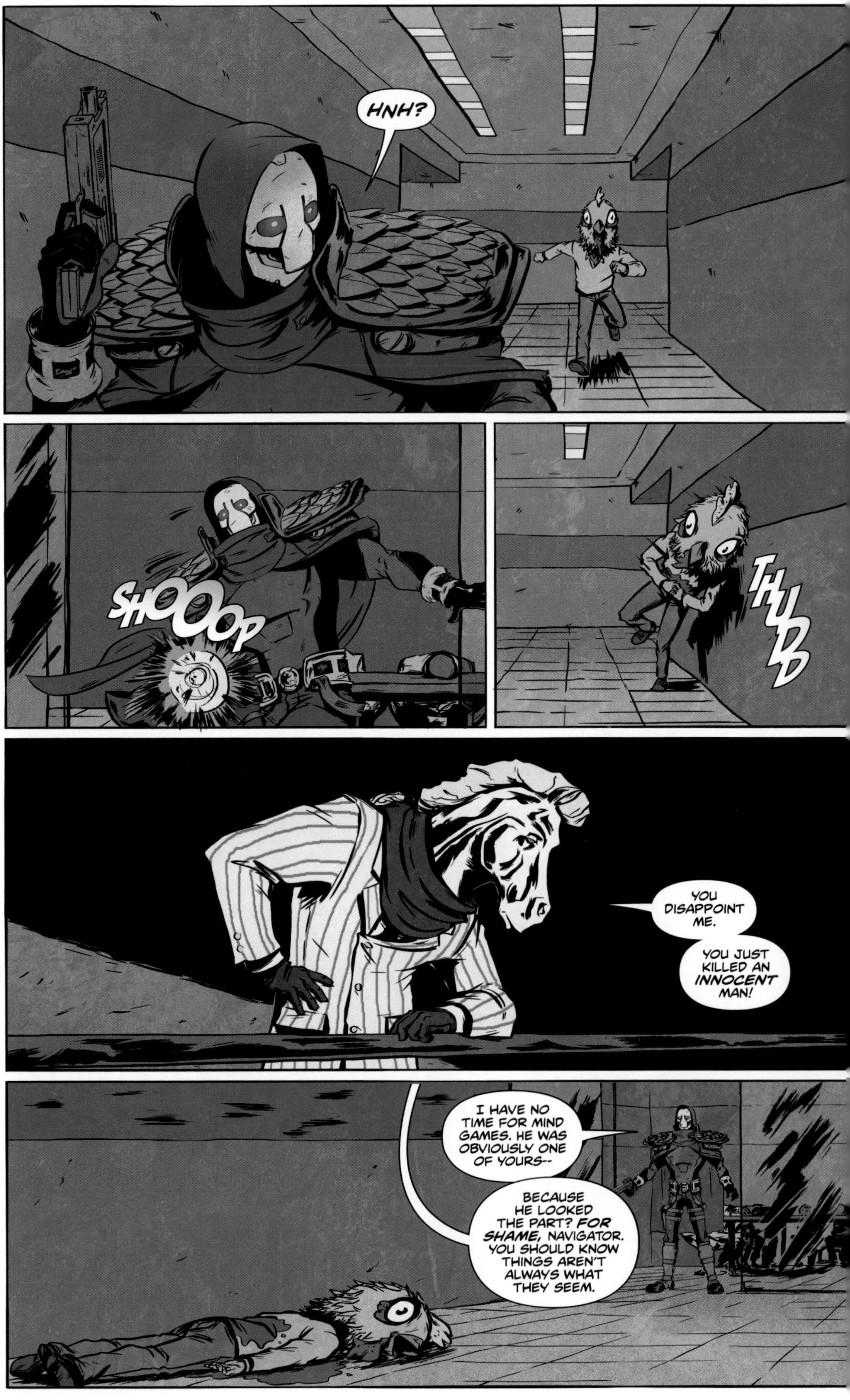
HNH?
SHOOOP
THUD
YOU DISAPPOINT ME.
YOU JUST KILLED AN INNOCENT MAN!
I HAVE NO TIME FOR MIND GAMES. HE WAS OBVIOUSLY ONE OF YOURS--
BECAUSE HE LOOKED THE PART? FOR SHAME, NAVIGATOR. YOU SHOULD KNOW THINGS AREN'T ALWAYS WHAT THEY SEEM.

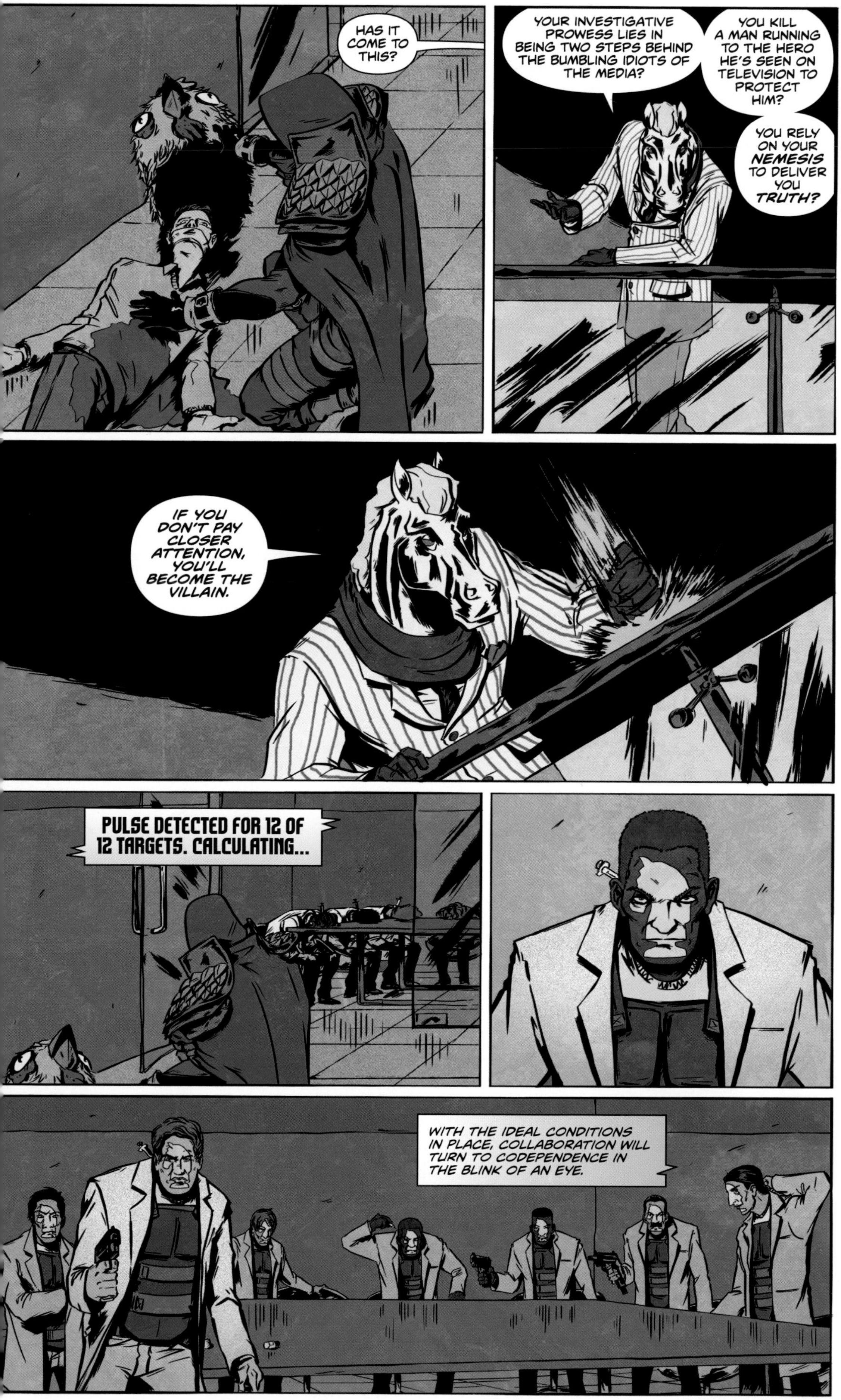
HAS IT COME TO THIS?
YOUR INVESTIGATIVE PROWESS LIES IN BEING TWO STEPS BEHIND THE BUMBLING IDIOTS OF THE MEDIA?
YOU KILL A MAN RUNNING TO THE HERO HE'S SEEN ON TELEVISION TO PROTECT HIM?
YOU RELY ON YOUR NEMESIS TO DELIVER YOU TRUTH?
IF YOU DON'T PAY CLOSER ATTENTION, YOU'LL BECOME THE VILLAIN.
PULSE DETECTED FOR 12 OF 12 TARGETS. CALCULATING...
WITH THE IDEAL CONDITIONS IN PLACE, COLLABORATION WILL TURN TO CODEPENDENCE IN THE BLINK OF AN EYE.

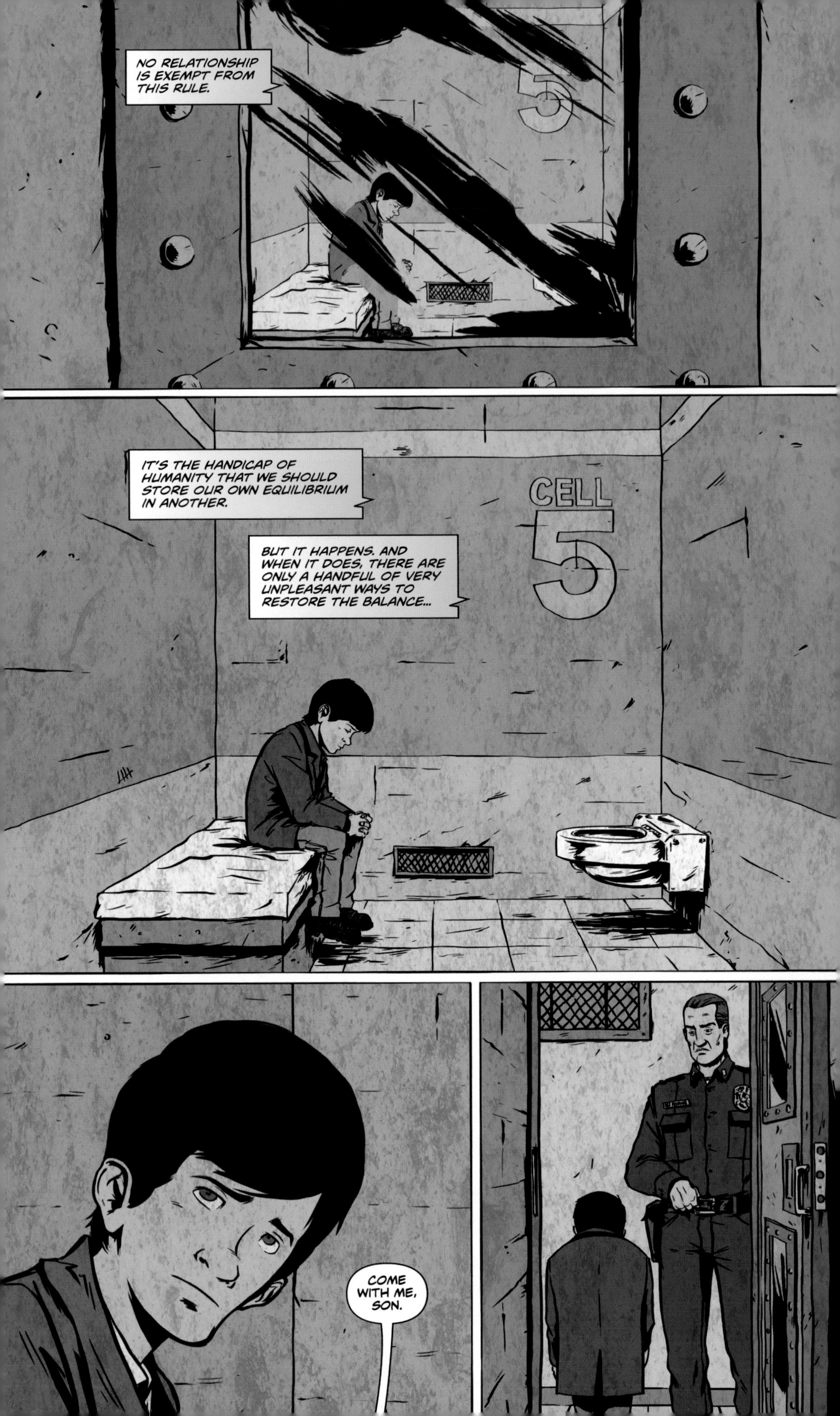
NO RELATIONSHIP IS EXEMPT FROM THIS RULE.
5
IT'S THE HANDICAP OF HUMANITY THAT WE SHOULD STORE OUR OWN EQUILIBRIUM IN ANOTHER.
CELL 5
BUT IT HAPPENS. AND WHEN IT DOES, THERE ARE ONLY A HANDFUL OF VERY UNPLEASANT WAYS TO RESTORE THE BALANCE...
COME WITH ME, SON.

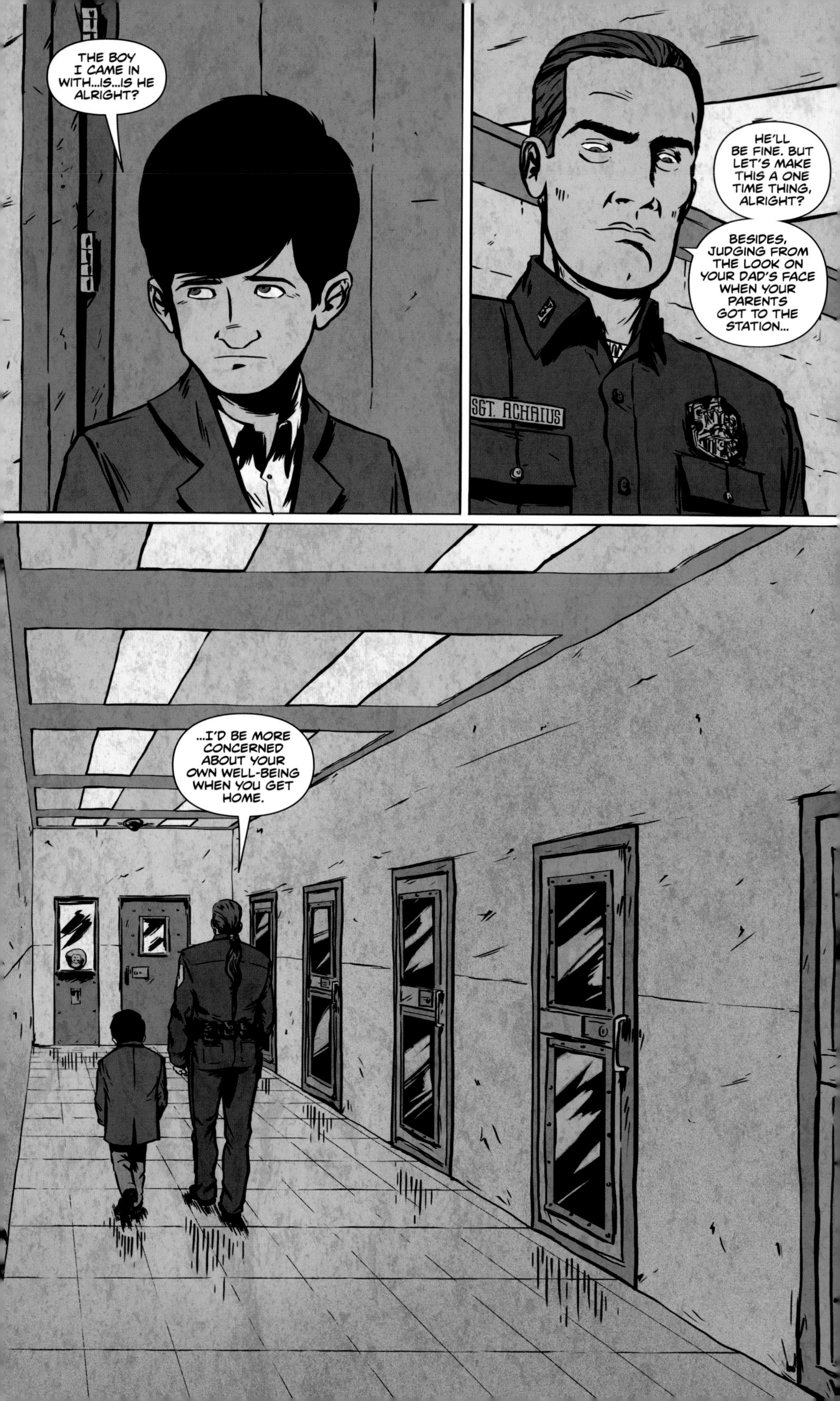
THE BOY I CAME IN WITH...IS...IS HE ALRIGHT?
HE'LL BE FINE. BUT LET'S MAKE THIS A ONE TIME THING, ALRIGHT?
BESIDES, JUDGING FROM THE LOOK ON YOUR DAD'S FACE WHEN YOUR PARENTS GOT TO THE STATION...
SGT. ACHAIUS
...I'D BE MORE CONCERNED ABOUT YOUR OWN WELL-BEING WHEN YOU GET HOME.

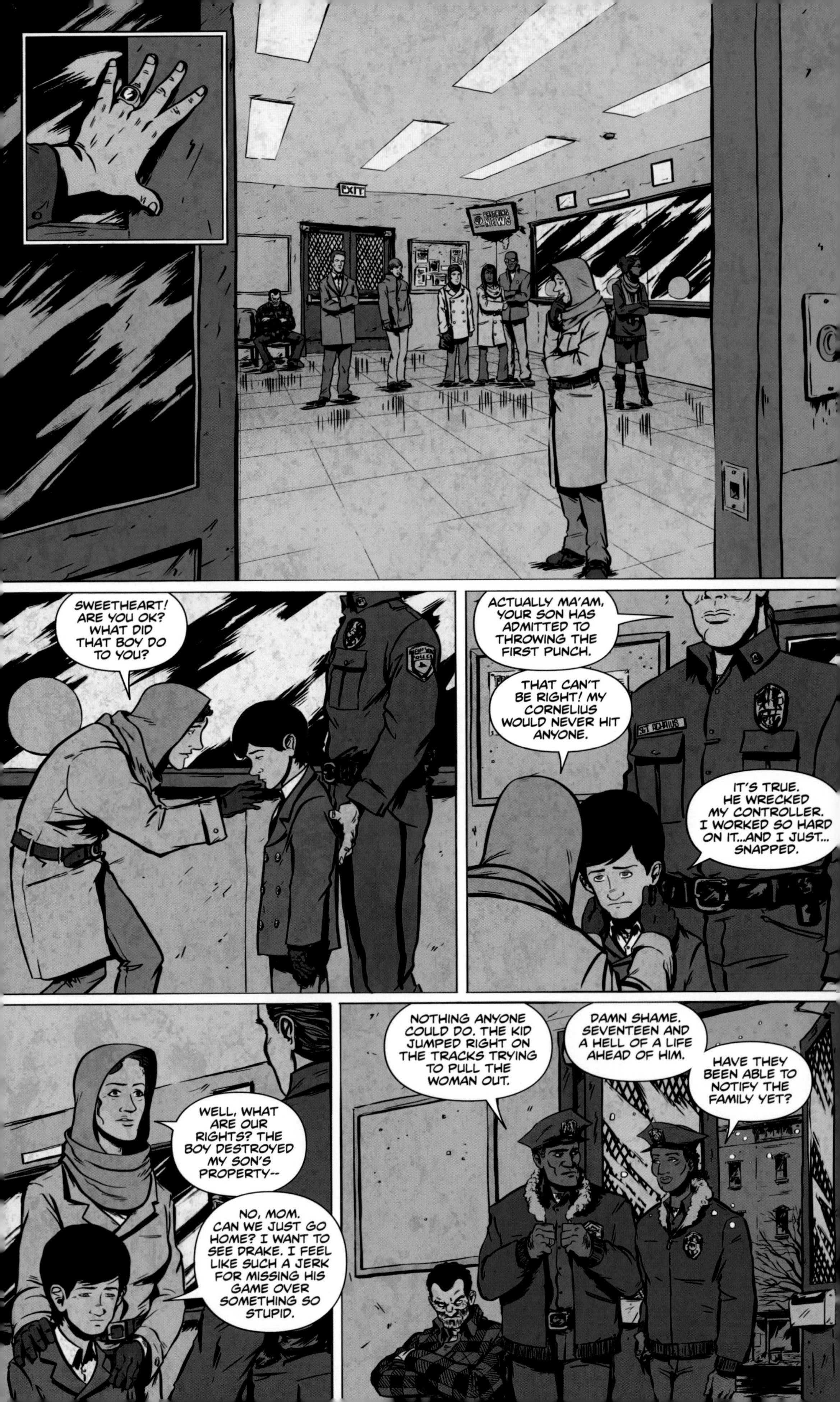

EXIT
NEWS
SWEETHEART! ARE YOU OK? WHAT DID THAT BOY DO TO YOU?
ACTUALLY MA'AM, YOUR SON HAS ADMITTED TO THROWING THE FIRST PUNCH.
THAT CAN'T BE RIGHT! MY CORNELIUS WOULD NEVER HIT ANYONE.
IT'S TRUE. HE WRECKED MY CONTROLLER. I WORKED SO HARD ON IT...AND I JUST... SNAPPED.
WELL, WHAT ARE OUR RIGHTS? THE BOY DESTROYED MY SON'S PROPERTY--
NO, MOM. CAN WE JUST GO HOME? I WANT TO SEE DRAKE. I FEEL LIKE SUCH A JERK FOR MISSING HIS GAME OVER SOMETHING SO STUPID.
NOTHING ANYONE COULD DO. THE KID JUMPED RIGHT ON THE TRACKS TRYING TO PULL THE WOMAN OUT.
DAMN SHAME. SEVENTEEN AND A HELL OF A LIFE AHEAD OF HIM.
HAVE THEY BEEN ABLE TO NOTIFY THE FAMILY YET?

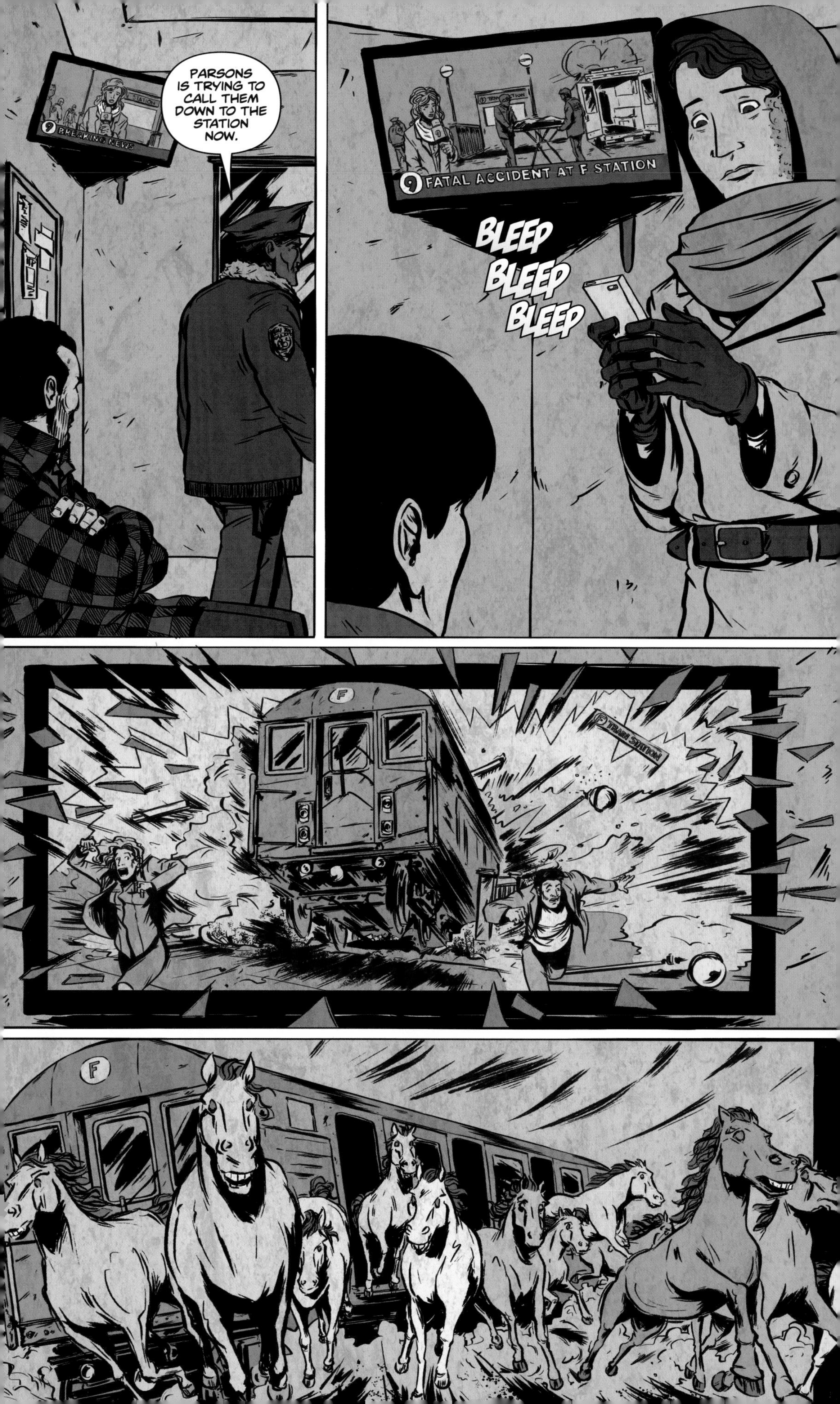
BREAKING NEWS
PARSONS IS TRYING TO CALL THEM DOWN TO THE STATION NOW.
FATAL ACCIDENT AT F STATION
BLEEP
BLEEP
BLEEP
TRAIN STATION

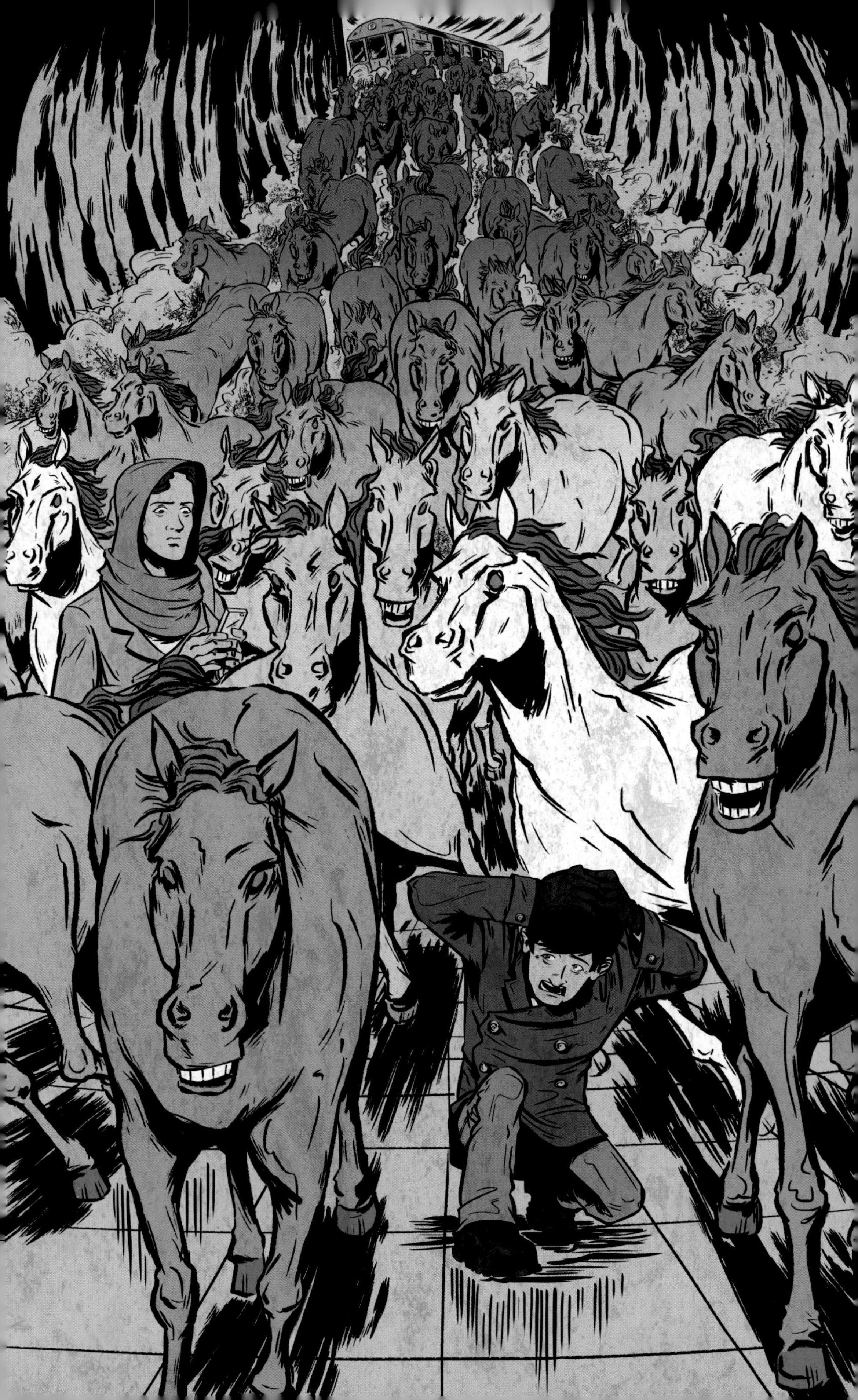

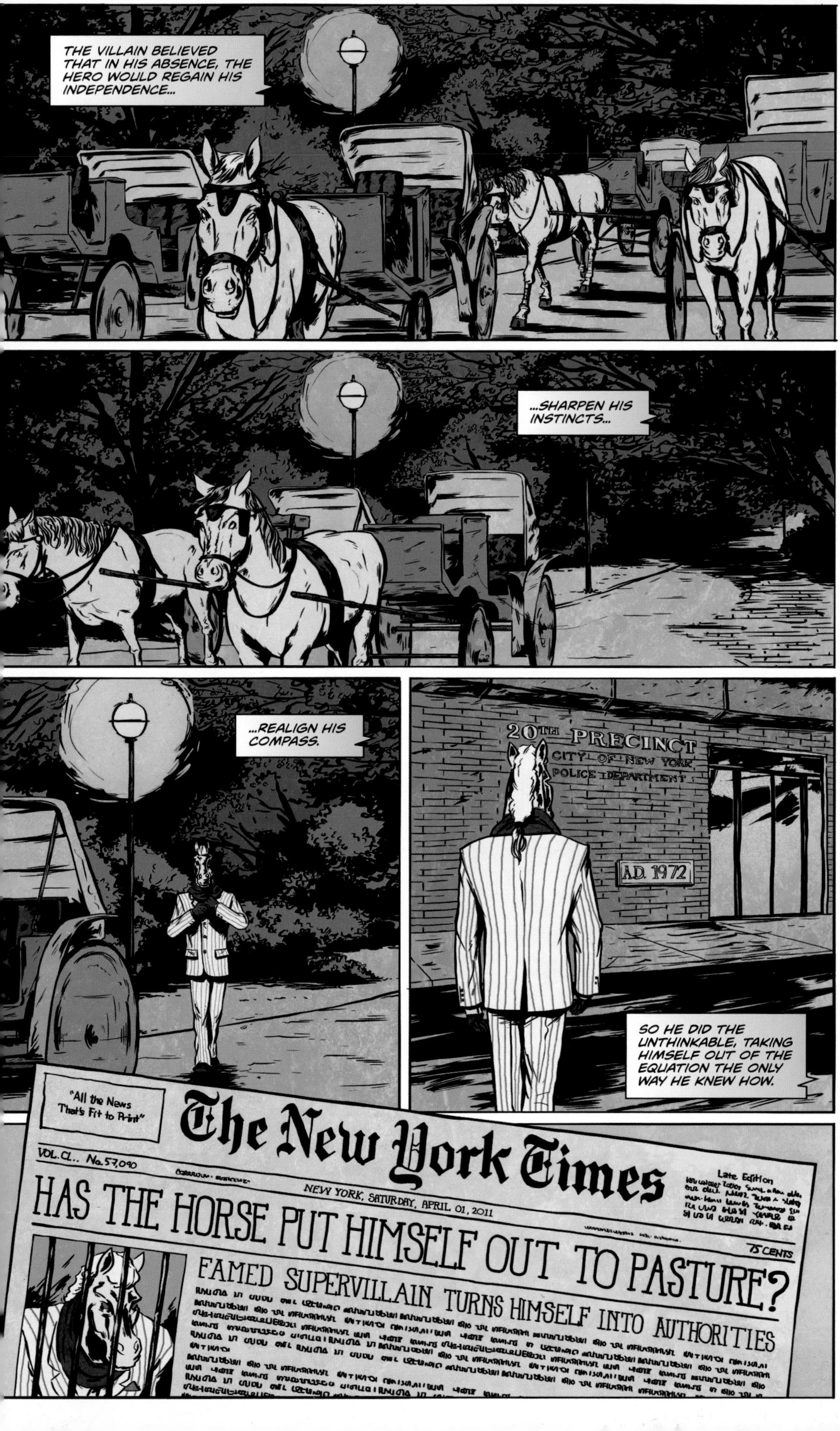
THE VILLAIN BELIEVED THAT IN HIS ABSENCE, THE HERO WOULD REGAIN HIS INDEPENDENCE...
...SHARPEN HIS INSTINCTS...
...REALIGN HIS COMPASS.
20TH PRECINCT
CITY OF NEW YORK
POLICE DEPARTMENT
A.D. 1972
SO HE DID THE UNTHINKABLE, TAKING HIMSELF OUT OF THE EQUATION THE ONLY WAY HE KNEW HOW.
"All the News That's Fit to Print"
The New York Times
VOL. CL.. No. 57,090
Late Edition
NEW YORK, SATURDAY, APRIL 01, 2011
75 CENTS
HAS THE HORSE PUT HIMSELF OUT TO PASTURE?
FAMED SUPERVILLAIN TURNS HIMSELF INTO AUTHORITIES

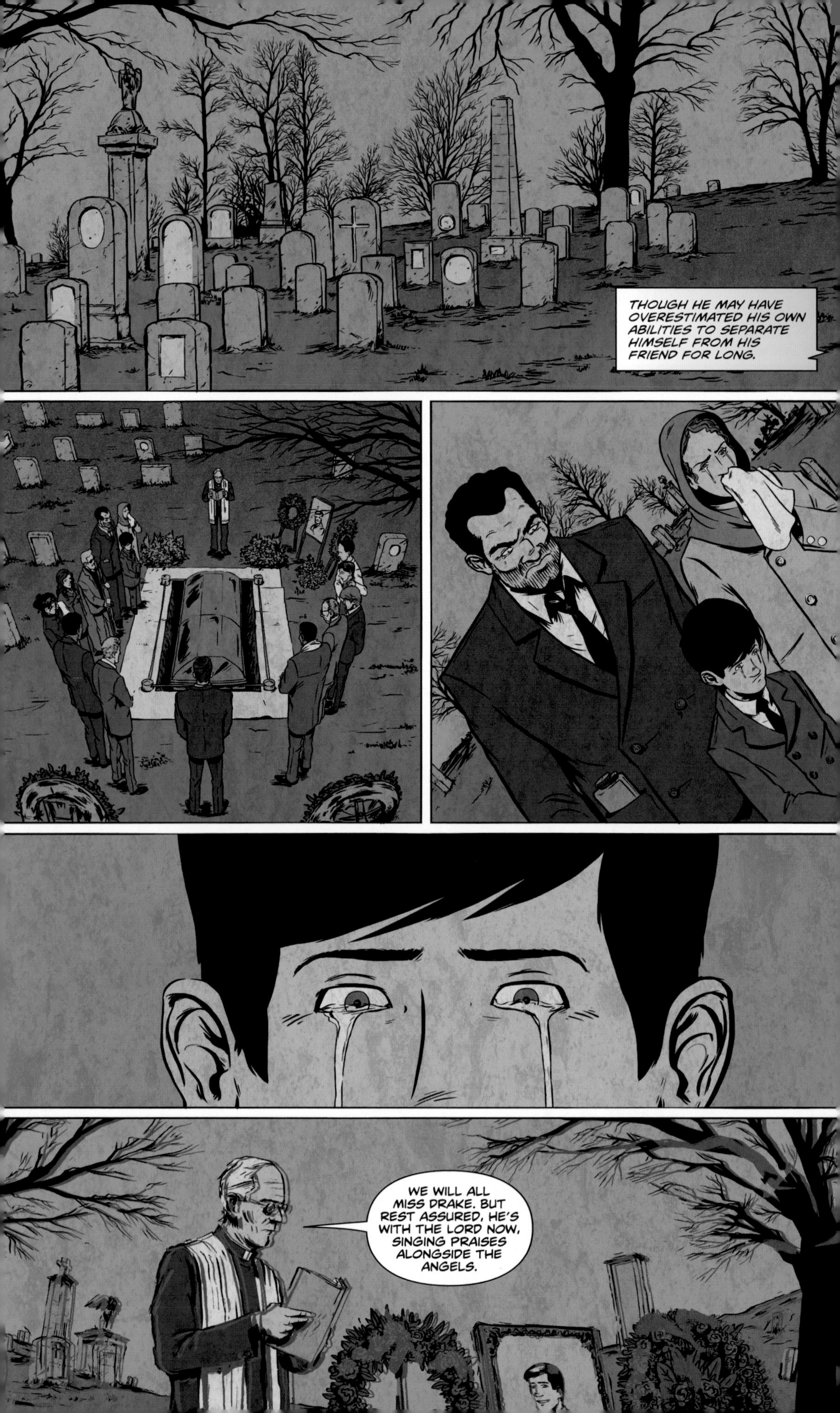
THOUGH HE MAY HAVE OVERESTIMATED HIS OWN ABILITIES TO SEPARATE HIMSELF FROM HIS FRIEND FOR LONG.
WE WILL ALL MISS DRAKE. BUT REST ASSURED, HE'S WITH THE LORD NOW, SINGING PRAISES ALONGSIDE THE ANGELS.

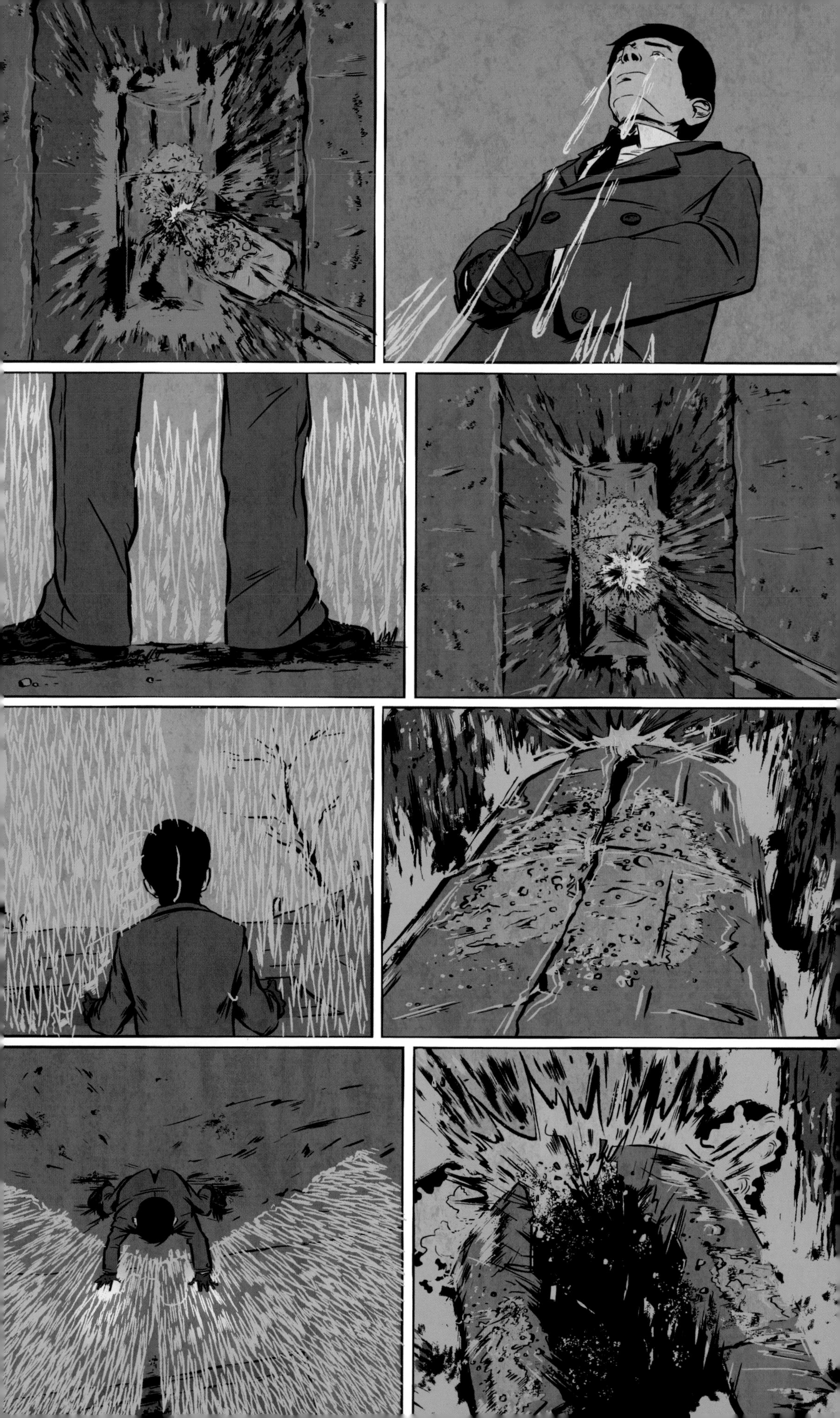

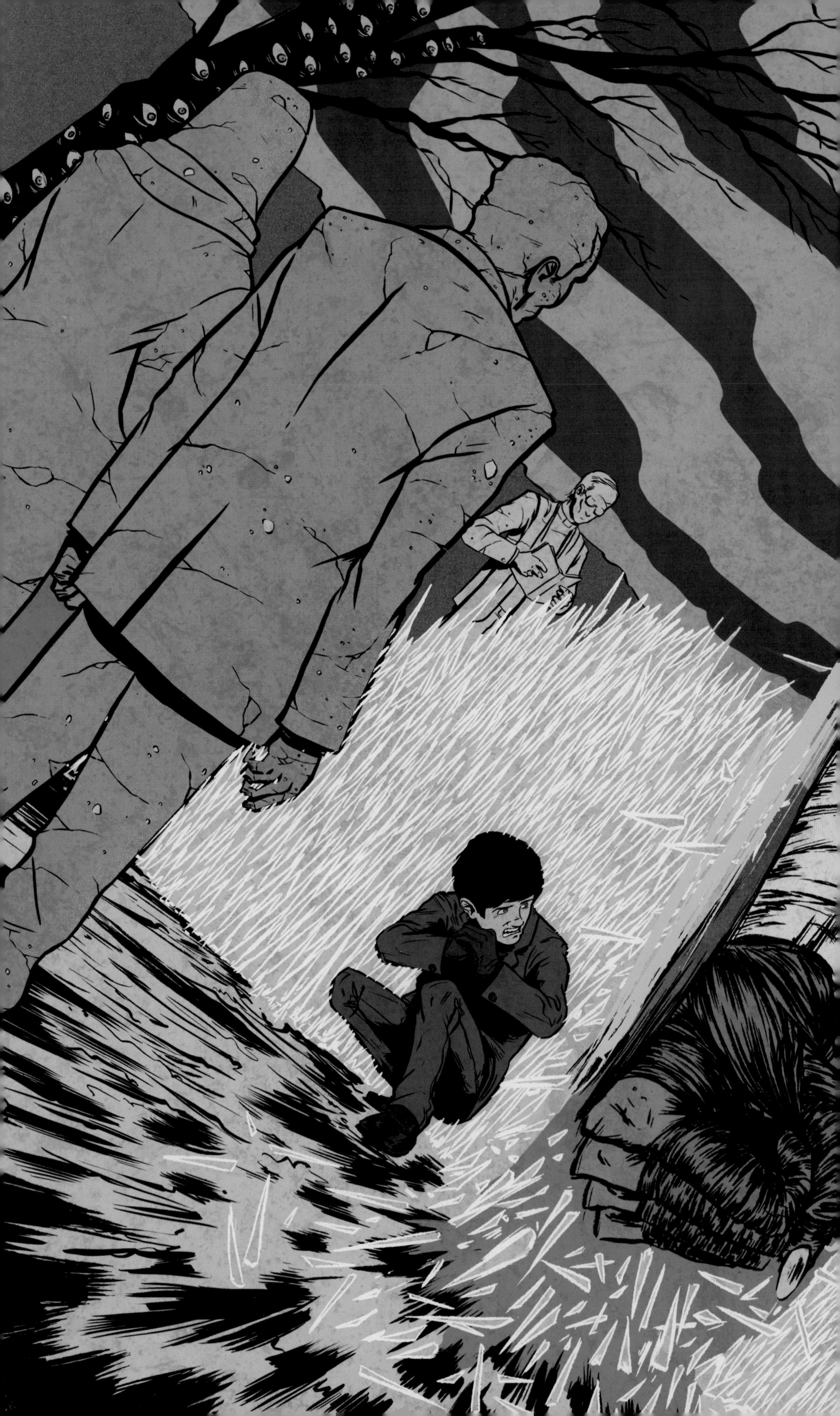

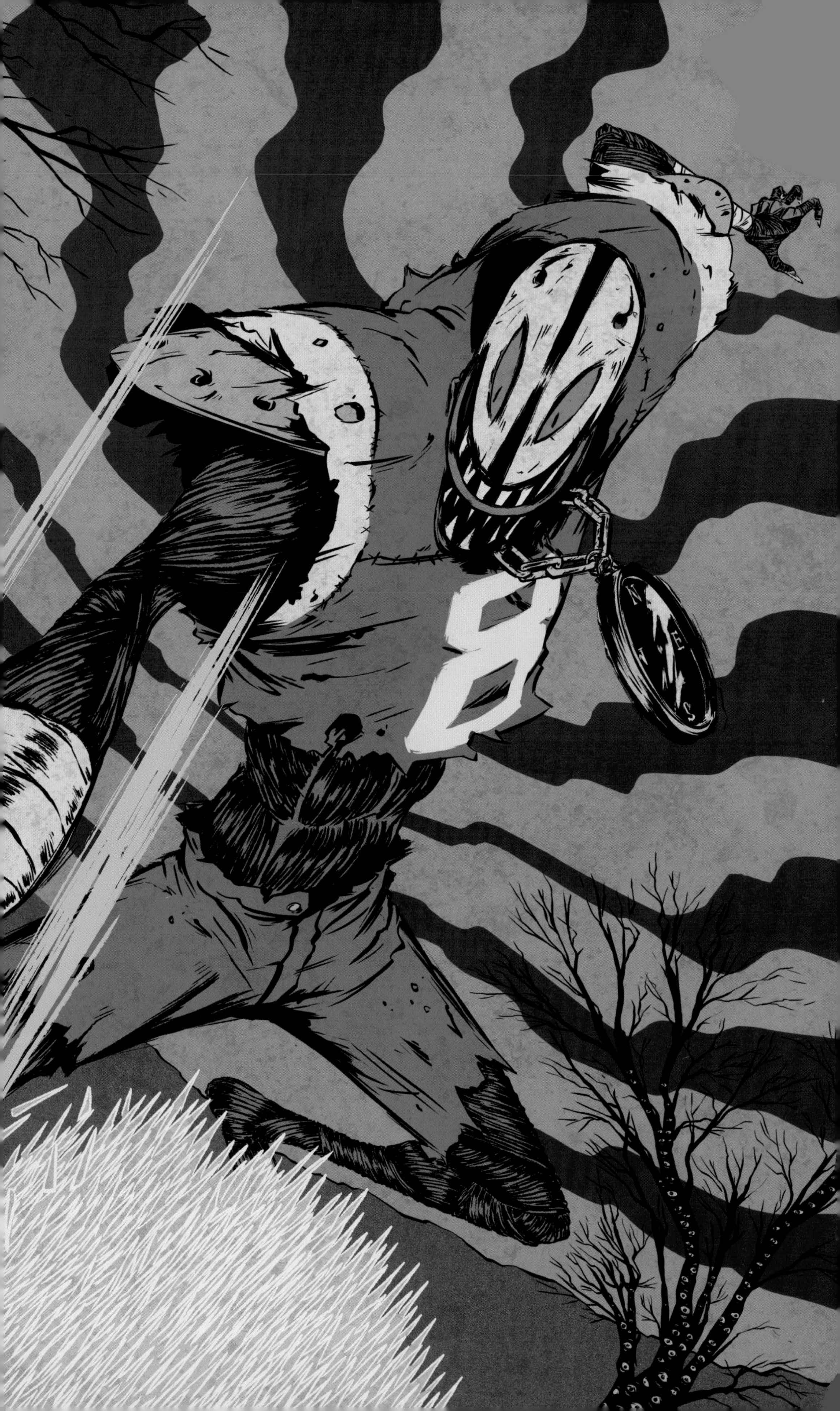
8

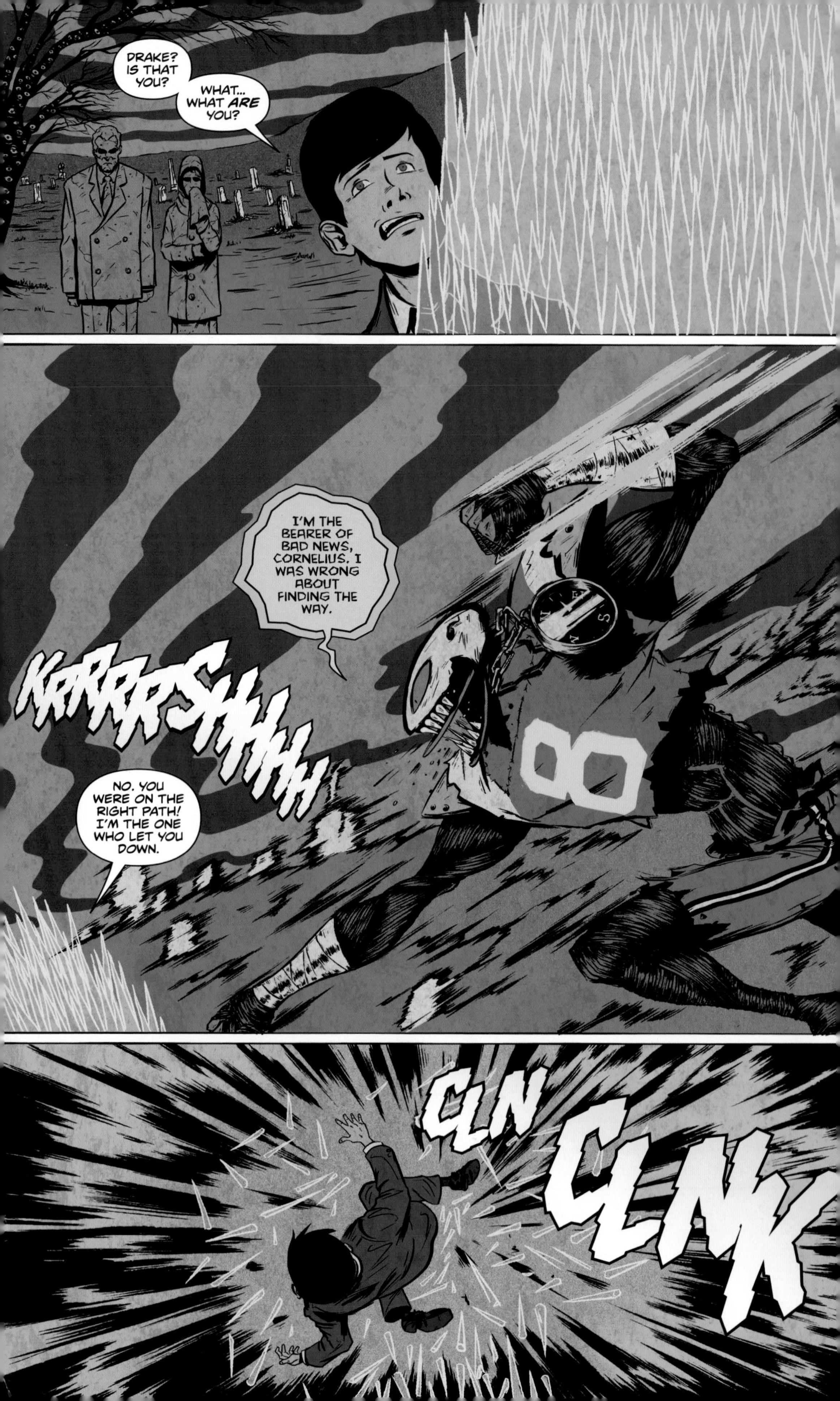
DRAKE? IS THAT YOU?
WHAT... WHAT ARE YOU?
I'M THE BEARER OF BAD NEWS, CORNELIUS. I WAS WRONG ABOUT FINDING THE WAY.
KRRRRSHHHHH
NO. YOU WERE ON THE RIGHT PATH! I'M THE ONE WHO LET YOU DOWN.
CLN
CLNK

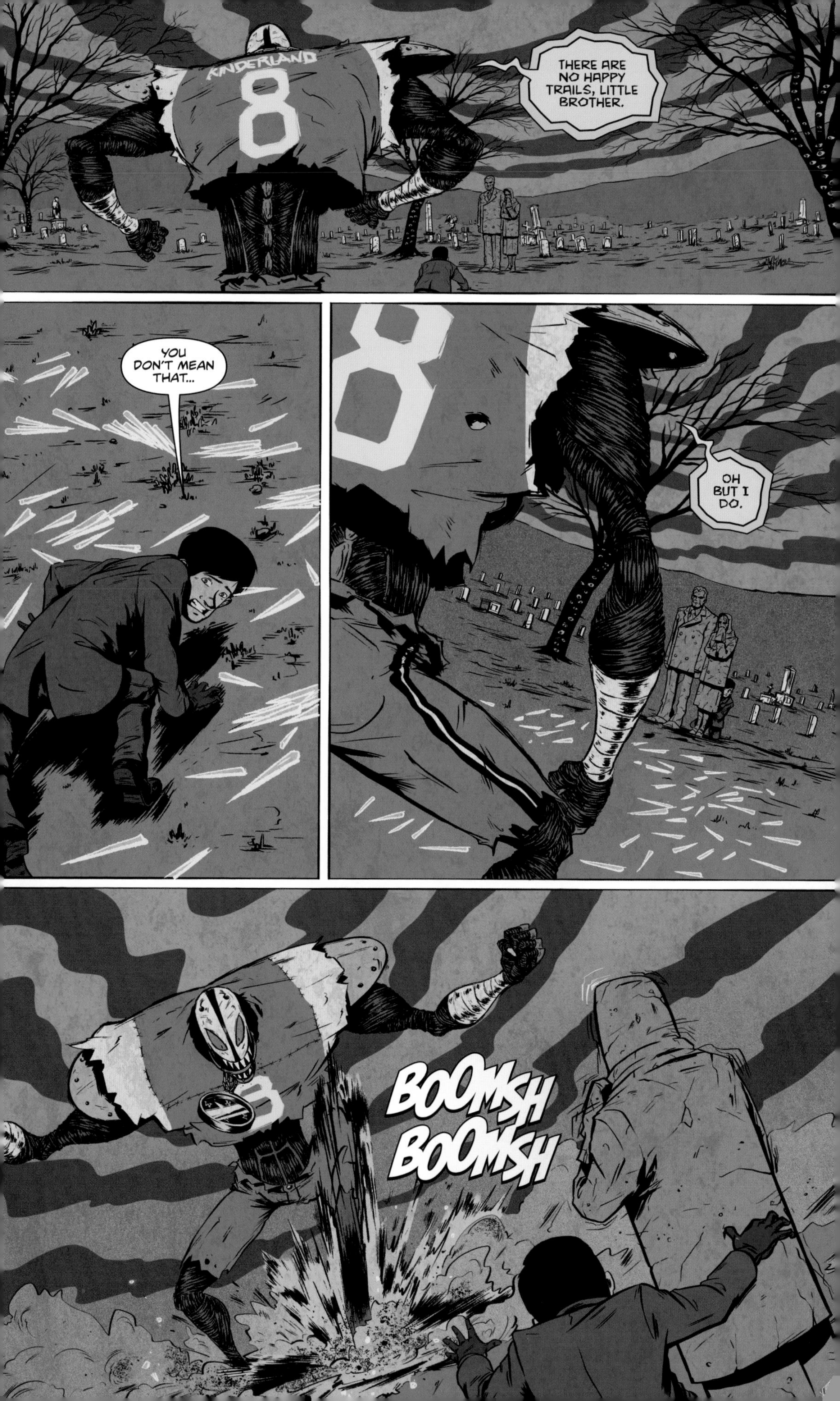
KINDERLAND
8
THERE ARE NO HAPPY TRAILS, LITTLE BROTHER.
YOU DON'T MEAN THAT...
OH BUT I DO.
BOOMSH
BOOMSH

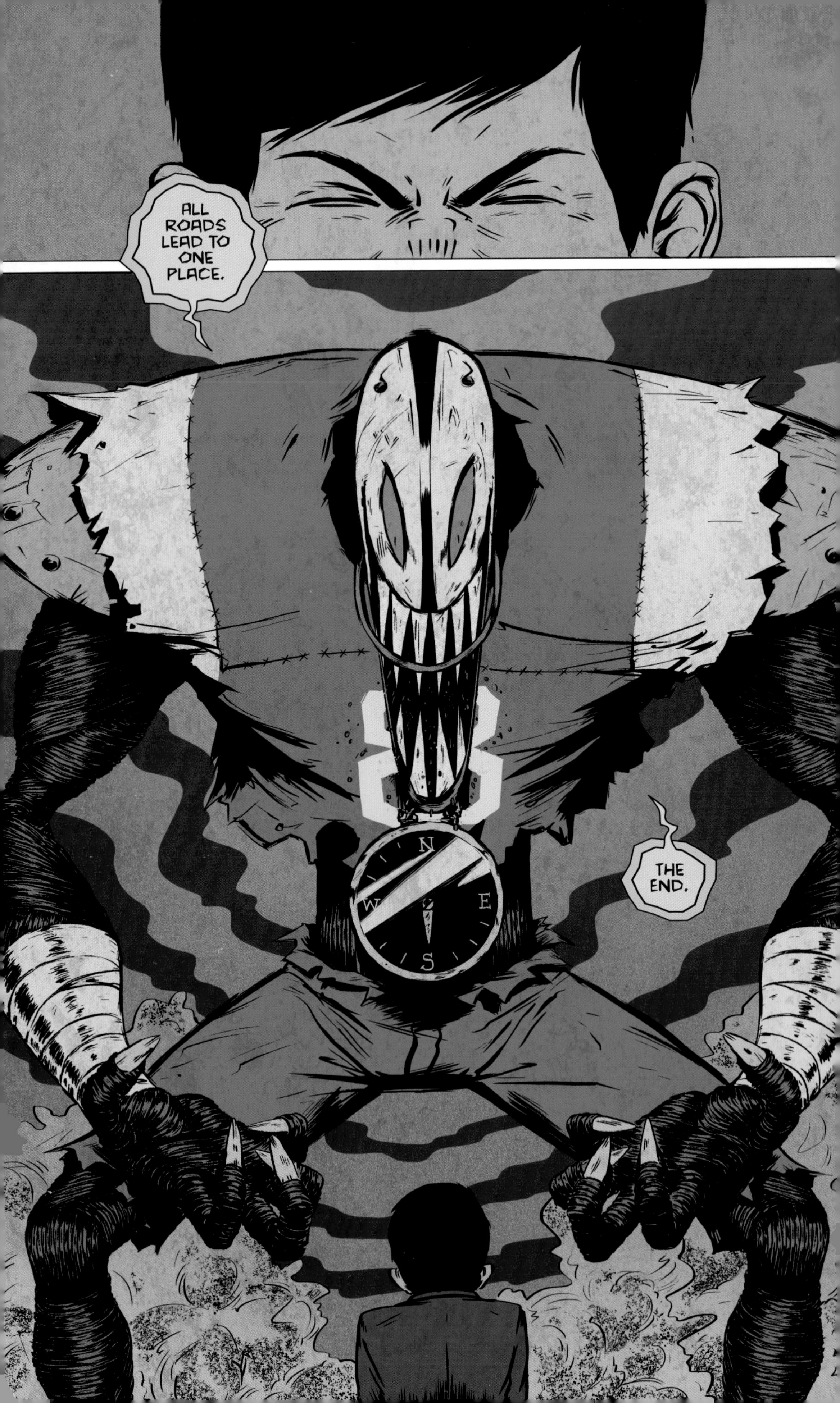
ALL ROADS LEAD TO ONE PLACE.
THE END.

ISSUE THREE BOOM! STUDIOS EXCLUSIVE COVER BY **FELIPE SMITH**

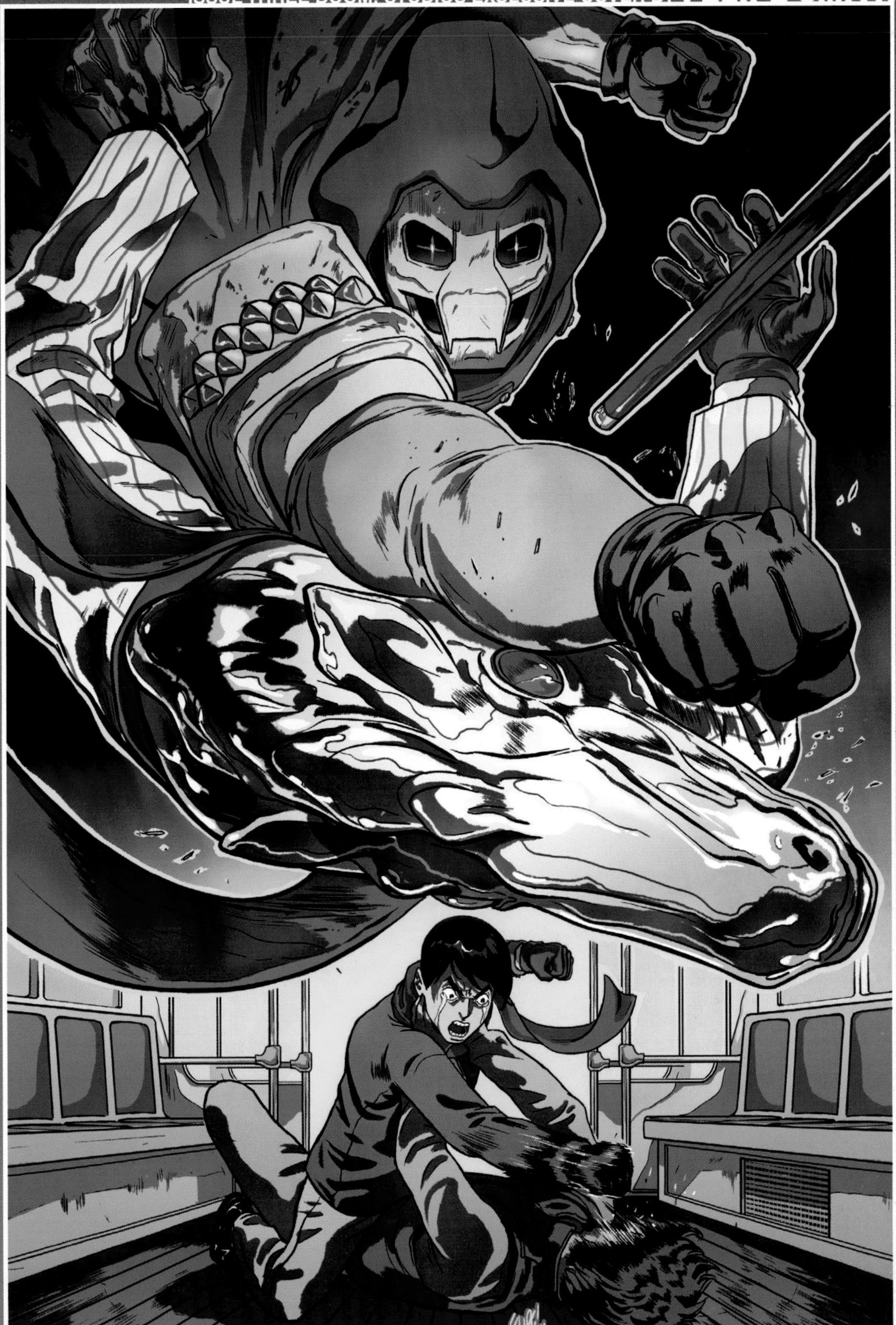

ISSUE FOUR COVER BY **JEFF STOKELY**

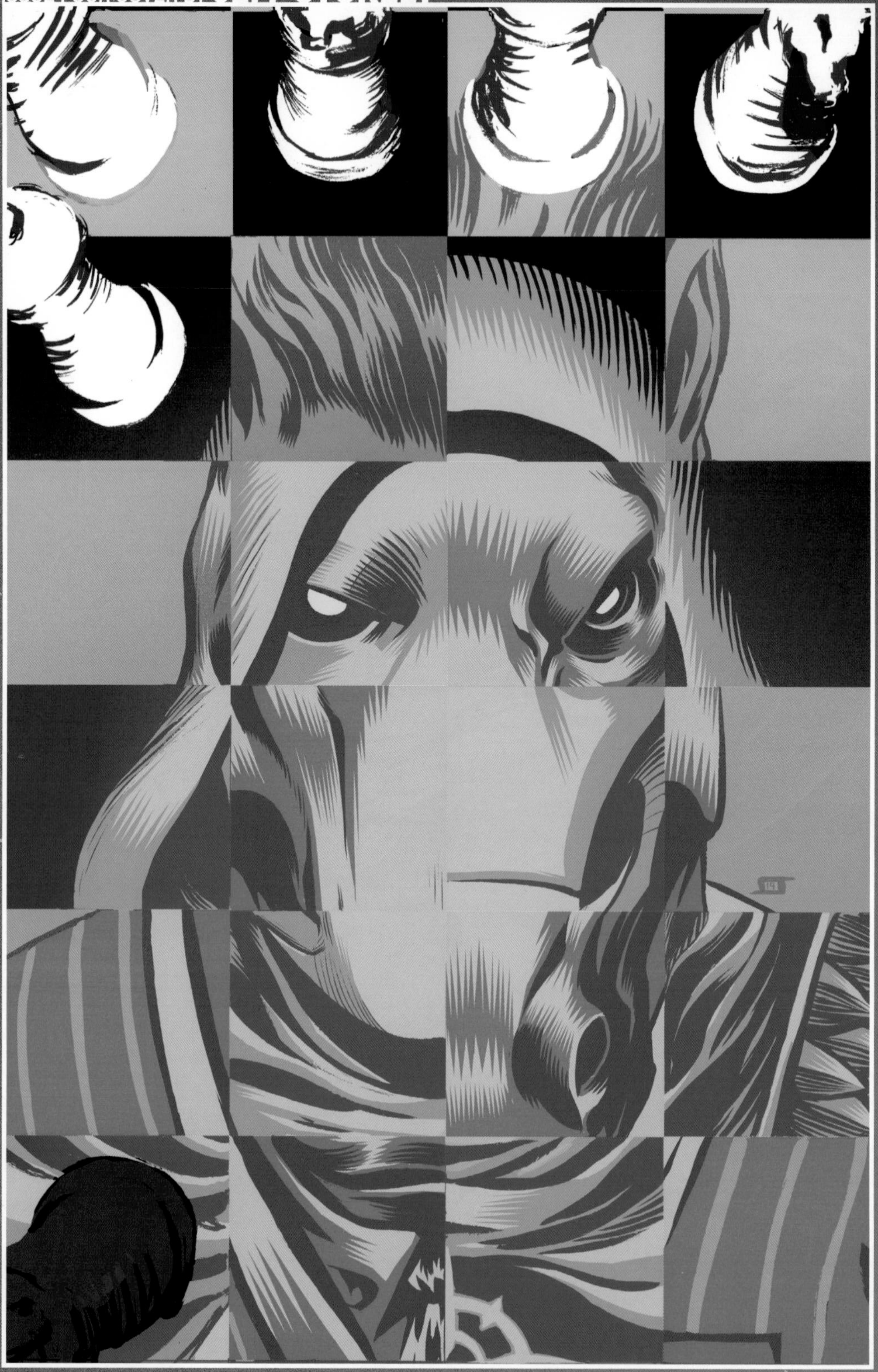

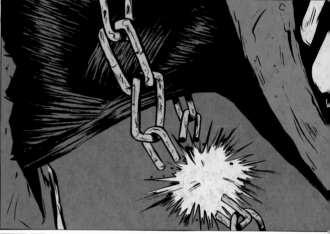

WHEREVER YOU ARE, DRAKE...I LOVE YOU.

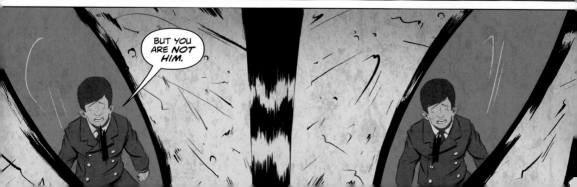

BUT YOU ARE *NOT* HIM.

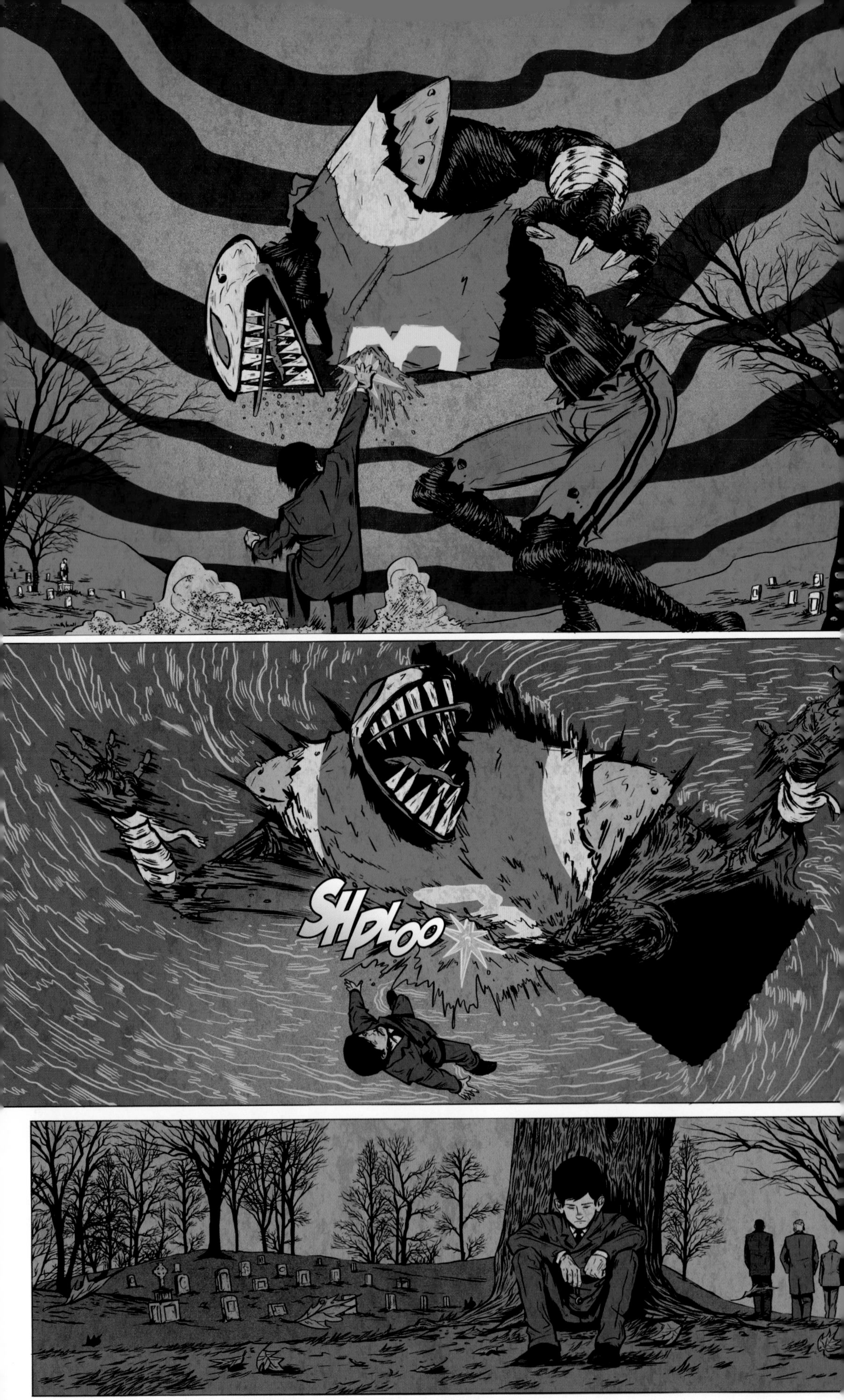
SHPLOO

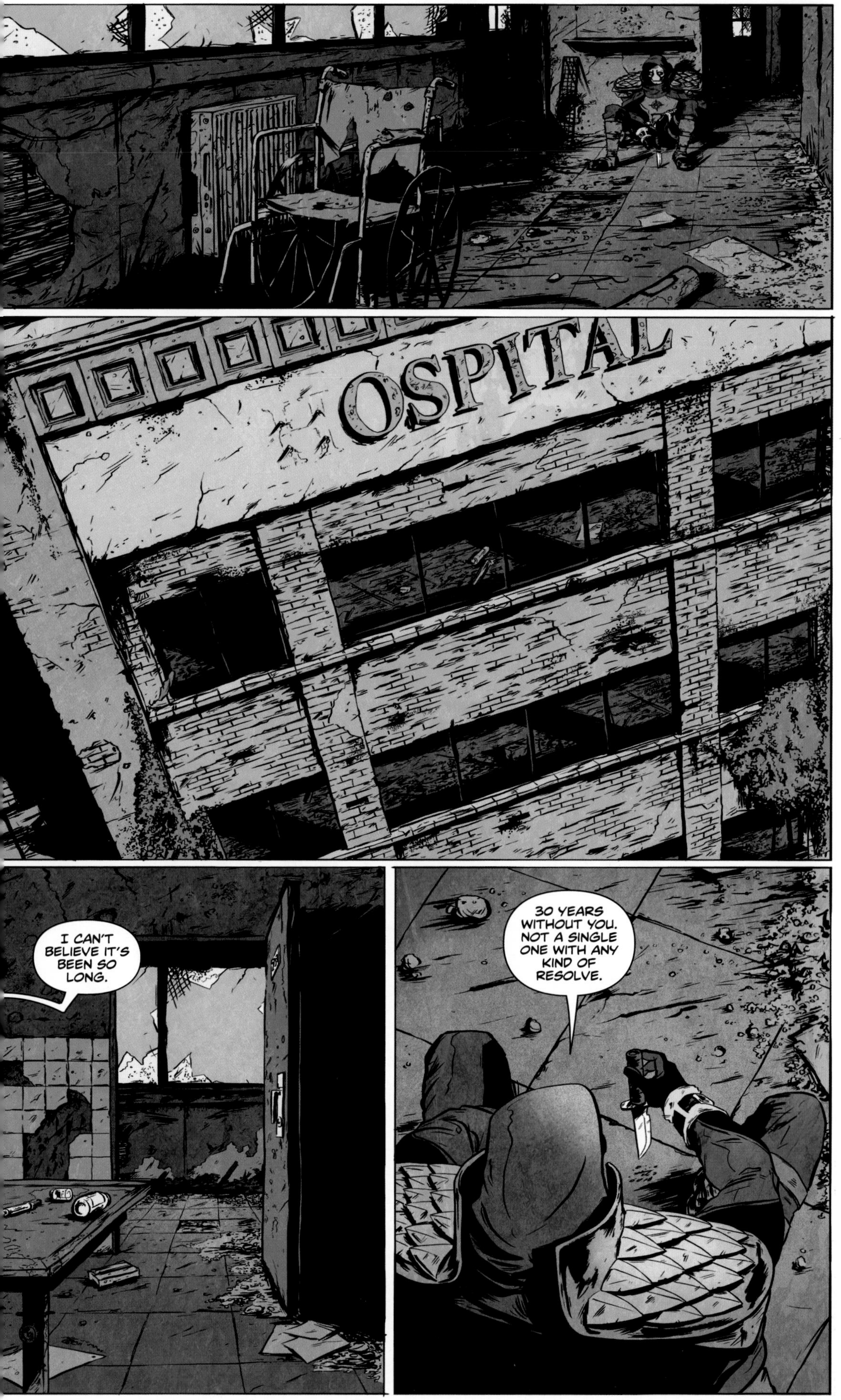
OSPITAL
I CAN'T BELIEVE IT'S BEEN SO LONG.
30 YEARS WITHOUT YOU. NOT A SINGLE ONE WITH ANY KIND OF RESOLVE.

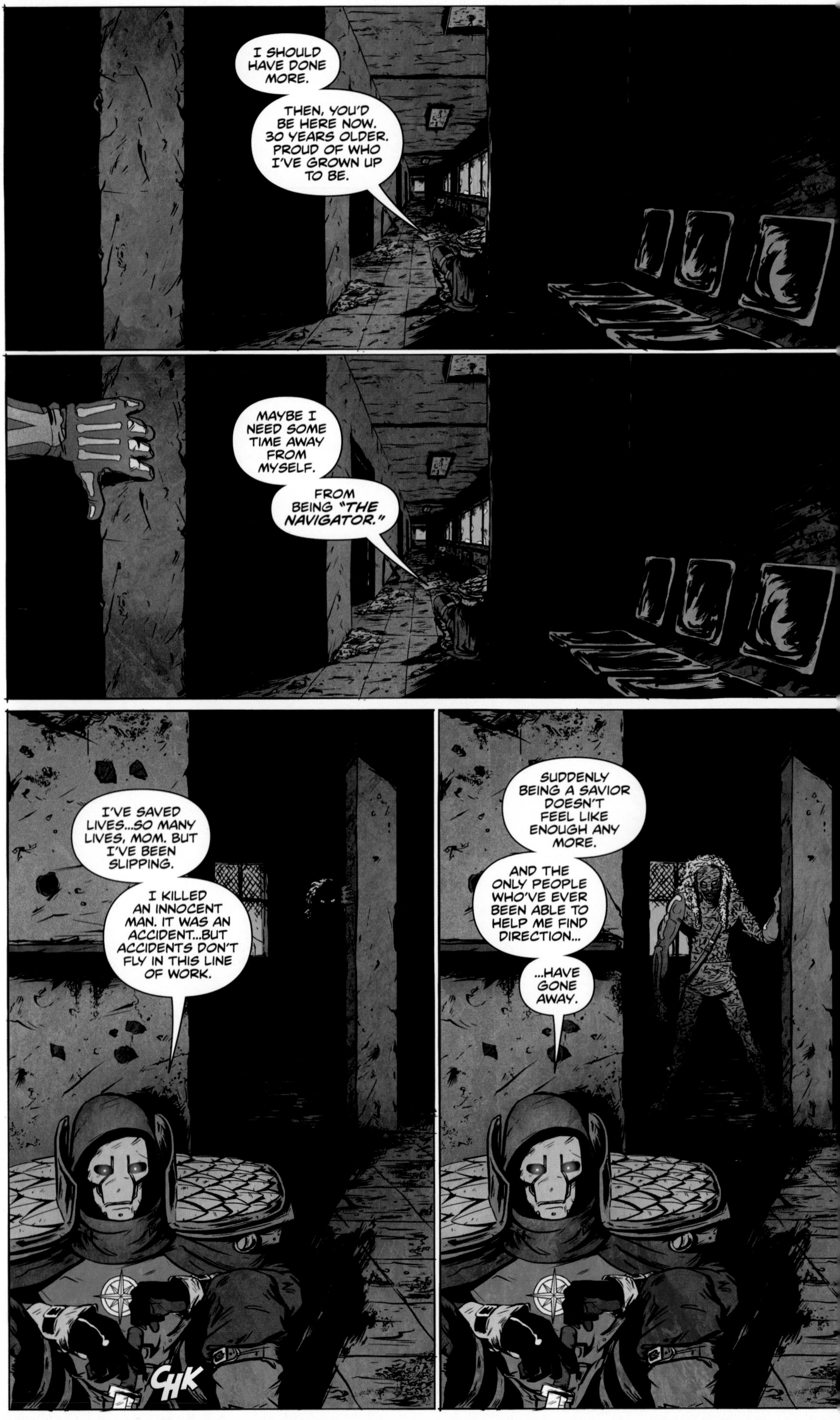
I SHOULD HAVE DONE MORE.
THEN, YOU'D BE HERE NOW. 30 YEARS OLDER. PROUD OF WHO I'VE GROWN UP TO BE.
MAYBE I NEED SOME TIME AWAY FROM MYSELF.
FROM BEING *"THE NAVIGATOR."*
I'VE SAVED LIVES...SO MANY LIVES, MOM. BUT I'VE BEEN SLIPPING.
I KILLED AN INNOCENT MAN. IT WAS AN ACCIDENT...BUT ACCIDENTS DON'T FLY IN THIS LINE OF WORK.
CHK
SUDDENLY BEING A SAVIOR DOESN'T FEEL LIKE ENOUGH ANY MORE.
AND THE ONLY PEOPLE WHO'VE EVER BEEN ABLE TO HELP ME FIND DIRECTION...
...HAVE GONE AWAY.

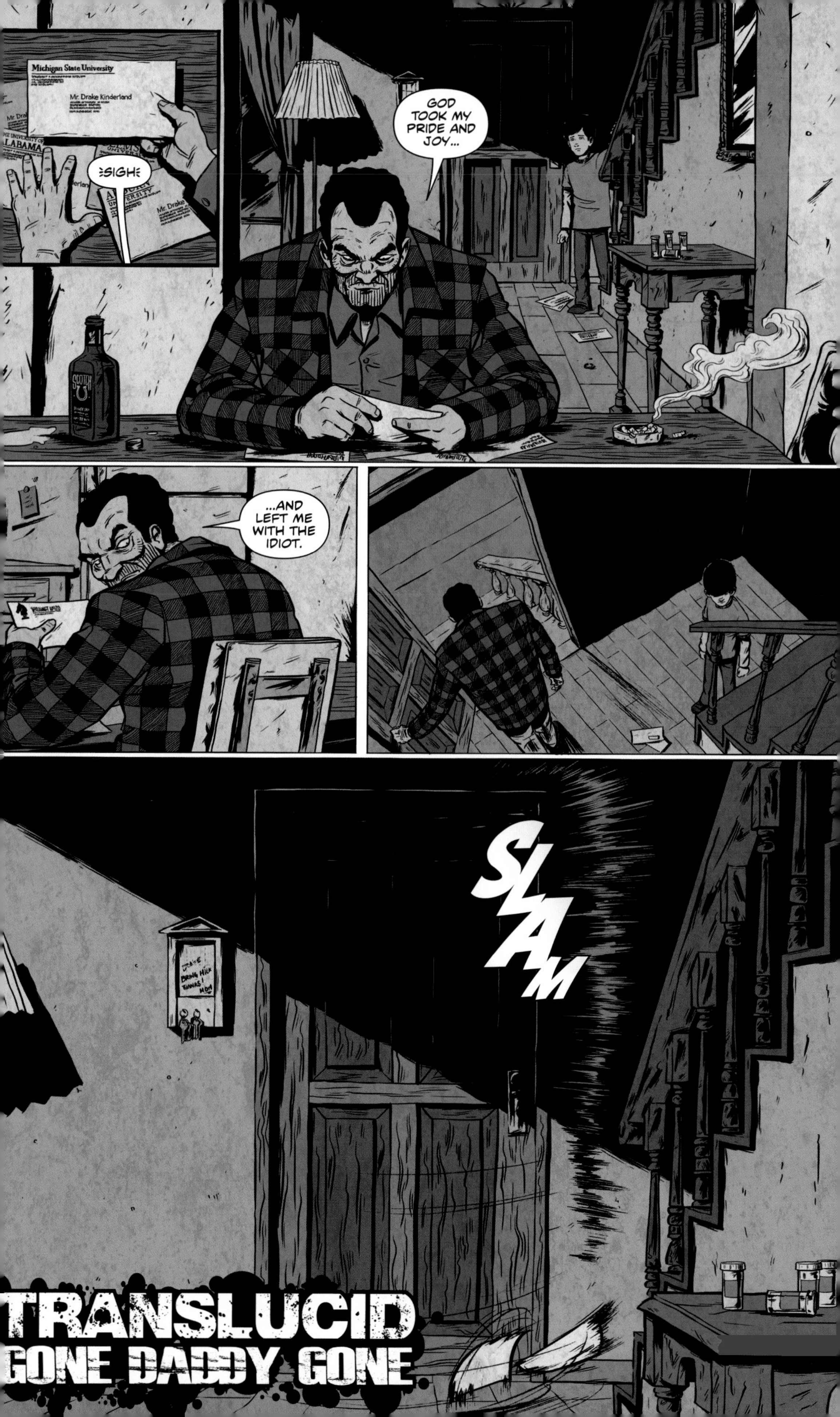
Michigan State University
Mr. Drake Kinderland
SIGH
GOD TOOK MY PRIDE AND JOY...
...AND LEFT ME WITH THE IDIOT.
SLAM
TRANSLUCID
GONE DADDY GONE

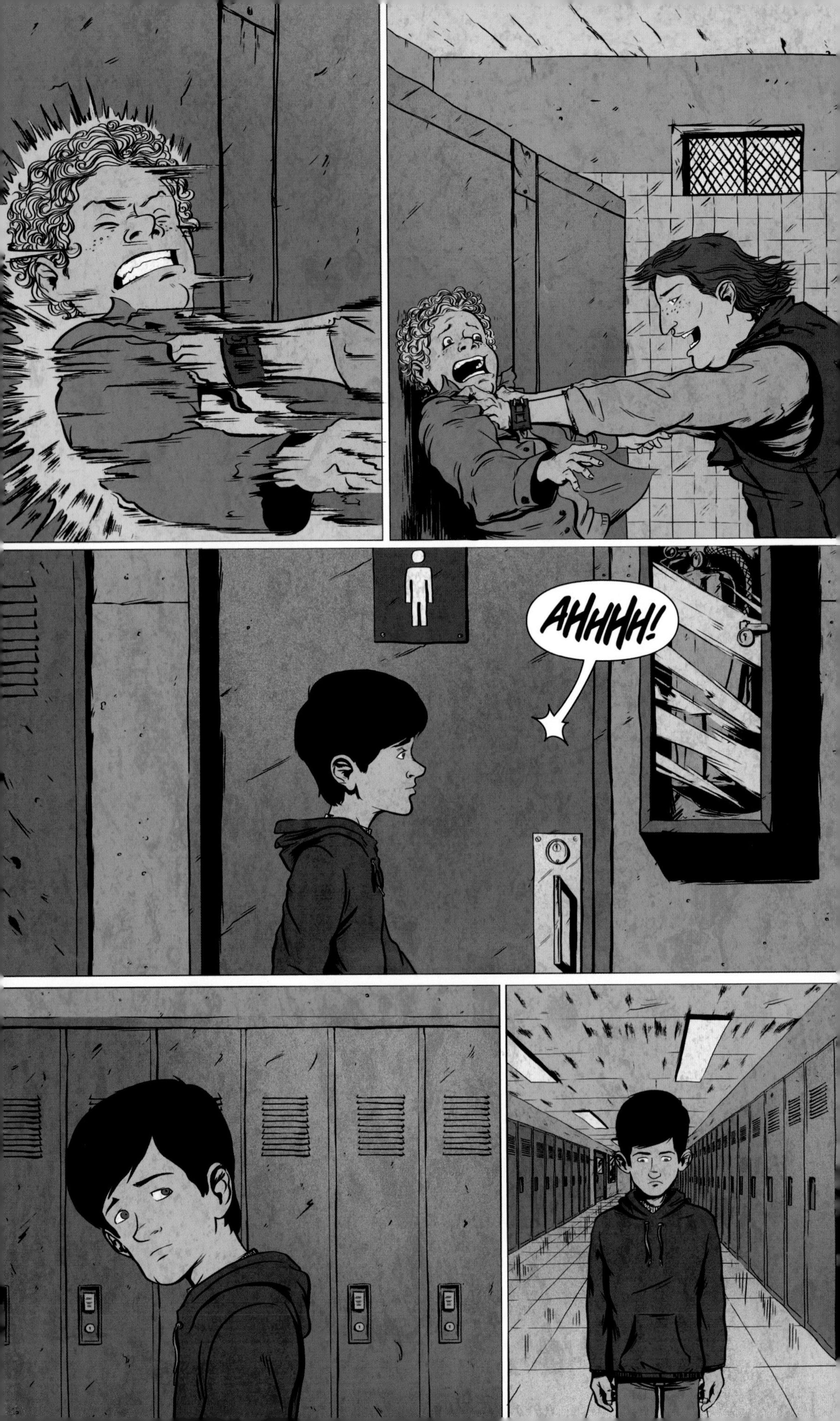
AHHHH!

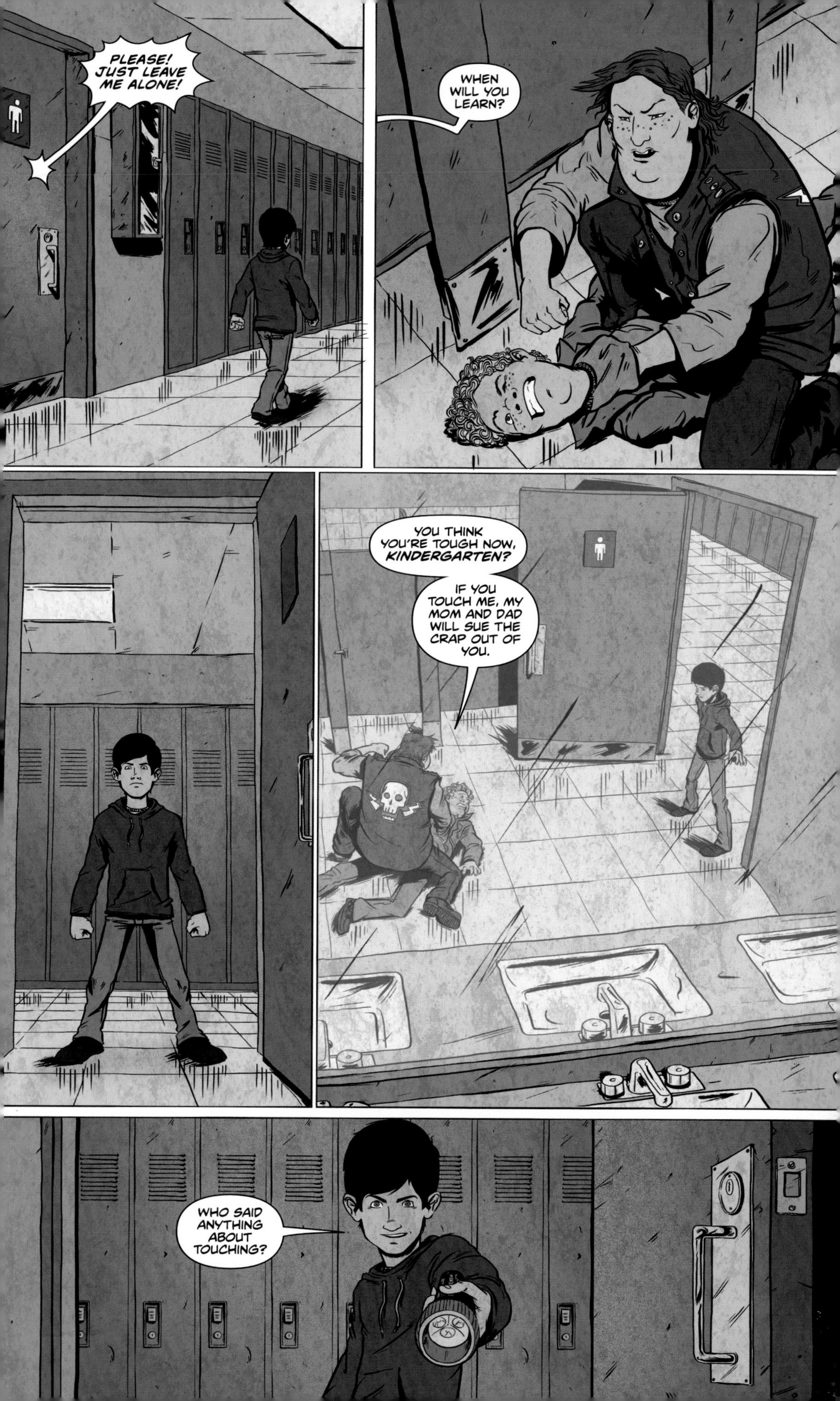
PLEASE! JUST LEAVE ME ALONE!
WHEN WILL YOU LEARN?
YOU THINK YOU'RE TOUGH NOW, KINDERGARTEN?
IF YOU TOUCH ME, MY MOM AND DAD WILL SUE THE CRAP OUT OF YOU.
WHO SAID ANYTHING ABOUT TOUCHING?

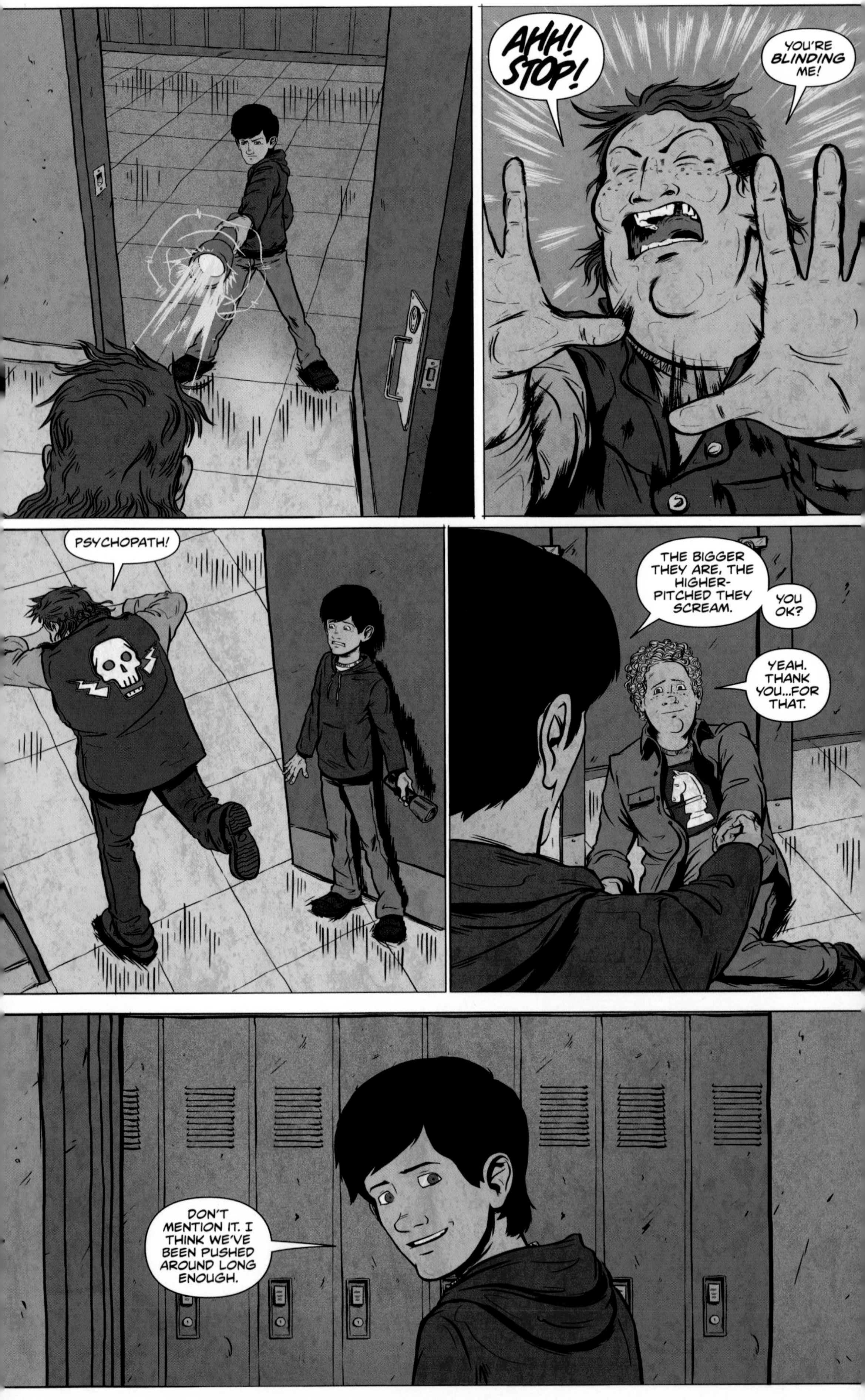
AHH! STOP!
YOU'RE BLINDING ME!
PSYCHOPATH!
THE BIGGER THEY ARE, THE HIGHER-PITCHED THEY SCREAM.
YOU OK?
YEAH. THANK YOU...FOR THAT.
DON'T MENTION IT. I THINK WE'VE BEEN PUSHED AROUND LONG ENOUGH.

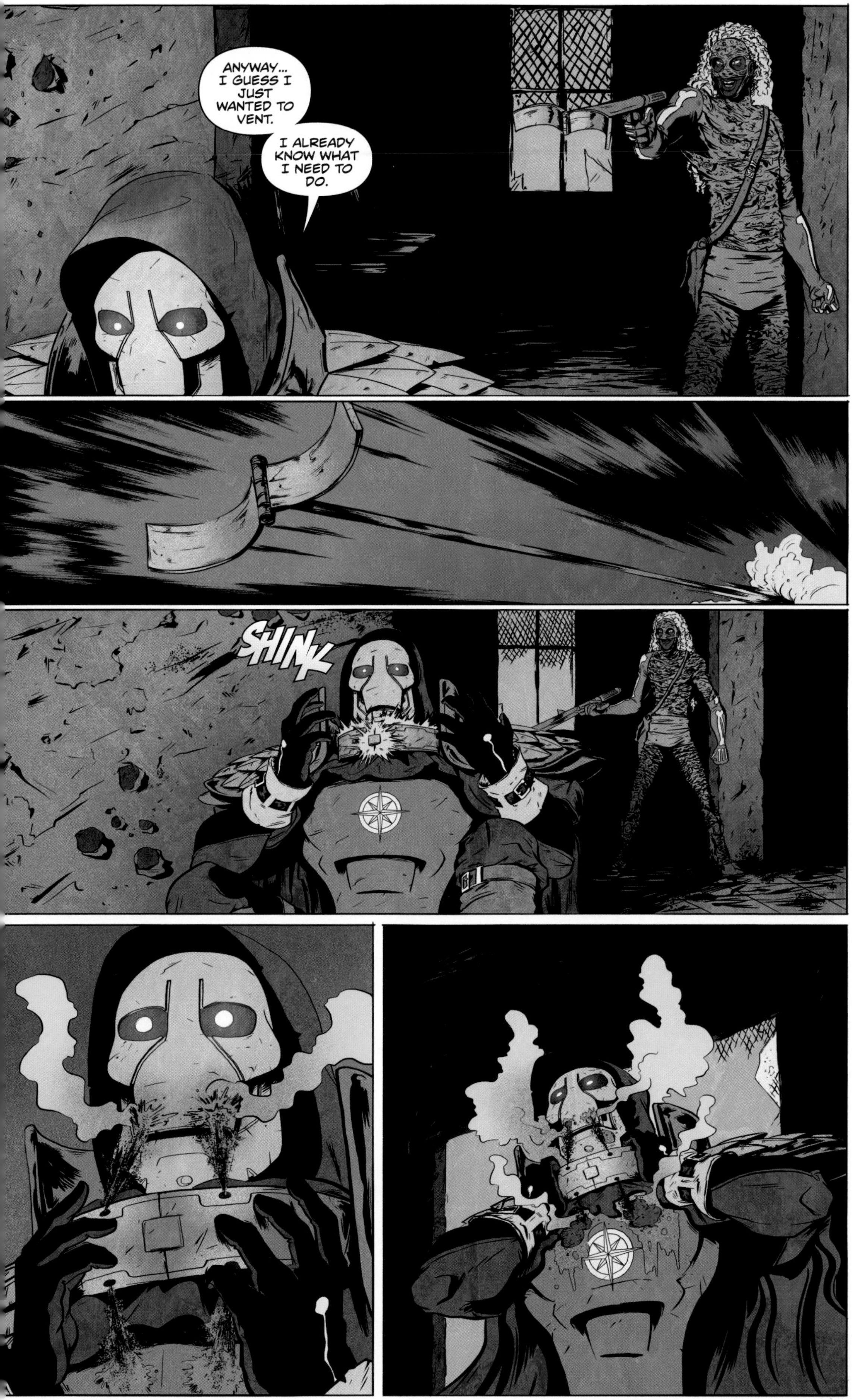
ANYWAY... I GUESS I JUST WANTED TO VENT.
I ALREADY KNOW WHAT I NEED TO DO.
SHINK

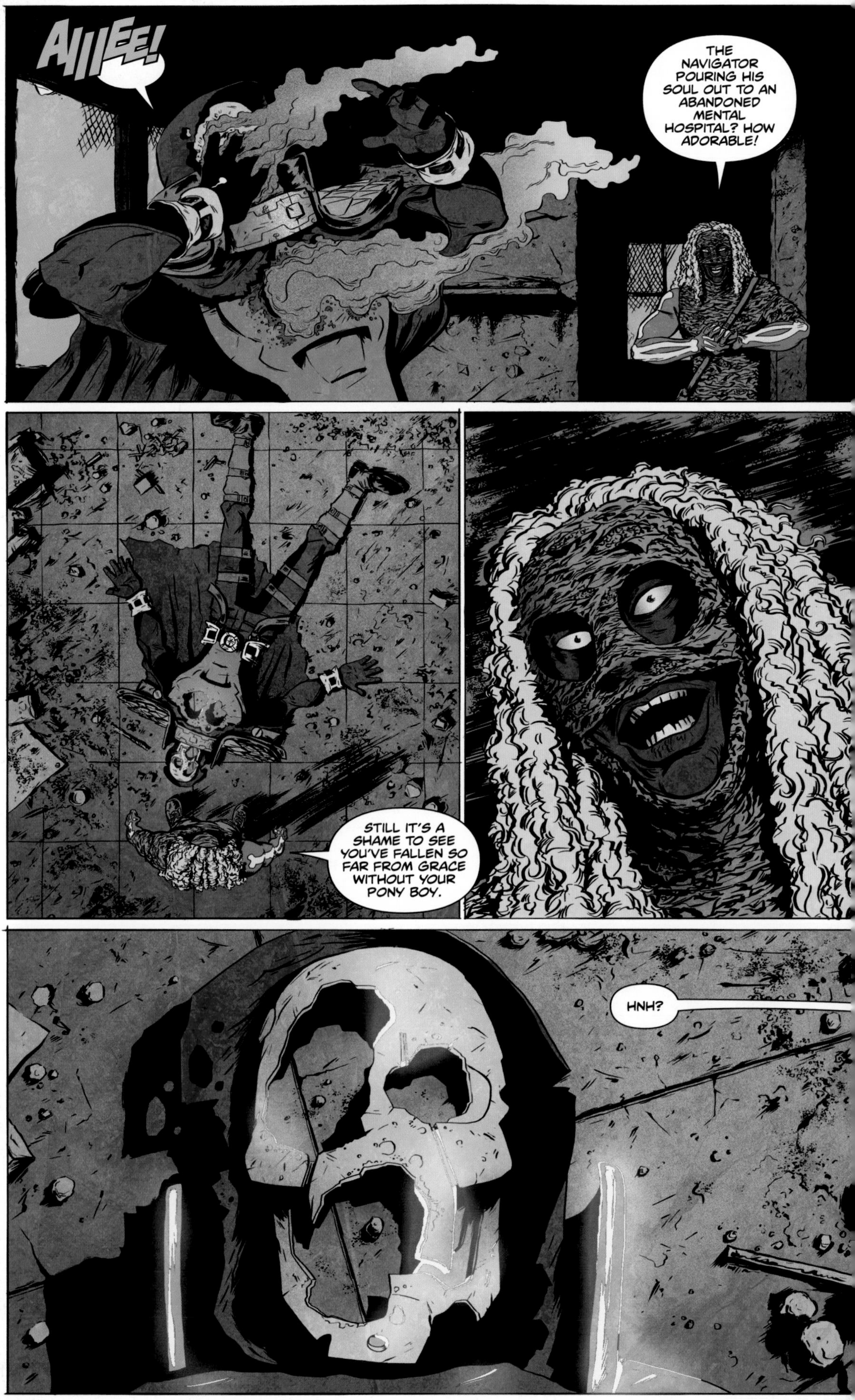
AIIIEE!
THE NAVIGATOR POURING HIS SOUL OUT TO AN ABANDONED MENTAL HOSPITAL? HOW ADORABLE!
STILL IT'S A SHAME TO SEE YOU'VE FALLEN SO FAR FROM GRACE WITHOUT YOUR PONY BOY.
HNH?

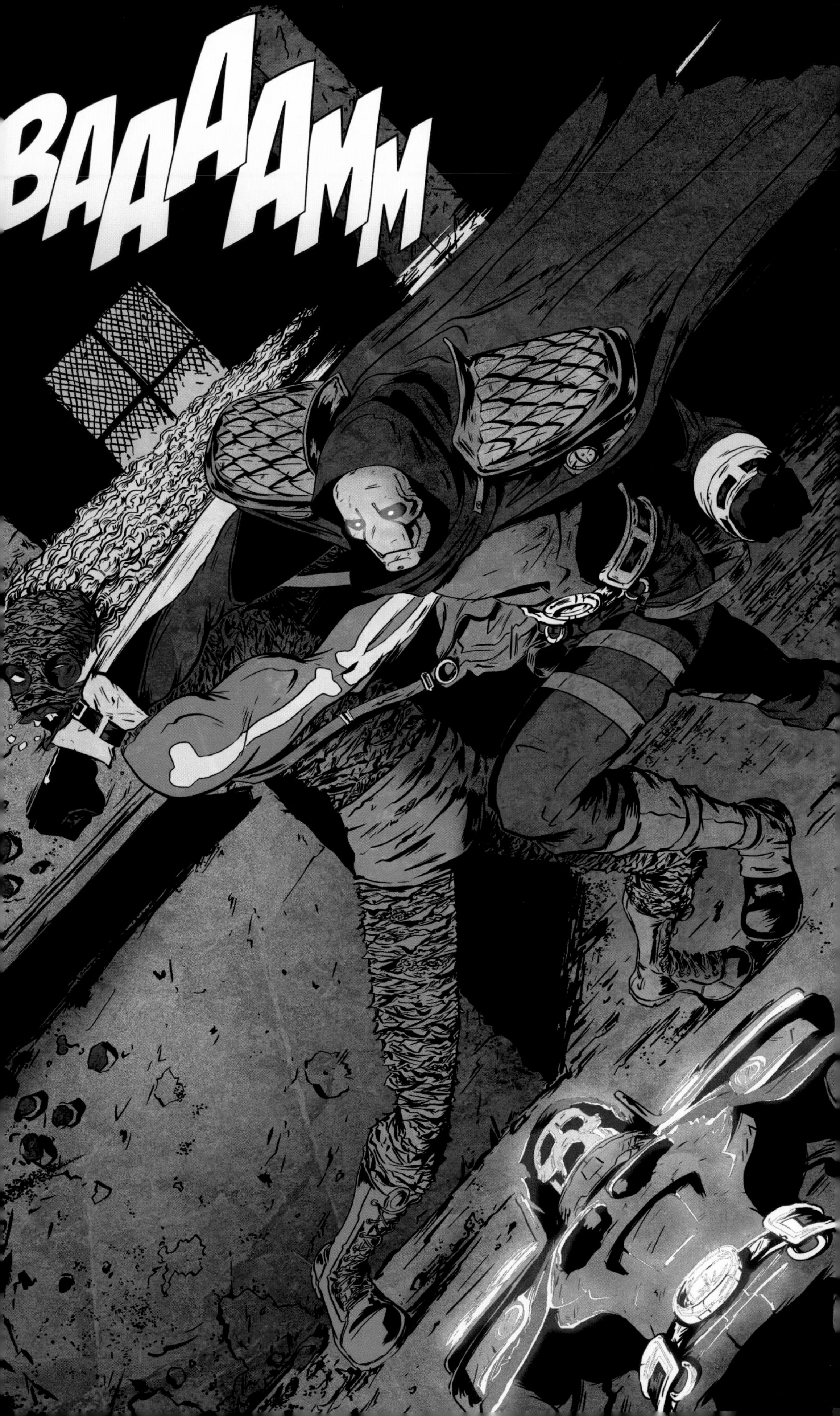
BAAAAMM

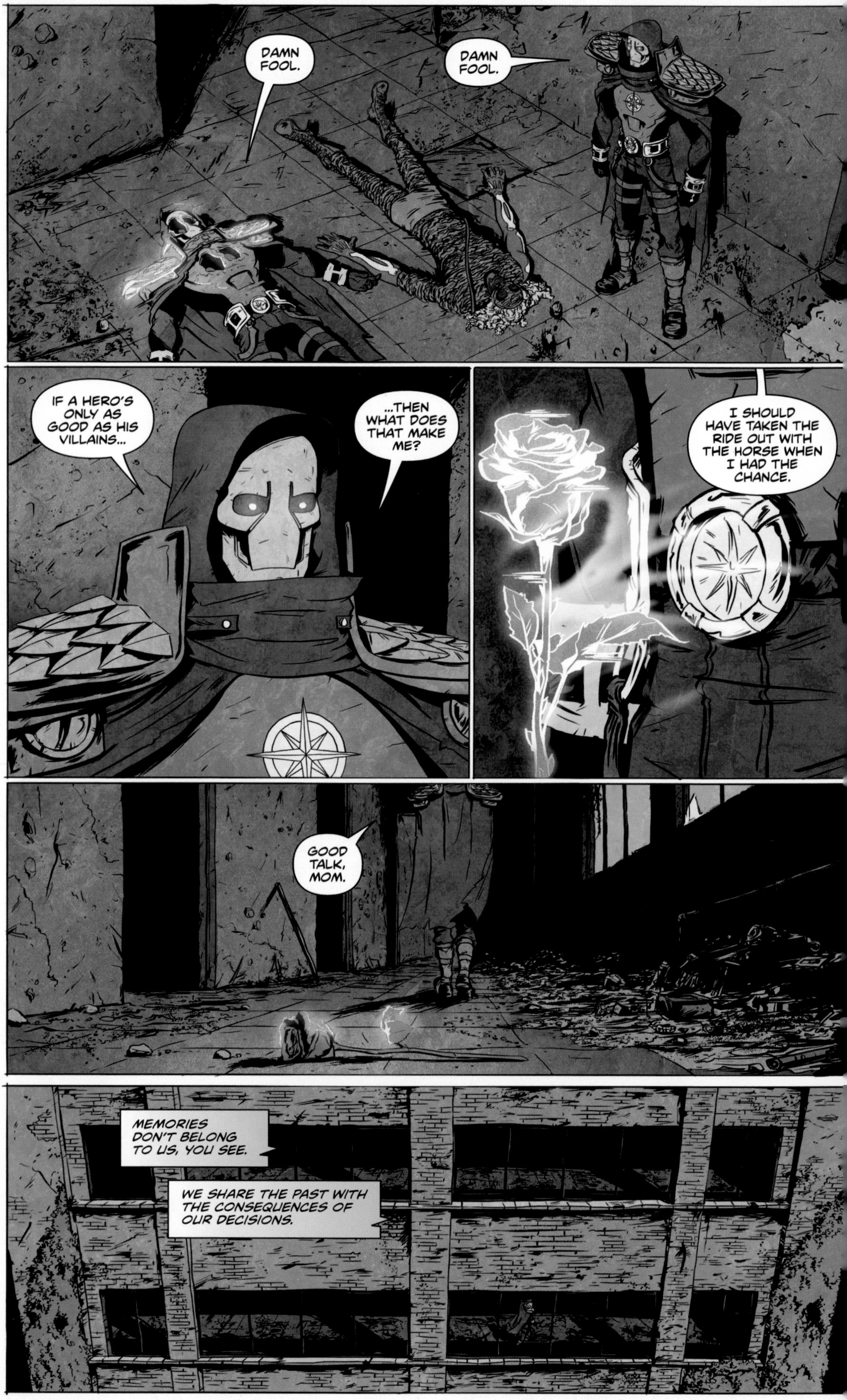
DAMN FOOL.
DAMN FOOL.
IF A HERO'S ONLY AS GOOD AS HIS VILLAINS...
...THEN WHAT DOES THAT MAKE ME?
I SHOULD HAVE TAKEN THE RIDE OUT WITH THE HORSE WHEN I HAD THE CHANCE.
GOOD TALK, MOM.
MEMORIES DON'T BELONG TO US, YOU SEE.
WE SHARE THE PAST WITH THE CONSEQUENCES OF OUR DECISIONS.

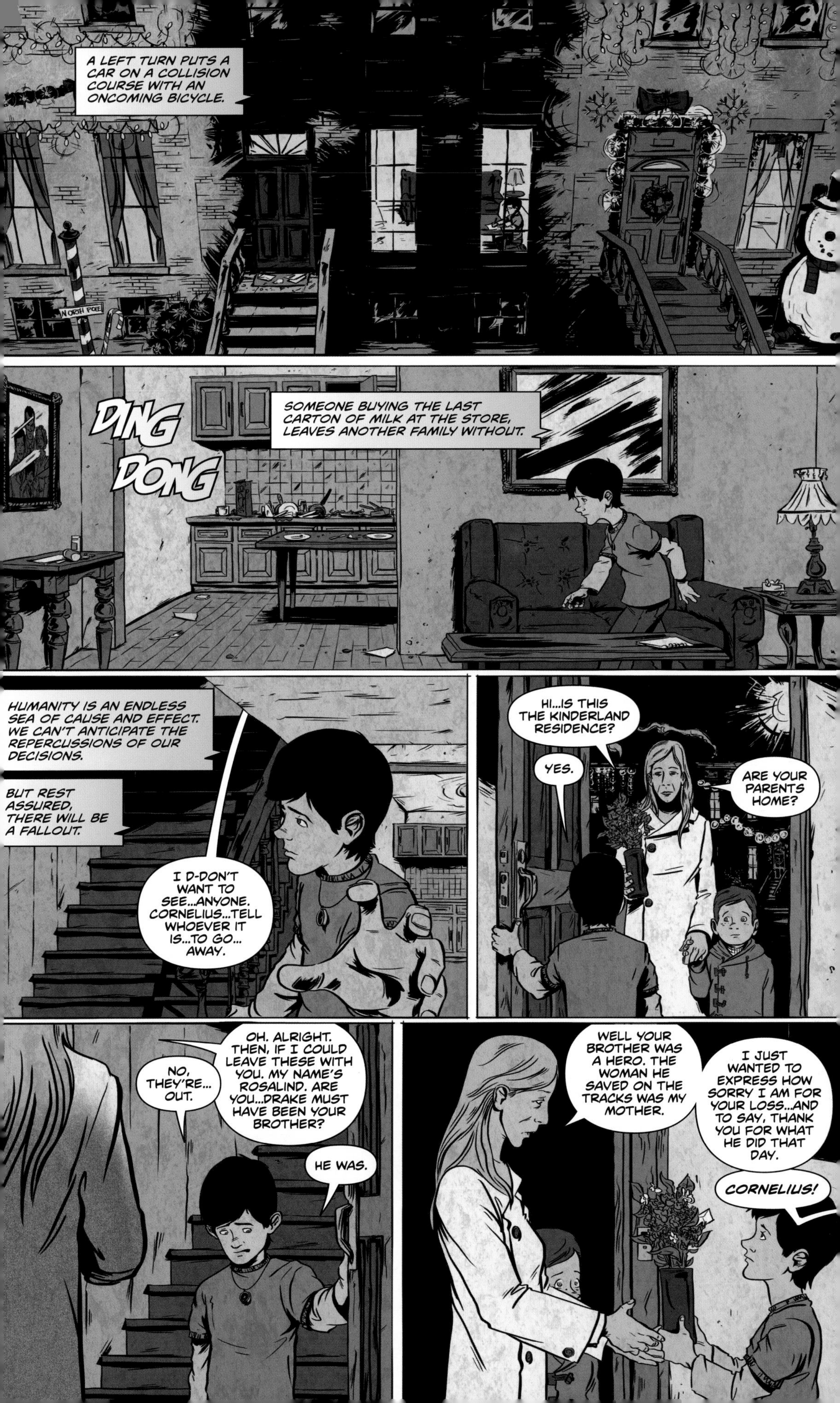

A LEFT TURN PUTS A CAR ON A COLLISION COURSE WITH AN ONCOMING BICYCLE.
NORTH POLE
DING DONG
SOMEONE BUYING THE LAST CARTON OF MILK AT THE STORE, LEAVES ANOTHER FAMILY WITHOUT.
HUMANITY IS AN ENDLESS SEA OF CAUSE AND EFFECT. WE CAN'T ANTICIPATE THE REPERCUSSIONS OF OUR DECISIONS.
BUT REST ASSURED, THERE WILL BE A FALLOUT.
I D-DON'T WANT TO SEE...ANYONE. CORNELIUS...TELL WHOEVER IT IS...TO GO... AWAY.
HI...IS THIS THE KINDERLAND RESIDENCE?
YES.
ARE YOUR PARENTS HOME?
NO, THEY'RE... OUT.
OH. ALRIGHT. THEN, IF I COULD LEAVE THESE WITH YOU. MY NAME'S ROSALIND. ARE YOU...DRAKE MUST HAVE BEEN YOUR BROTHER?
HE WAS.
WELL YOUR BROTHER WAS A HERO. THE WOMAN HE SAVED ON THE TRACKS WAS MY MOTHER.
I JUST WANTED TO EXPRESS HOW SORRY I AM FOR YOUR LOSS...AND TO SAY, THANK YOU FOR WHAT HE DID THAT DAY.
CORNELIUS!

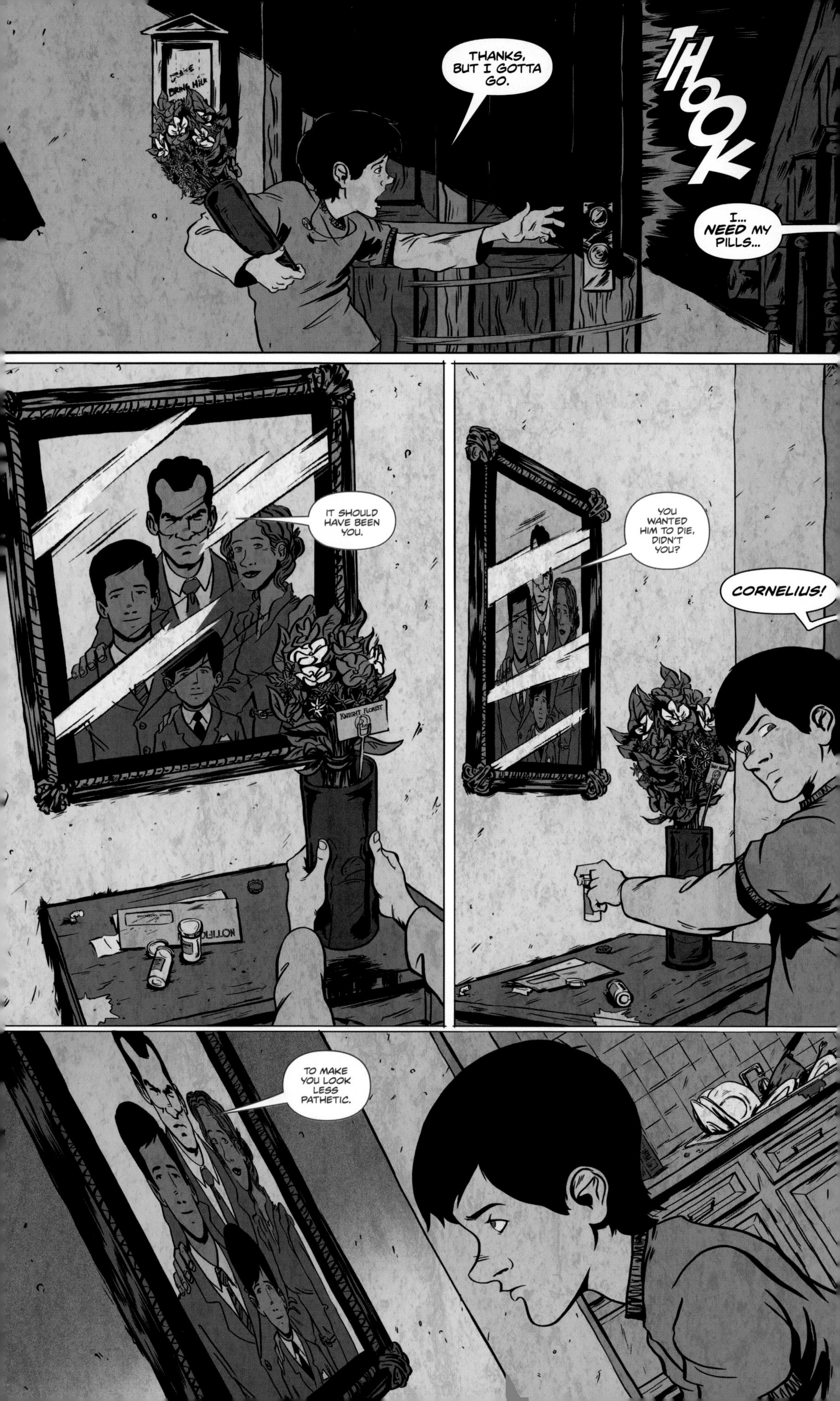
THANKS, BUT I GOTTA GO.
THOOK
I... NEED MY PILLS...
IT SHOULD HAVE BEEN YOU.
KNIGHT FLORIST
YOU WANTED HIM TO DIE, DIDN'T YOU?
CORNELIUS!
TO MAKE YOU LOOK LESS PATHETIC.

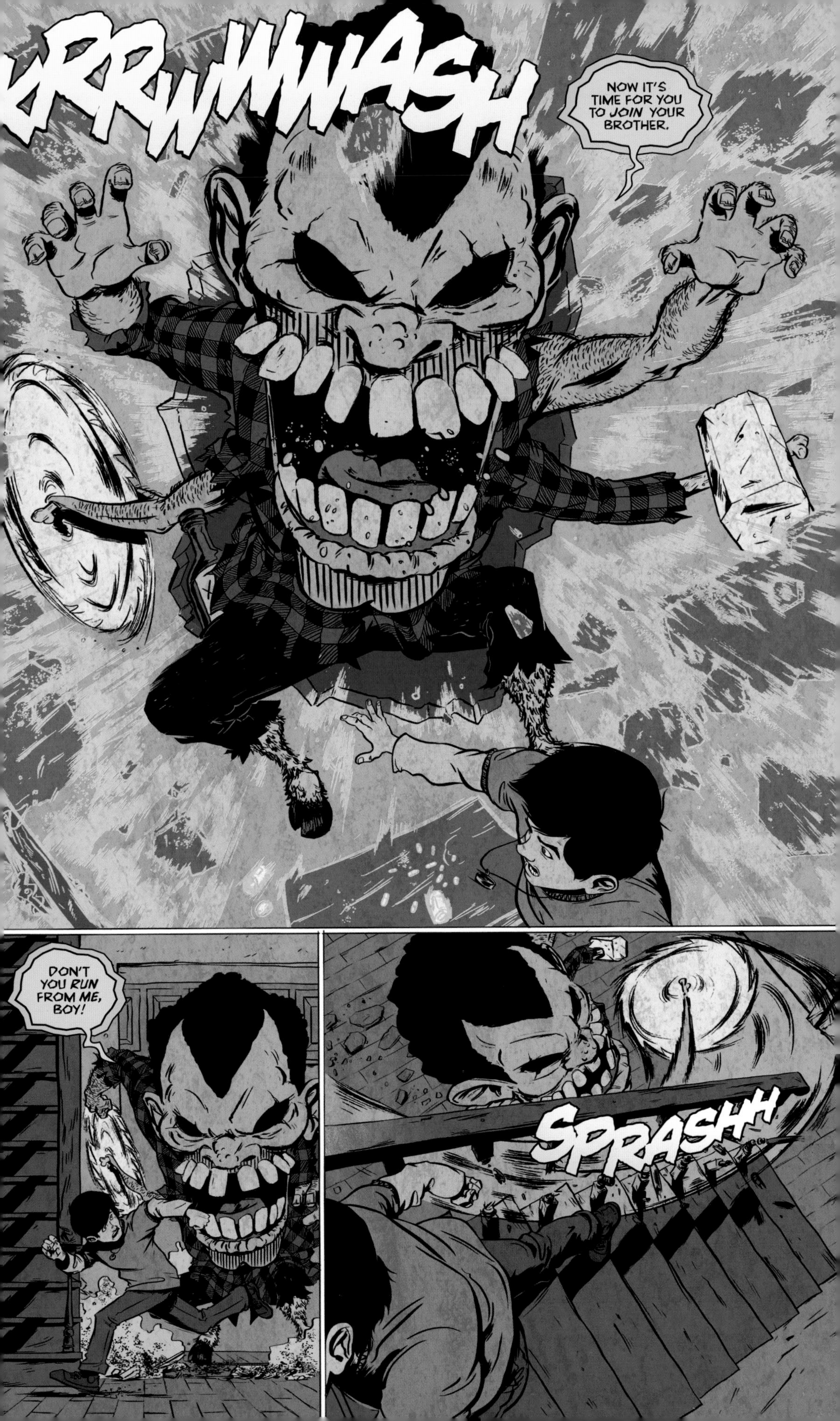
KRRWWWASH
NOW IT'S TIME FOR YOU TO JOIN YOUR BROTHER.
DON'T YOU RUN FROM ME, BOY!
SPRASHH

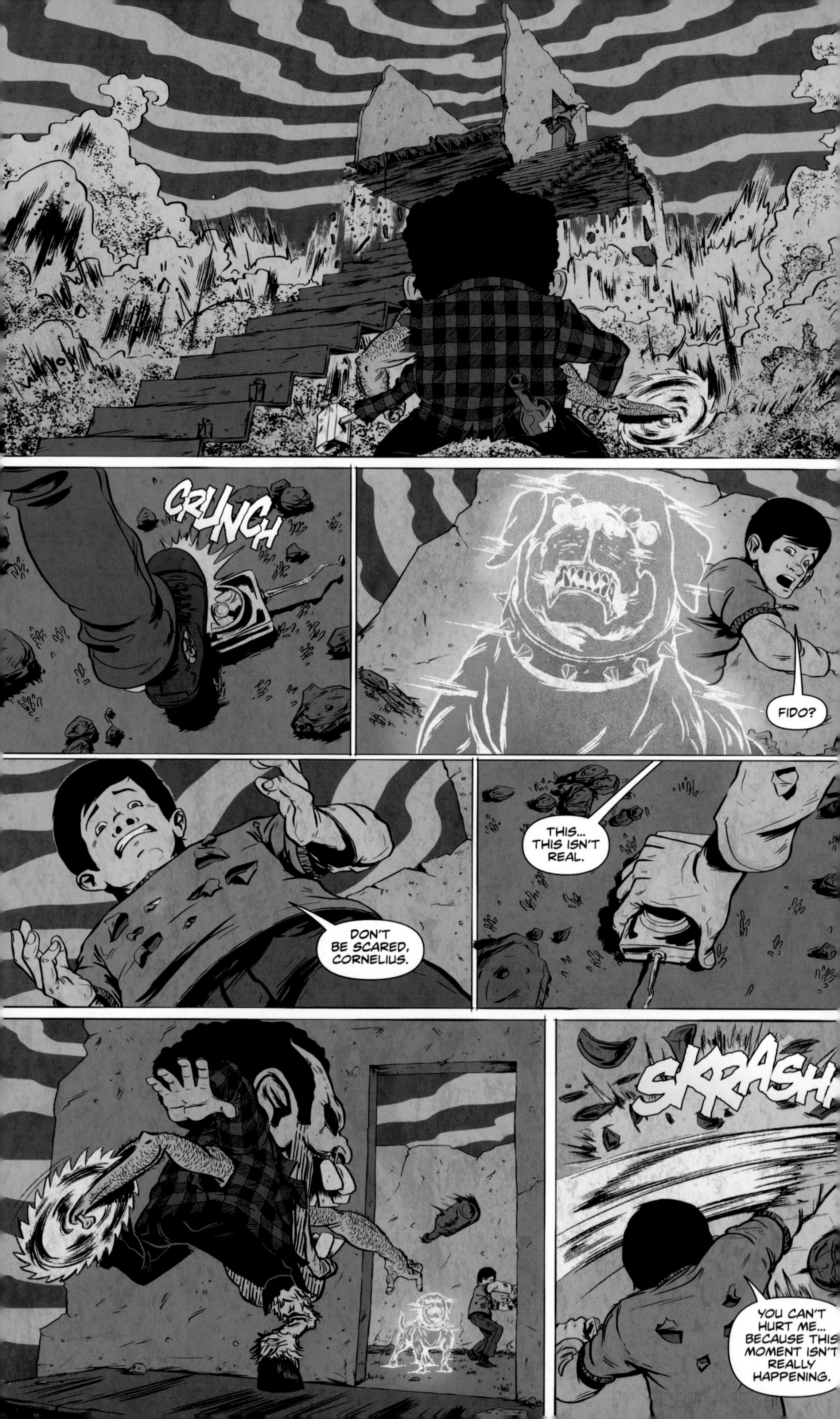
CRUNCH
FIDO?
DON'T BE SCARED, CORNELIUS.
THIS... THIS ISN'T REAL.
SKRASH
YOU CAN'T HURT ME... BECAUSE THIS MOMENT ISN'T REALLY HAPPENING.

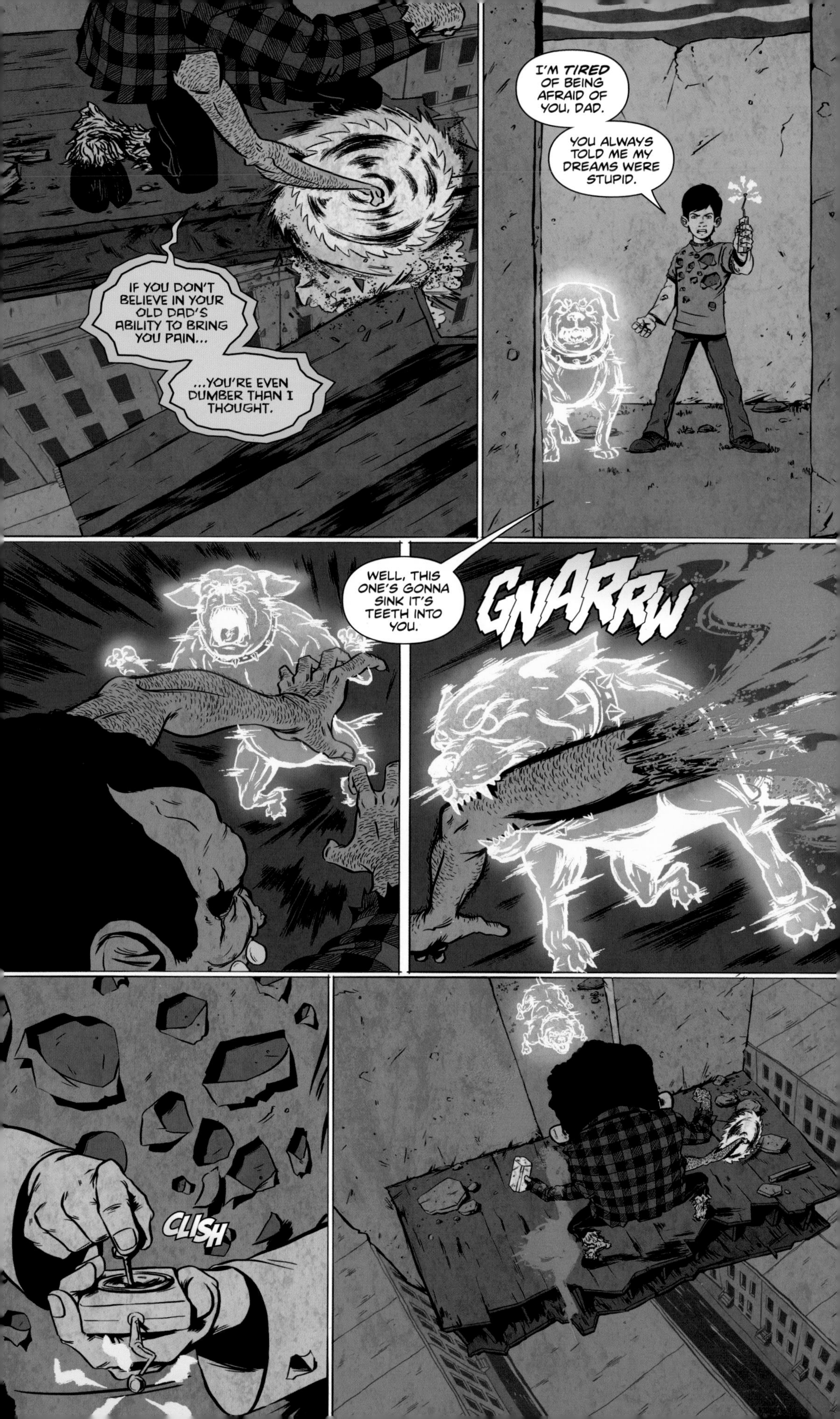
IF YOU DON'T BELIEVE IN YOUR OLD DAD'S ABILITY TO BRING YOU PAIN...
...YOU'RE EVEN DUMBER THAN I THOUGHT.
I'M *TIRED* OF BEING AFRAID OF YOU, DAD.
YOU ALWAYS TOLD ME MY DREAMS WERE STUPID.
WELL, THIS ONE'S GONNA SINK IT'S TEETH INTO YOU.
GNARRW
CLISH

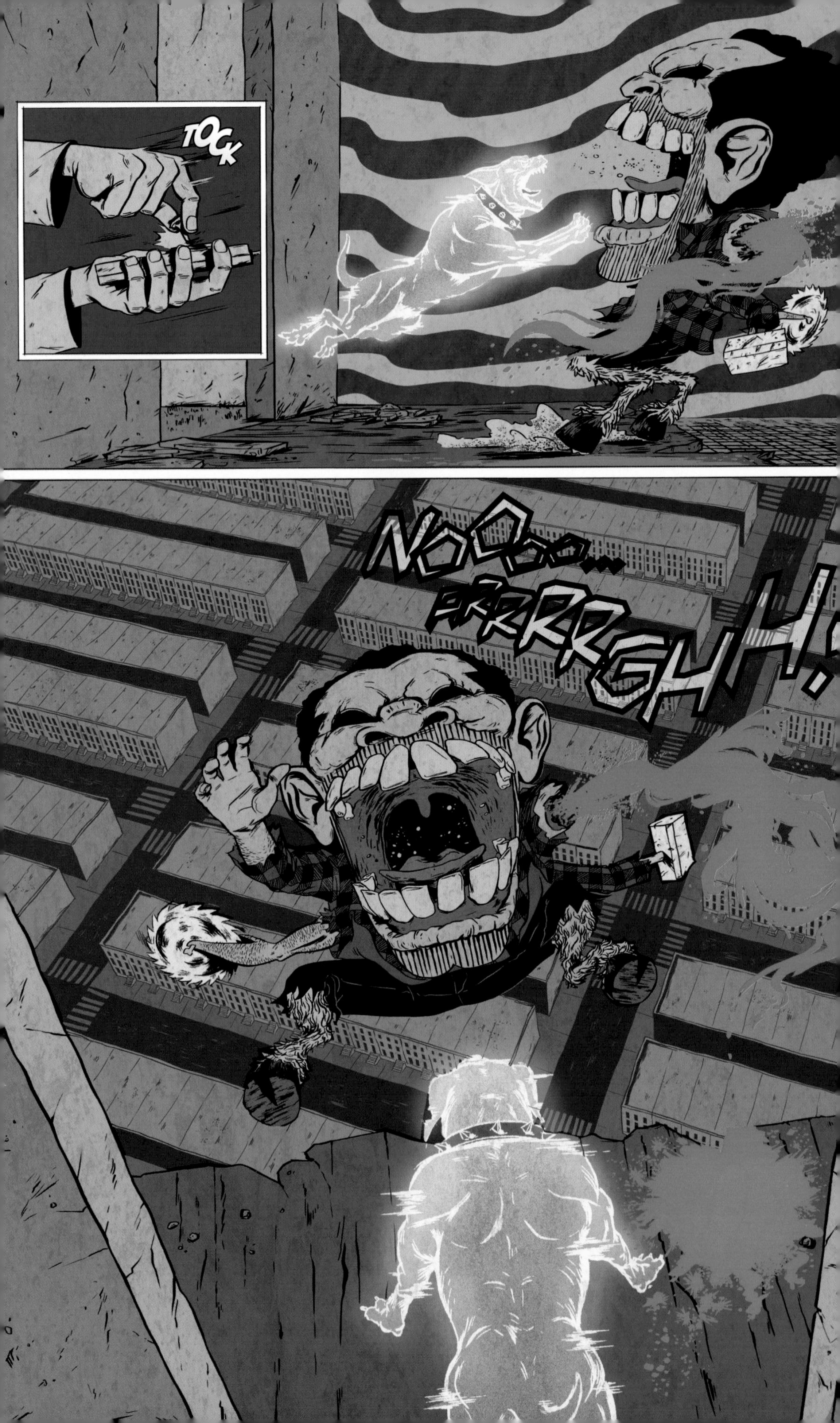
TOCK
NOOooo... ARRRRGH!

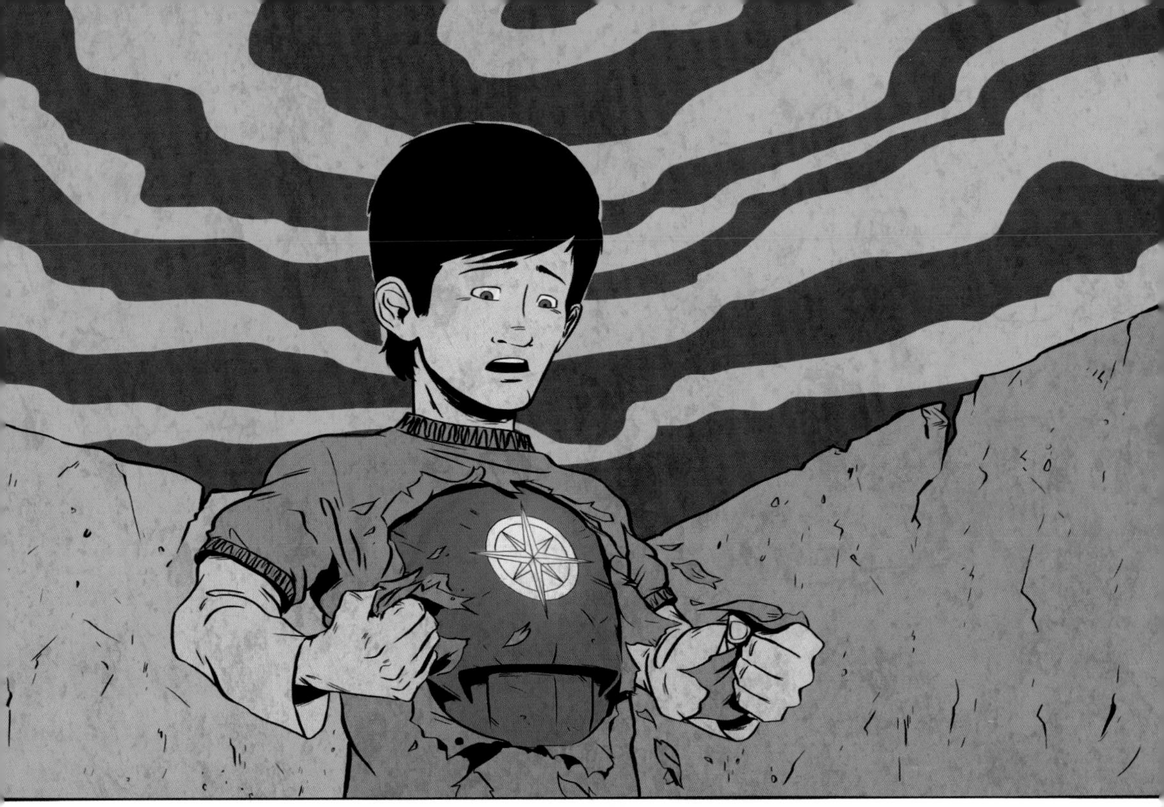
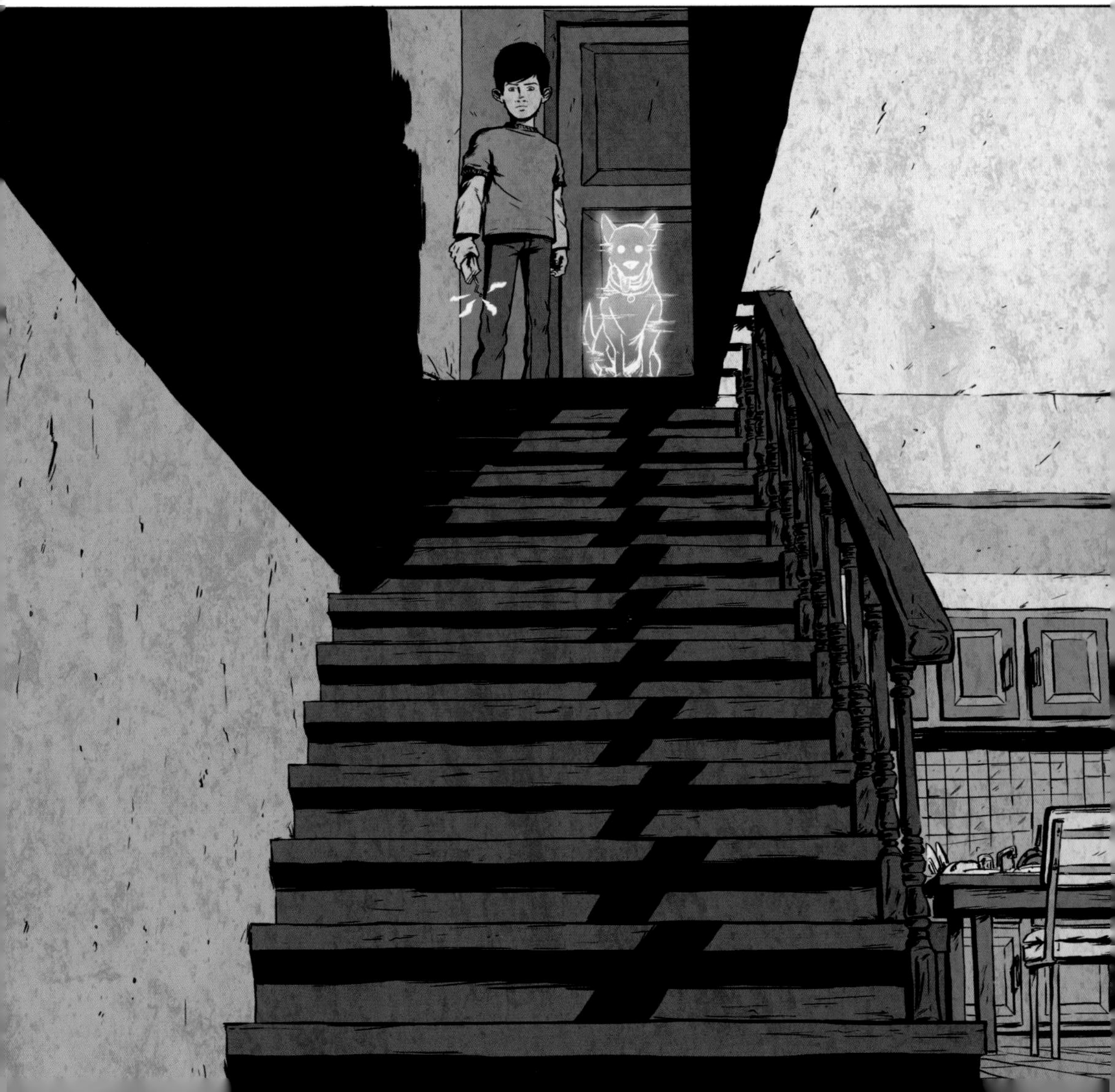

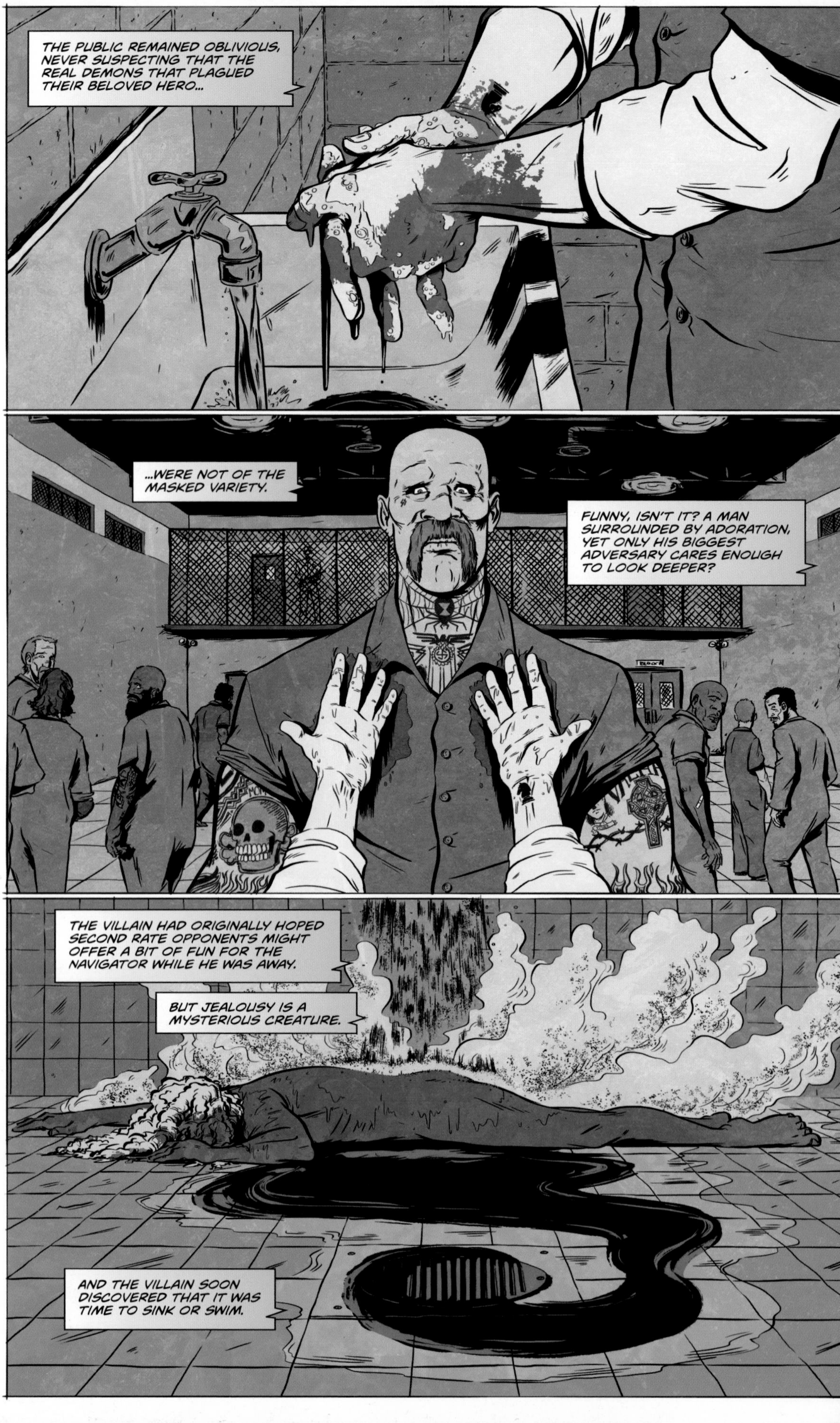

THE PUBLIC REMAINED OBLIVIOUS, NEVER SUSPECTING THAT THE REAL DEMONS THAT PLAGUED THEIR BELOVED HERO...
...WERE NOT OF THE MASKED VARIETY.
FUNNY, ISN'T IT? A MAN SURROUNDED BY ADORATION, YET ONLY HIS BIGGEST ADVERSARY CARES ENOUGH TO LOOK DEEPER?
THE VILLAIN HAD ORIGINALLY HOPED SECOND RATE OPPONENTS MIGHT OFFER A BIT OF FUN FOR THE NAVIGATOR WHILE HE WAS AWAY.
BUT JEALOUSY IS A MYSTERIOUS CREATURE.
AND THE VILLAIN SOON DISCOVERED THAT IT WAS TIME TO SINK OR SWIM.

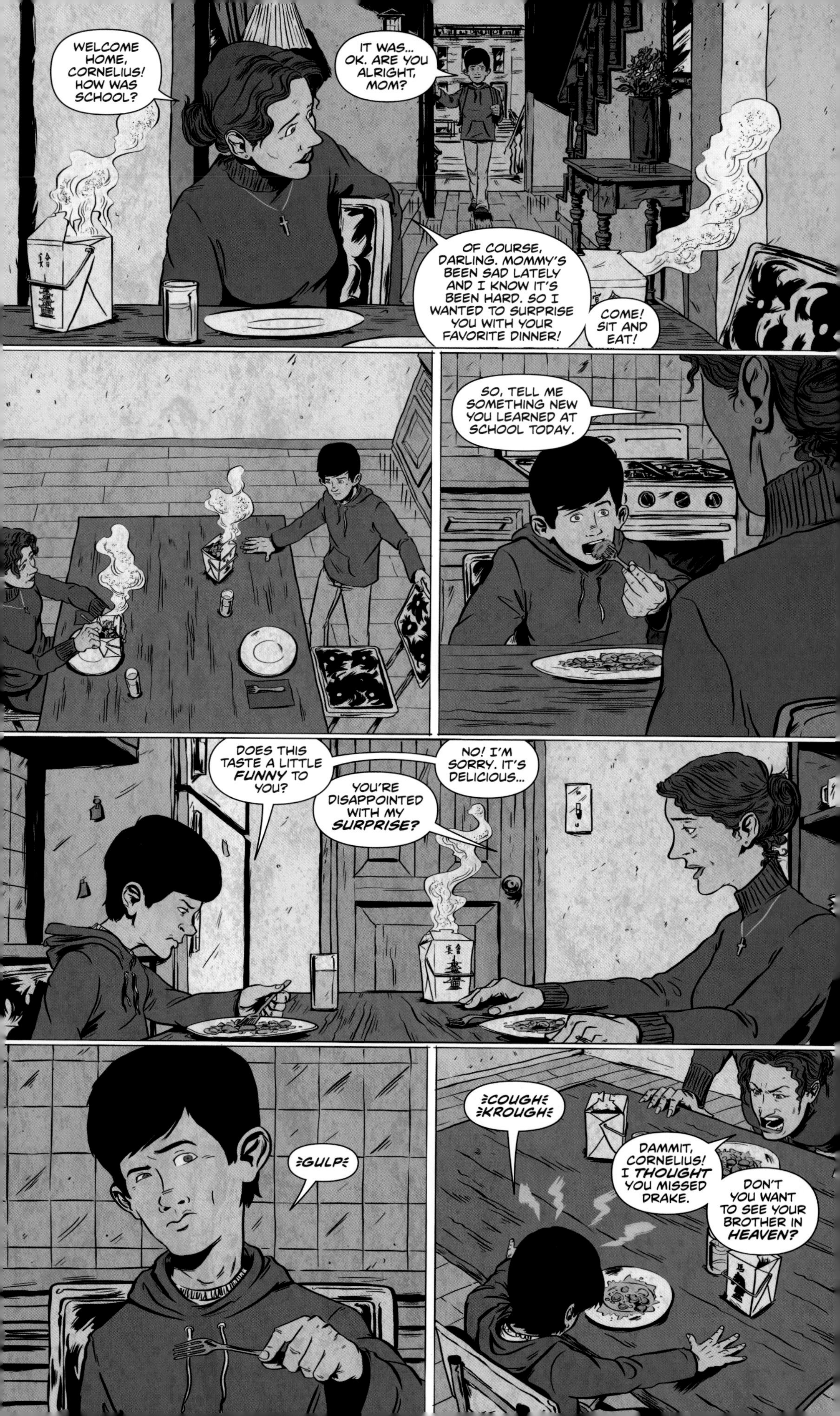
WELCOME HOME, CORNELIUS! HOW WAS SCHOOL?
IT WAS... OK. ARE YOU ALRIGHT, MOM?
OF COURSE, DARLING. MOMMY'S BEEN SAD LATELY AND I KNOW IT'S BEEN HARD. SO I WANTED TO SURPRISE YOU WITH YOUR FAVORITE DINNER!
COME! SIT AND EAT!
SO, TELL ME SOMETHING NEW YOU LEARNED AT SCHOOL TODAY.
DOES THIS TASTE A LITTLE *FUNNY* TO YOU?
YOU'RE DISAPPOINTED WITH MY *SURPRISE?*
NO! I'M SORRY. IT'S DELICIOUS...
GULP
COUGH KROUGH
DAMMIT, CORNELIUS! I *THOUGHT* YOU MISSED DRAKE.
DON'T YOU WANT TO SEE YOUR BROTHER IN *HEAVEN?*

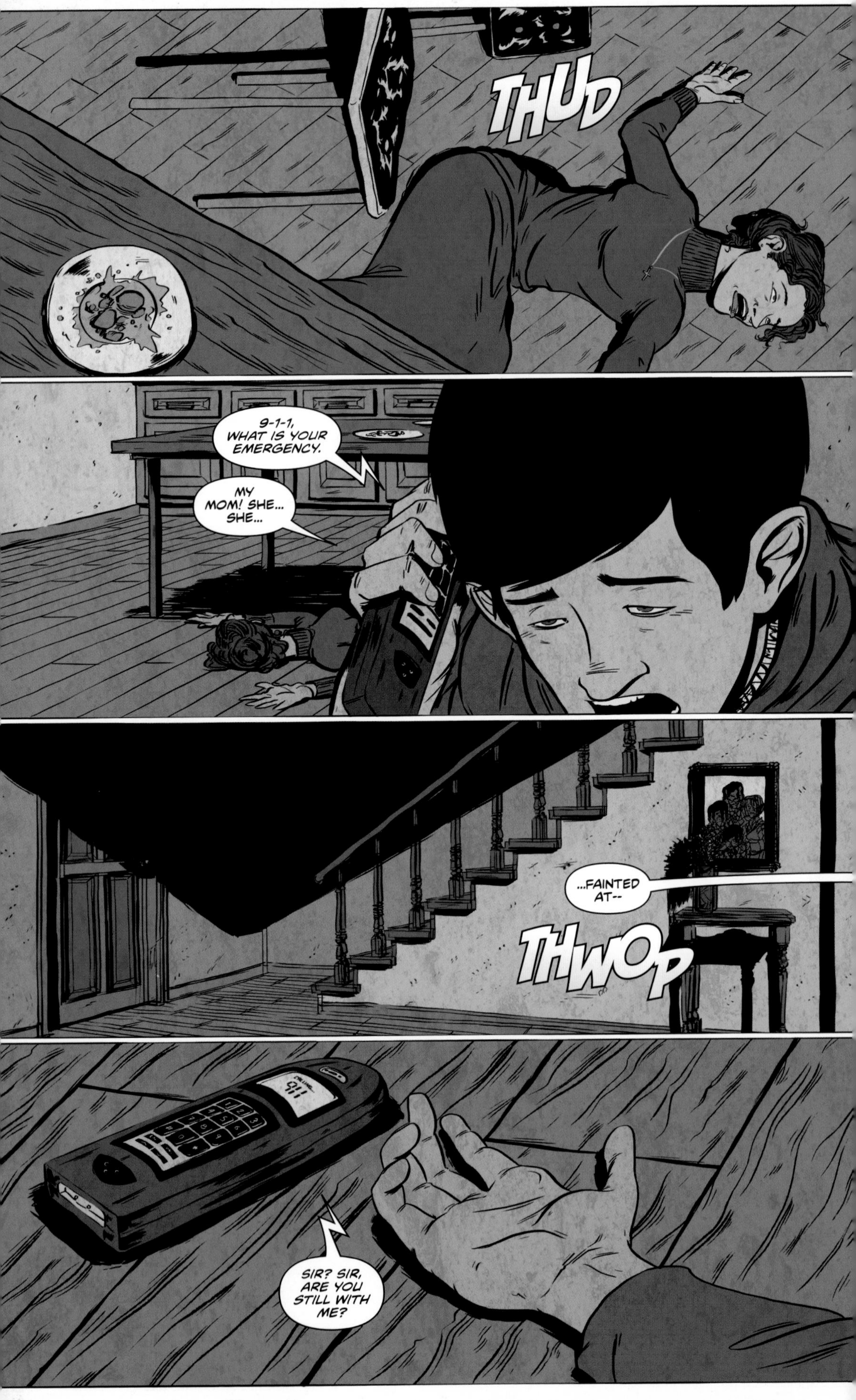
THUD
9-1-1, WHAT IS YOUR EMERGENCY.
MY MOM! SHE... SHE...
...FAINTED AT--
THWOP
SIR? SIR, ARE YOU STILL WITH ME?

ISSUE FOUR BOOM! STUDIOS EXCLUSIVE COVER BY **FELIPE SMITH**

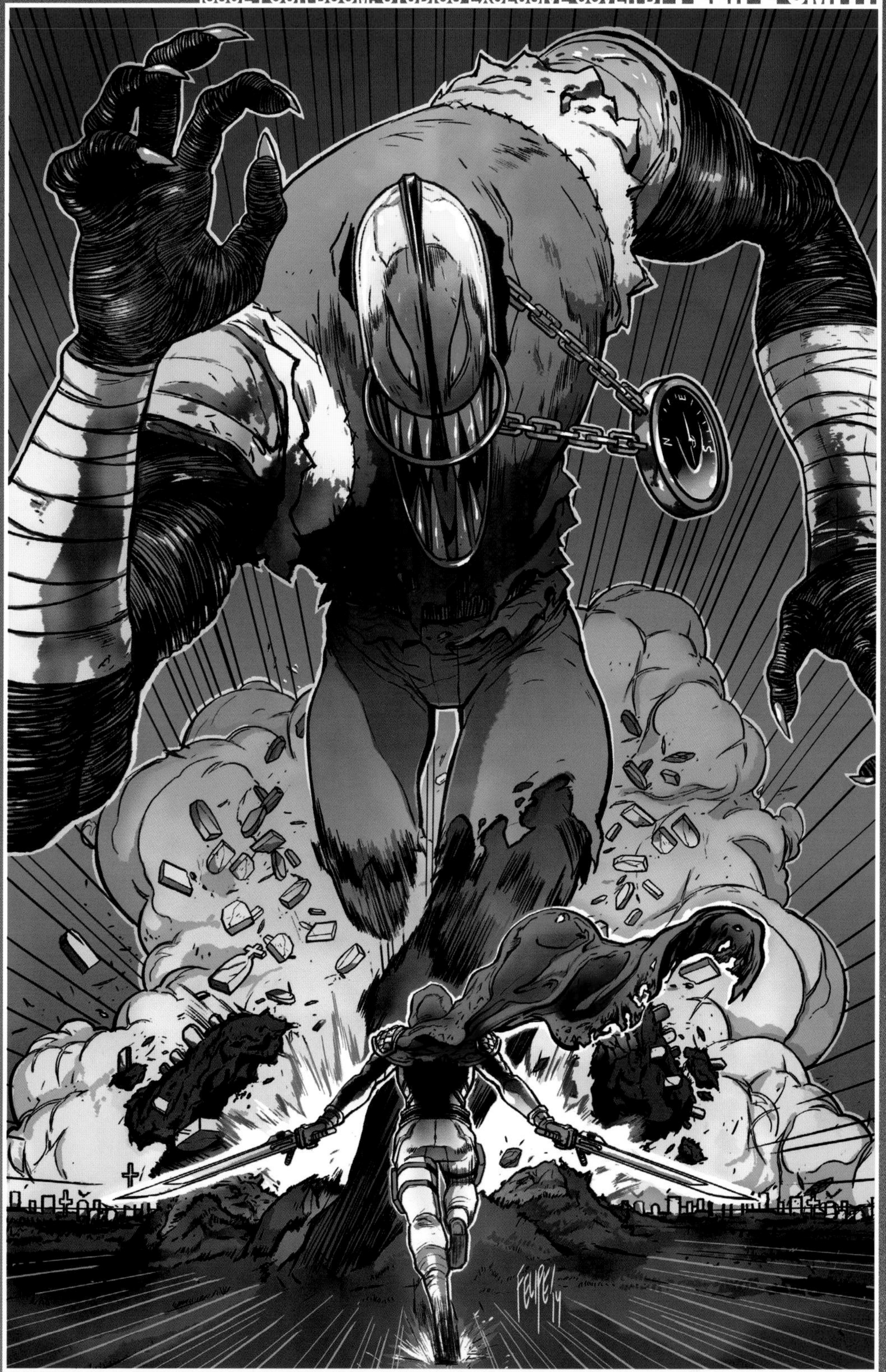
FELIPE '14

ISSUE FIVE COVER BY **JEFF STOKELY**

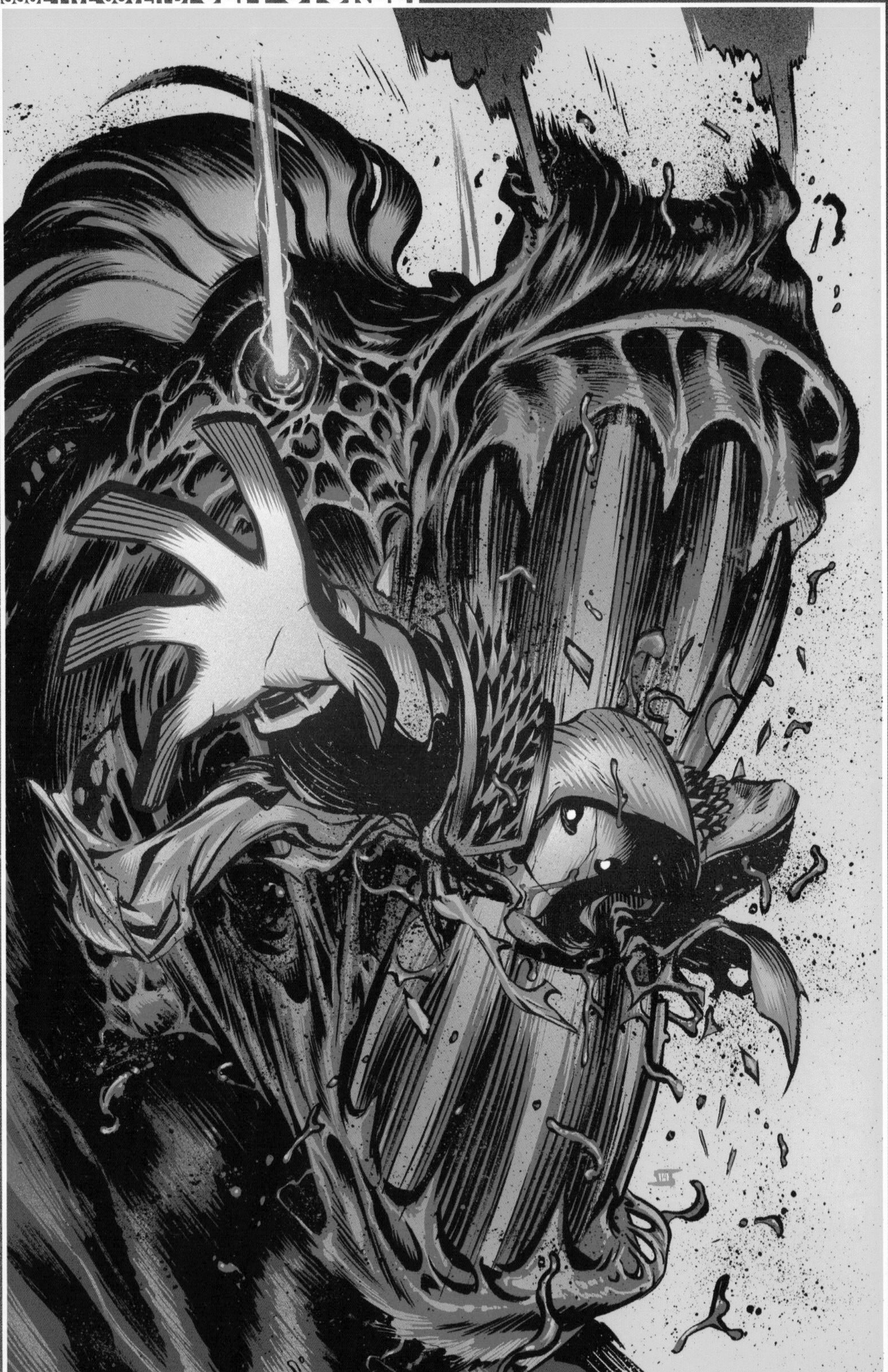

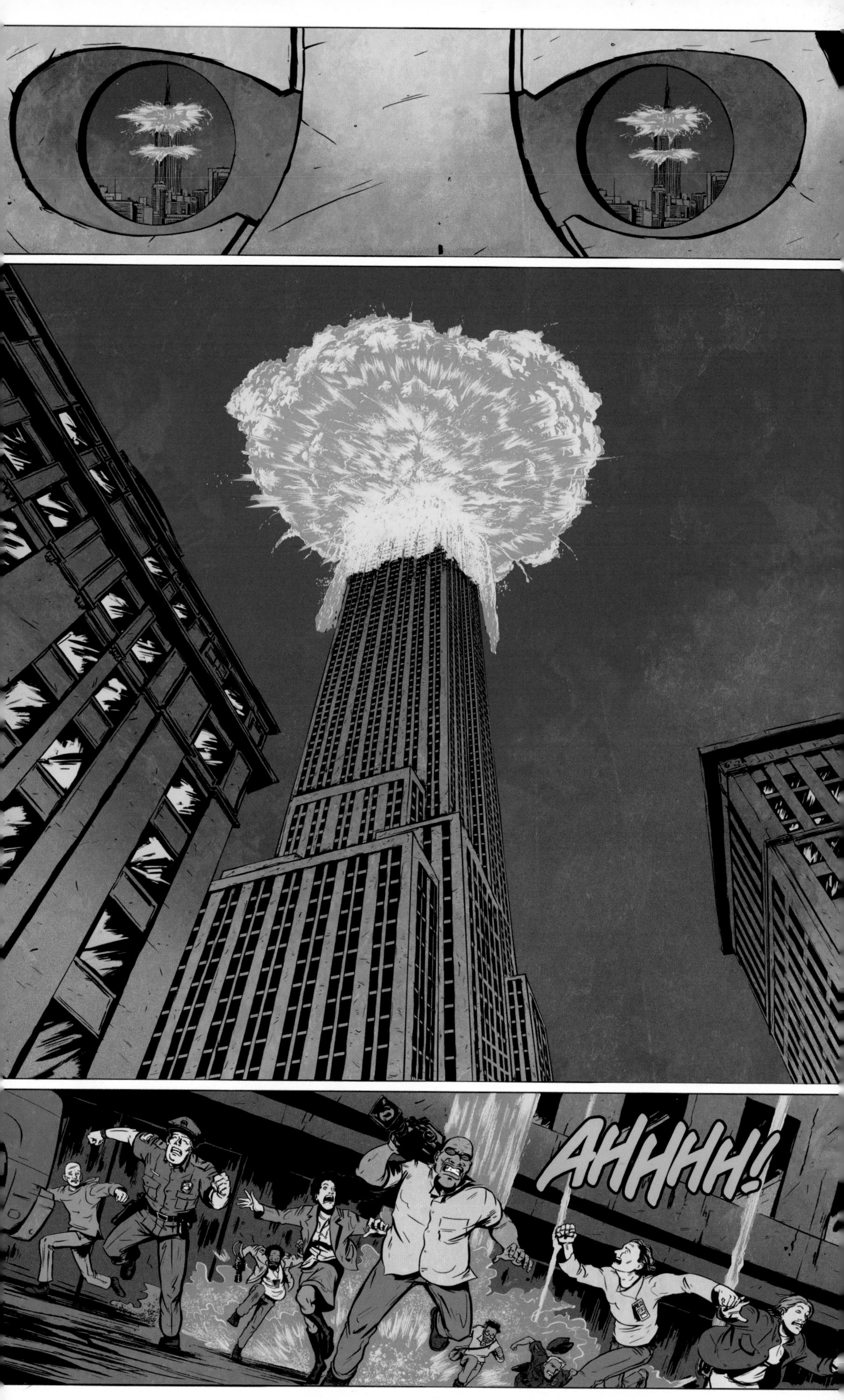
AHHHH!

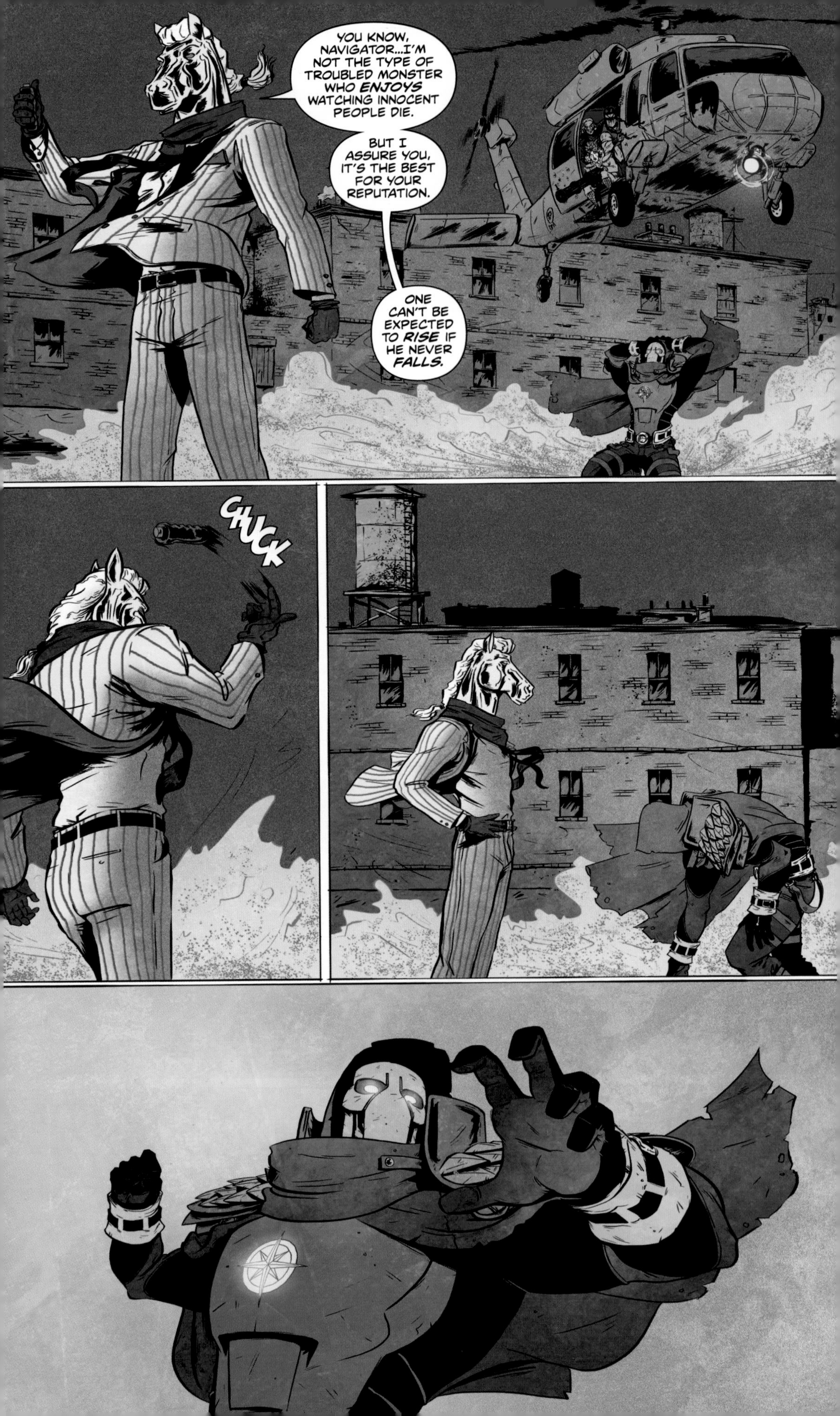

YOU KNOW, NAVIGATOR...I'M NOT THE TYPE OF TROUBLED MONSTER WHO *ENJOYS* WATCHING INNOCENT PEOPLE DIE.
BUT I ASSURE YOU, IT'S THE BEST FOR YOUR REPUTATION.
ONE CAN'T BE EXPECTED TO *RISE* IF HE NEVER *FALLS*.
CHUCK

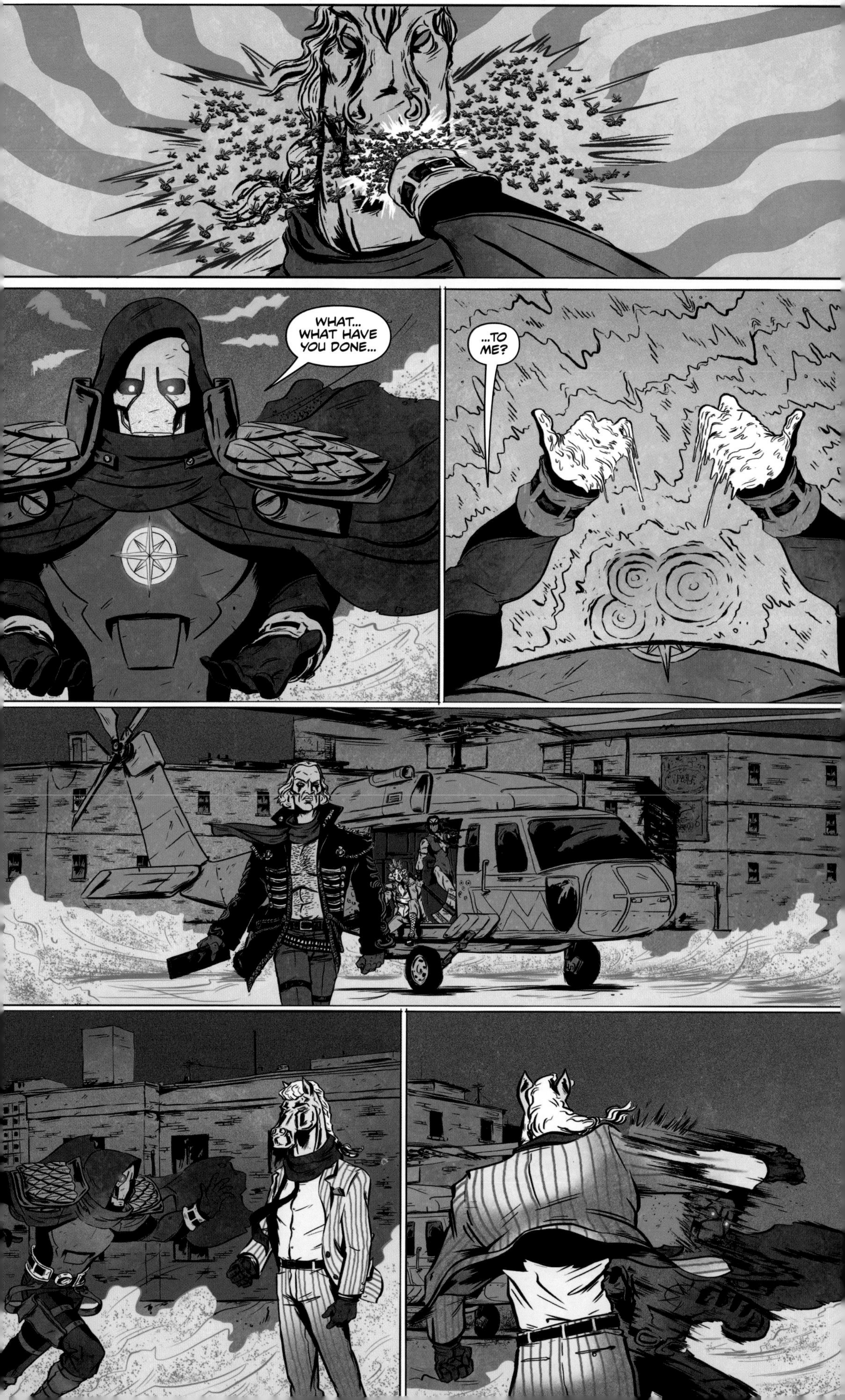
WHAT... WHAT HAVE YOU DONE...
...TO ME?

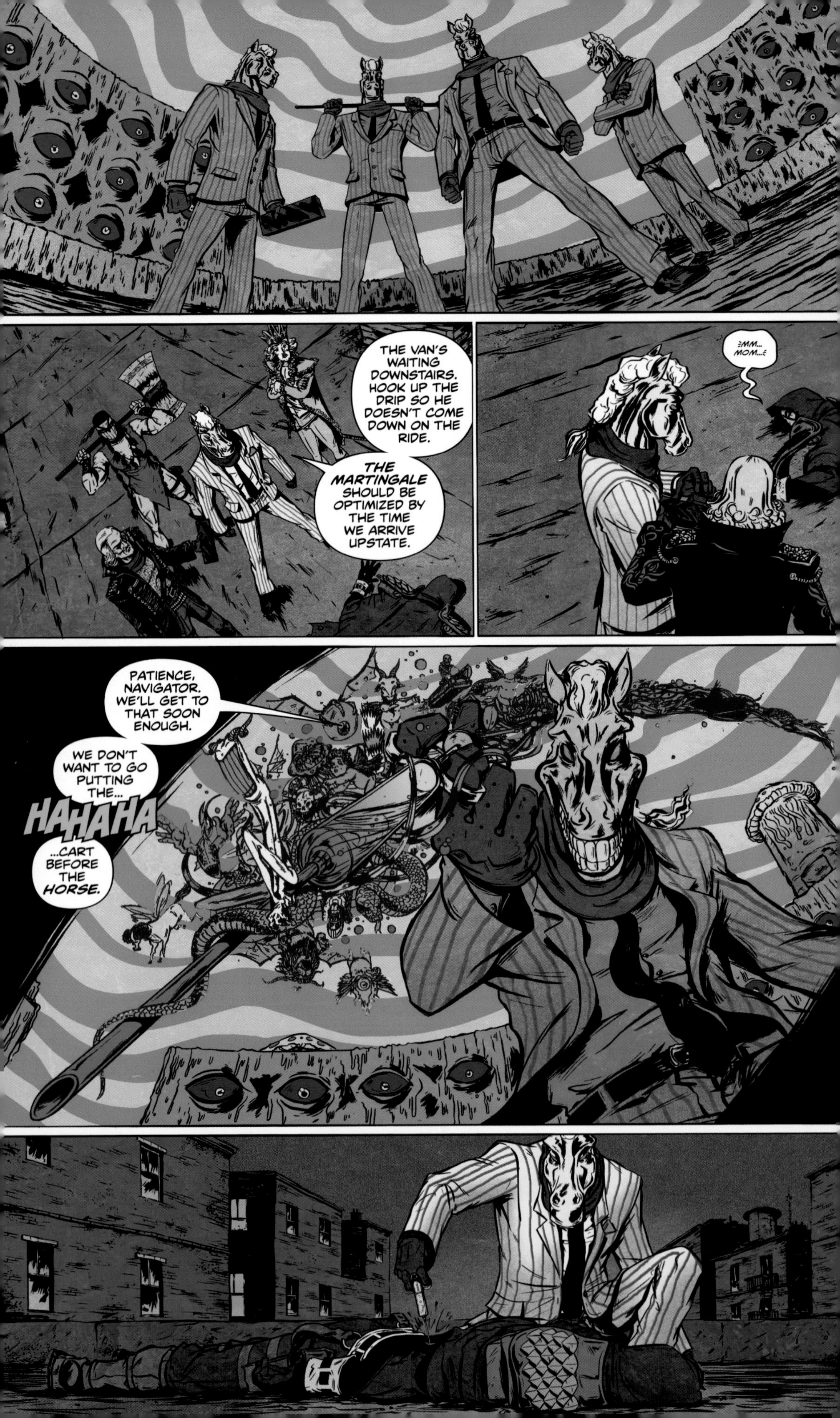
THE VAN'S WAITING DOWNSTAIRS. HOOK UP THE DRIP SO HE DOESN'T COME DOWN ON THE RIDE.
THE MARTINGALE SHOULD BE OPTIMIZED BY THE TIME WE ARRIVE UPSTATE.
MM... MOM...
PATIENCE, NAVIGATOR. WE'LL GET TO THAT SOON ENOUGH.
WE DON'T WANT TO GO PUTTING THE...
HAHAHA
...CART BEFORE THE HORSE.

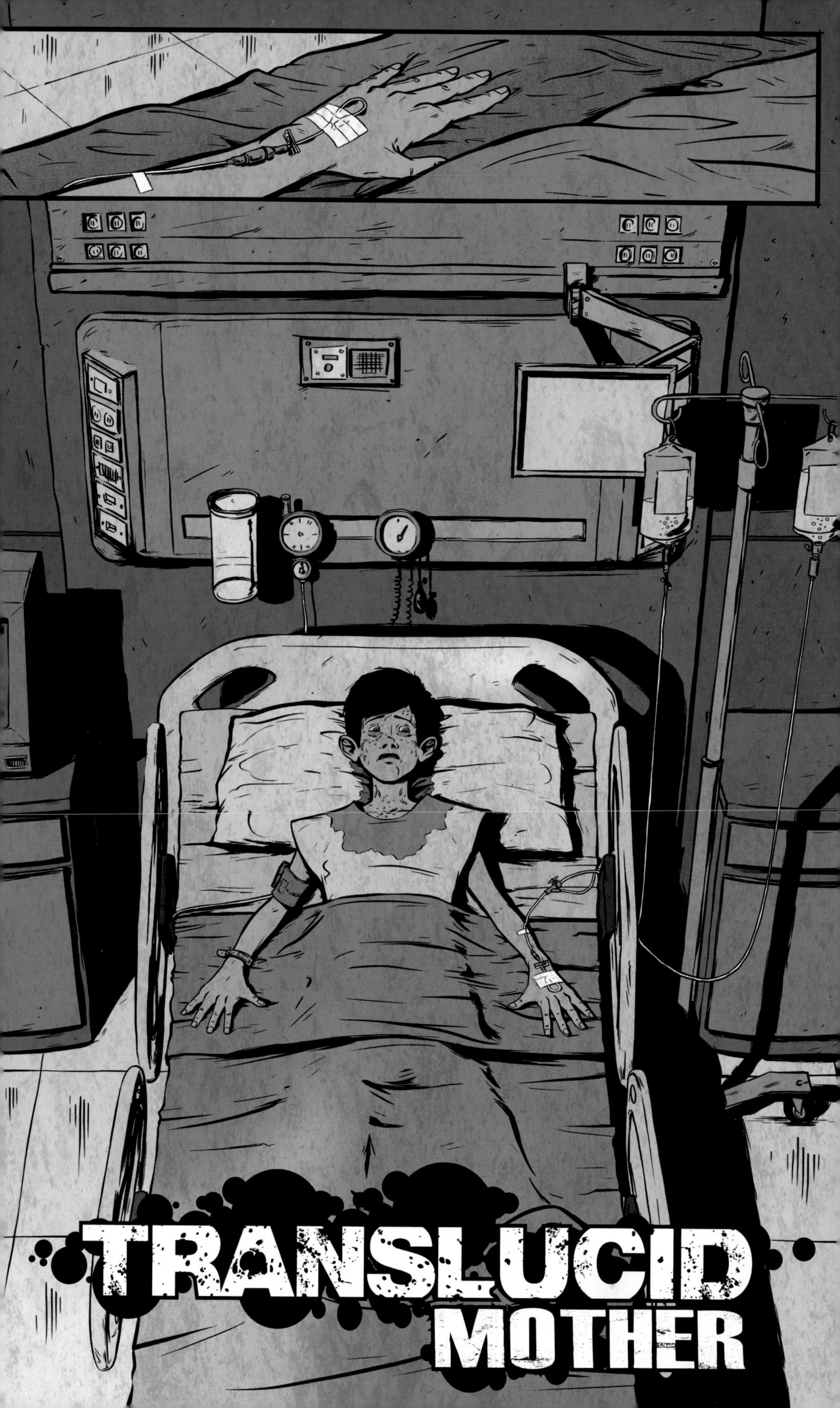
TRANSLUCID
MOTHER

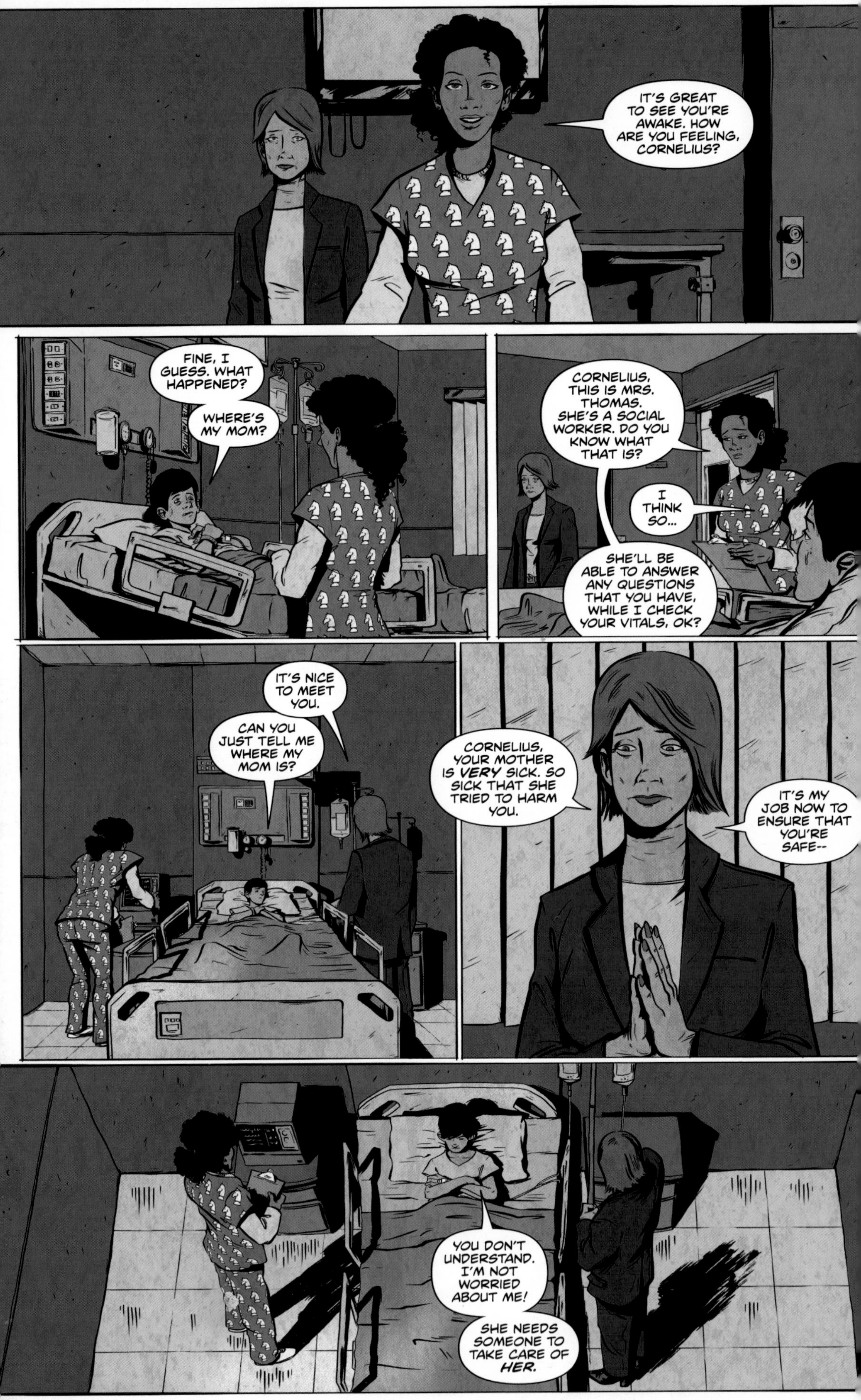
IT'S GREAT TO SEE YOU'RE AWAKE. HOW ARE YOU FEELING, CORNELIUS?
FINE, I GUESS. WHAT HAPPENED?
WHERE'S MY MOM?
CORNELIUS, THIS IS MRS. THOMAS. SHE'S A SOCIAL WORKER. DO YOU KNOW WHAT THAT IS?
I THINK SO...
SHE'LL BE ABLE TO ANSWER ANY QUESTIONS THAT YOU HAVE, WHILE I CHECK YOUR VITALS, OK?
IT'S NICE TO MEET YOU.
CAN YOU JUST TELL ME WHERE MY MOM IS?
CORNELIUS, YOUR MOTHER IS VERY SICK. SO SICK THAT SHE TRIED TO HARM YOU.
IT'S MY JOB NOW TO ENSURE THAT YOU'RE SAFE--
YOU DON'T UNDERSTAND. I'M NOT WORRIED ABOUT ME!
SHE NEEDS SOMEONE TO TAKE CARE OF HER.

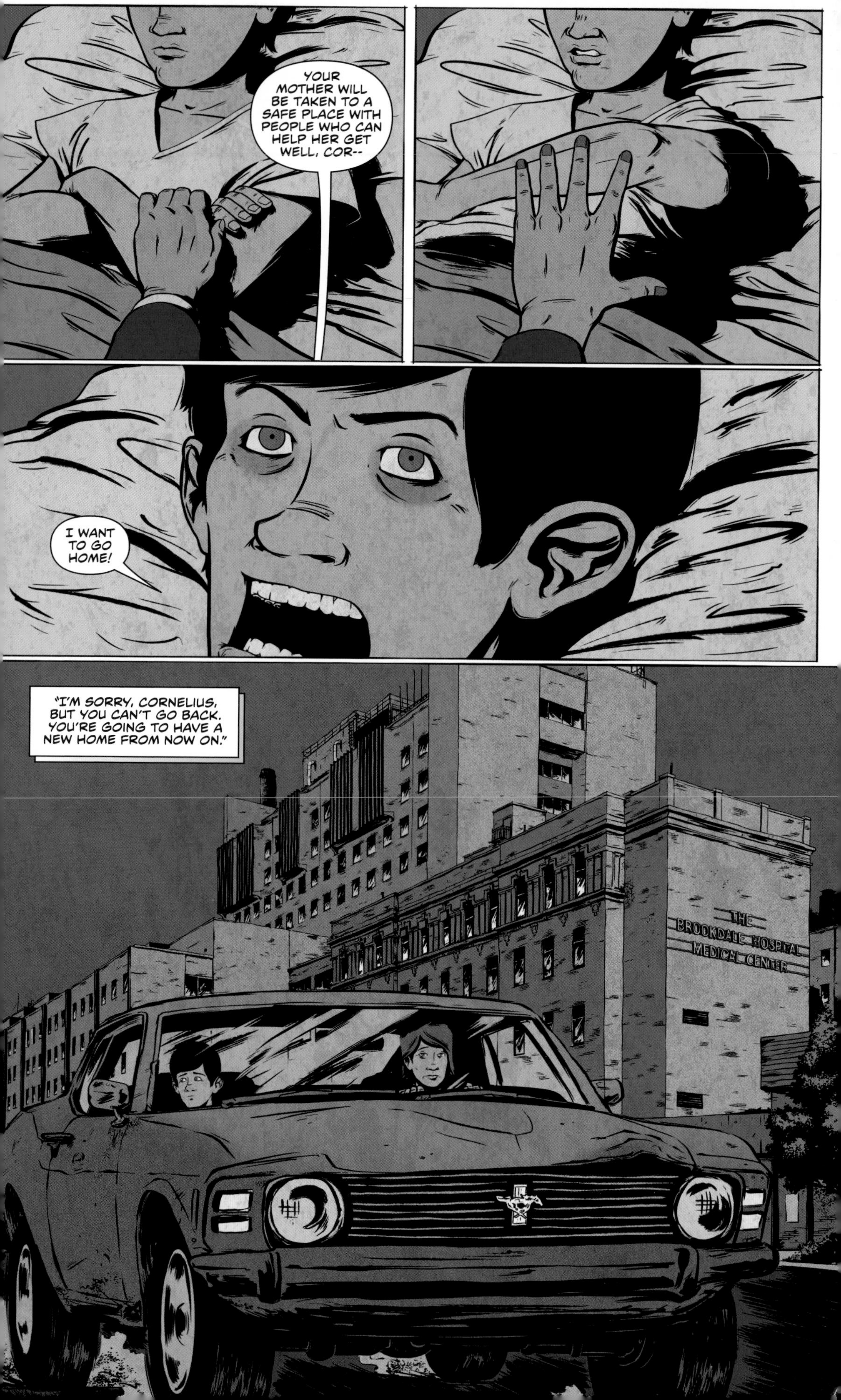
YOUR MOTHER WILL BE TAKEN TO A SAFE PLACE WITH PEOPLE WHO CAN HELP HER GET WELL, COR--
I WANT TO GO HOME!
"I'M SORRY, CORNELIUS, BUT YOU CAN'T GO BACK. YOU'RE GOING TO HAVE A NEW HOME FROM NOW ON."
THE BROOKDALE HOSPITAL MEDICAL CENTER

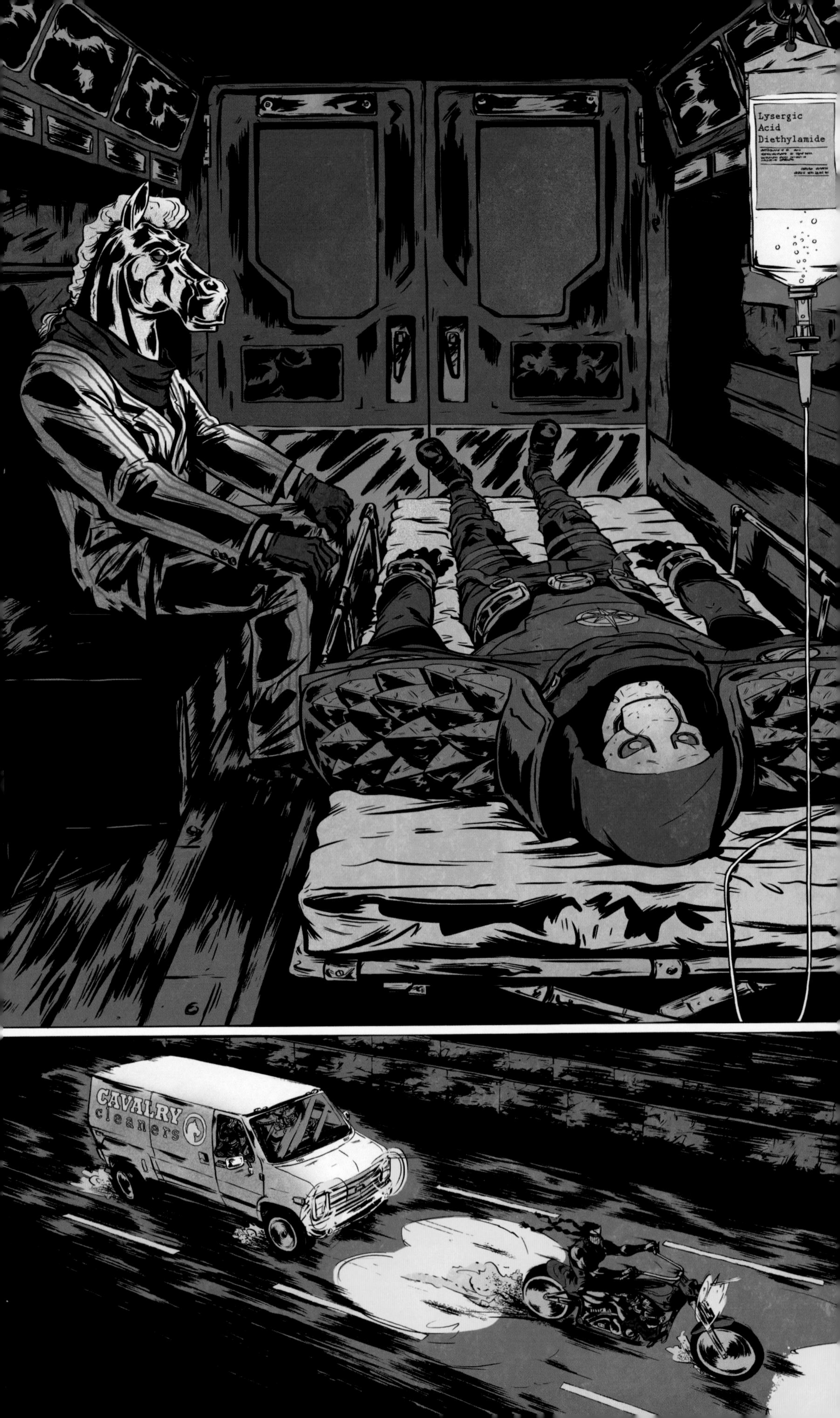
Lysergic
Acid
Diethylamide
CAVALRY
cleaners

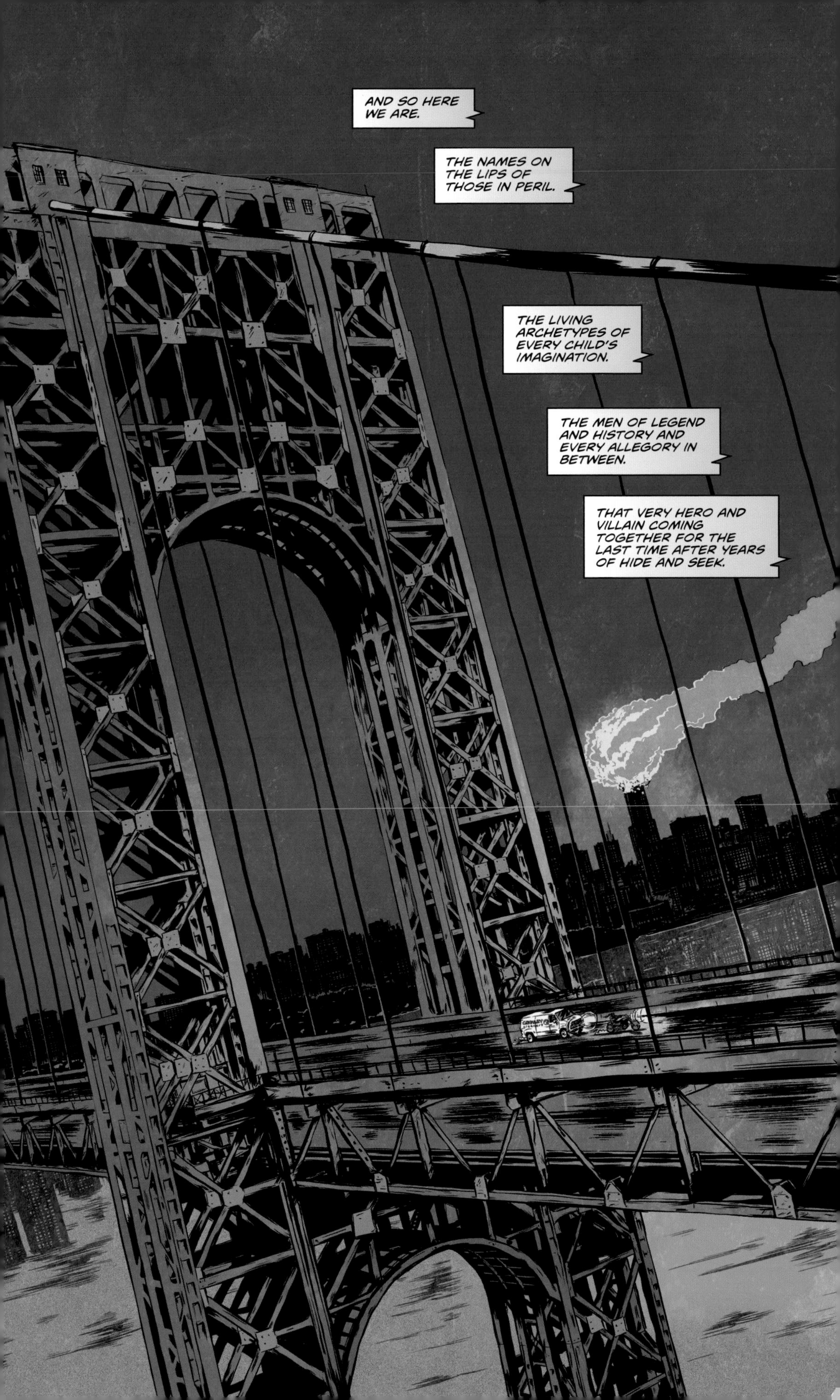
AND SO HERE WE ARE.
THE NAMES ON THE LIPS OF THOSE IN PERIL.
THE LIVING ARCHETYPES OF EVERY CHILD'S IMAGINATION.
THE MEN OF LEGEND AND HISTORY AND EVERY ALLEGORY IN BETWEEN.
THAT VERY HERO AND VILLAIN COMING TOGETHER FOR THE LAST TIME AFTER YEARS OF HIDE AND SEEK.

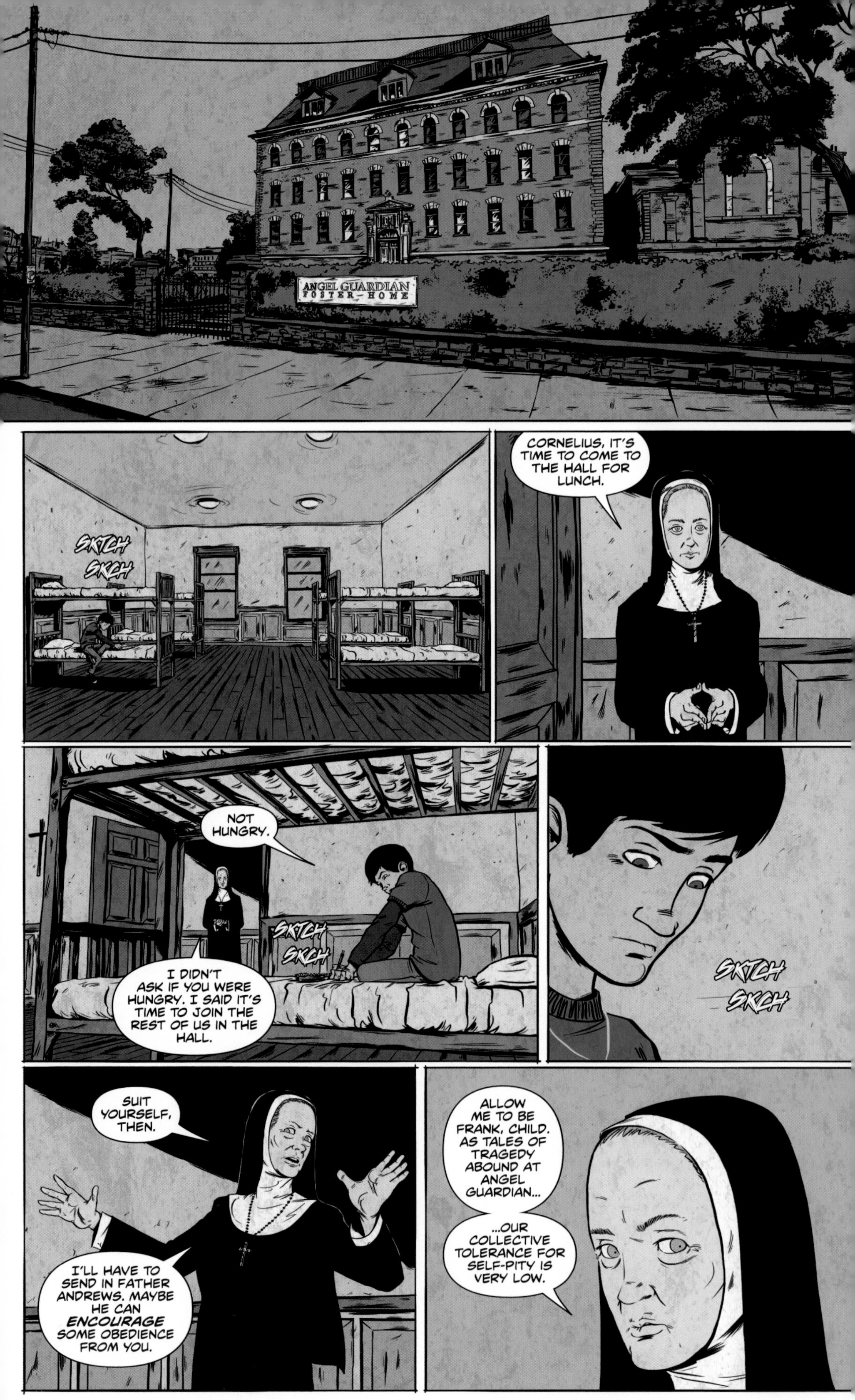
ANGEL GUARDIAN
FOSTER HOME
SKTCH
SKCH
CORNELIUS, IT'S TIME TO COME TO THE HALL FOR LUNCH.
NOT HUNGRY.
SKTCH
SKCH
I DIDN'T ASK IF YOU WERE HUNGRY. I SAID IT'S TIME TO JOIN THE REST OF US IN THE HALL.
SKTCH
SKCH
SUIT YOURSELF, THEN.
I'LL HAVE TO SEND IN FATHER ANDREWS. MAYBE HE CAN ENCOURAGE SOME OBEDIENCE FROM YOU.
ALLOW ME TO BE FRANK, CHILD. AS TALES OF TRAGEDY ABOUND AT ANGEL GUARDIAN...
...OUR COLLECTIVE TOLERANCE FOR SELF-PITY IS VERY LOW.

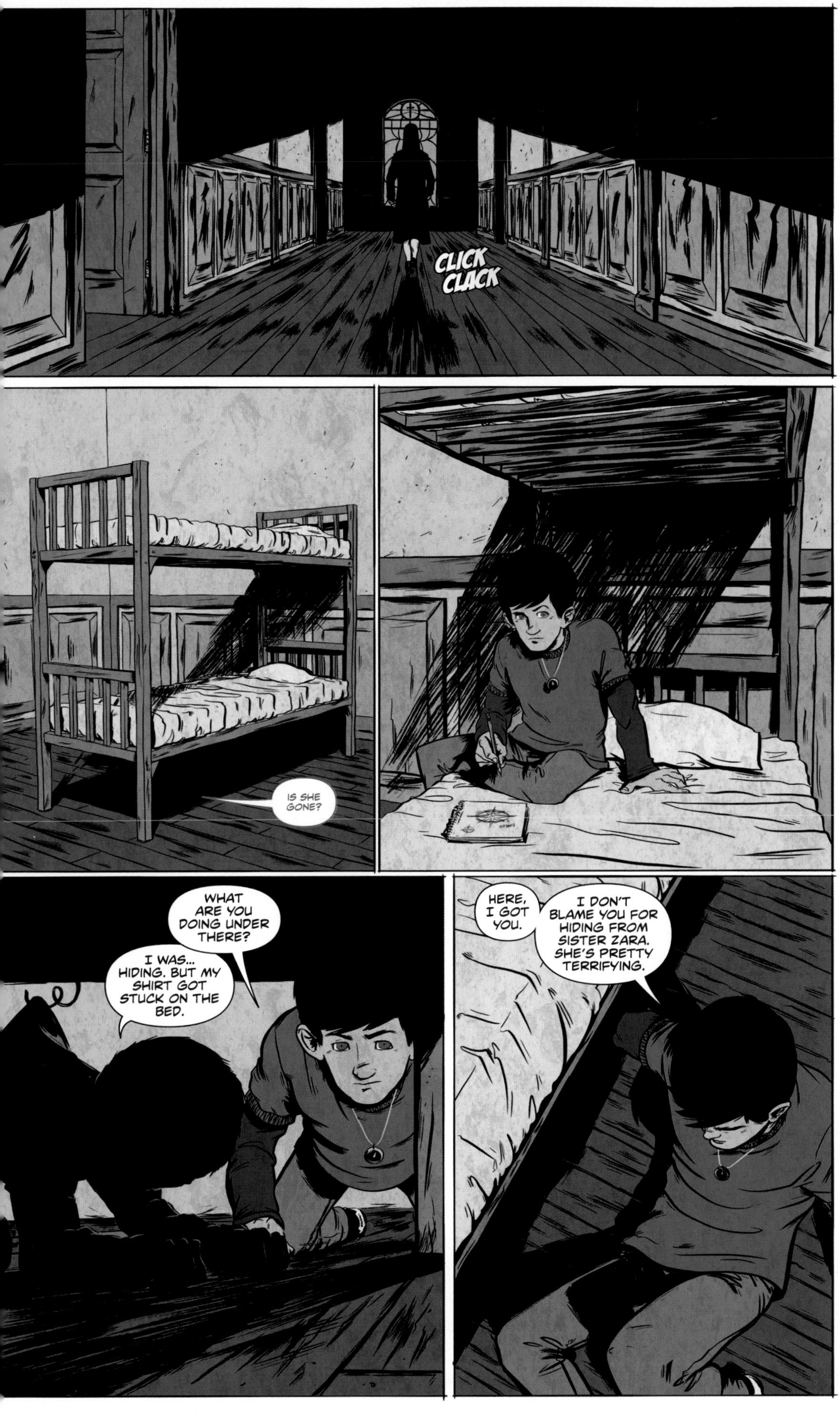
CLICK
CLACK
IS SHE GONE?
WHAT ARE YOU DOING UNDER THERE?
I WAS... HIDING. BUT MY SHIRT GOT STUCK ON THE BED.
HERE, I GOT YOU.
I DON'T BLAME YOU FOR HIDING FROM SISTER ZARA. SHE'S PRETTY TERRIFYING.

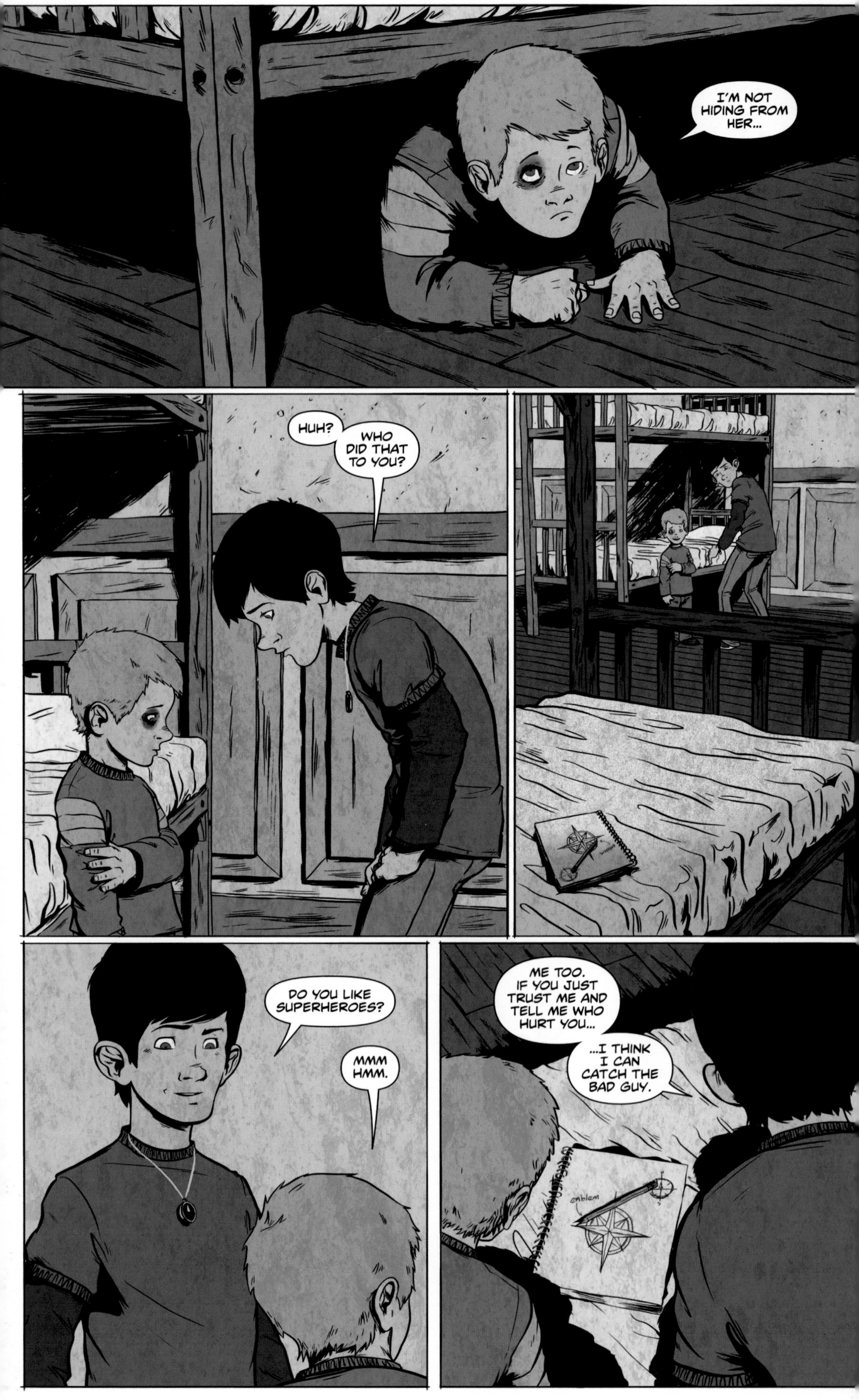
I'M NOT HIDING FROM HER...
HUH?
WHO DID THAT TO YOU?
DO YOU LIKE SUPERHEROES?
MMM HMM.
ME TOO. IF YOU JUST TRUST ME AND TELL ME WHO HURT YOU...
...I THINK I CAN CATCH THE BAD GUY.
emblem

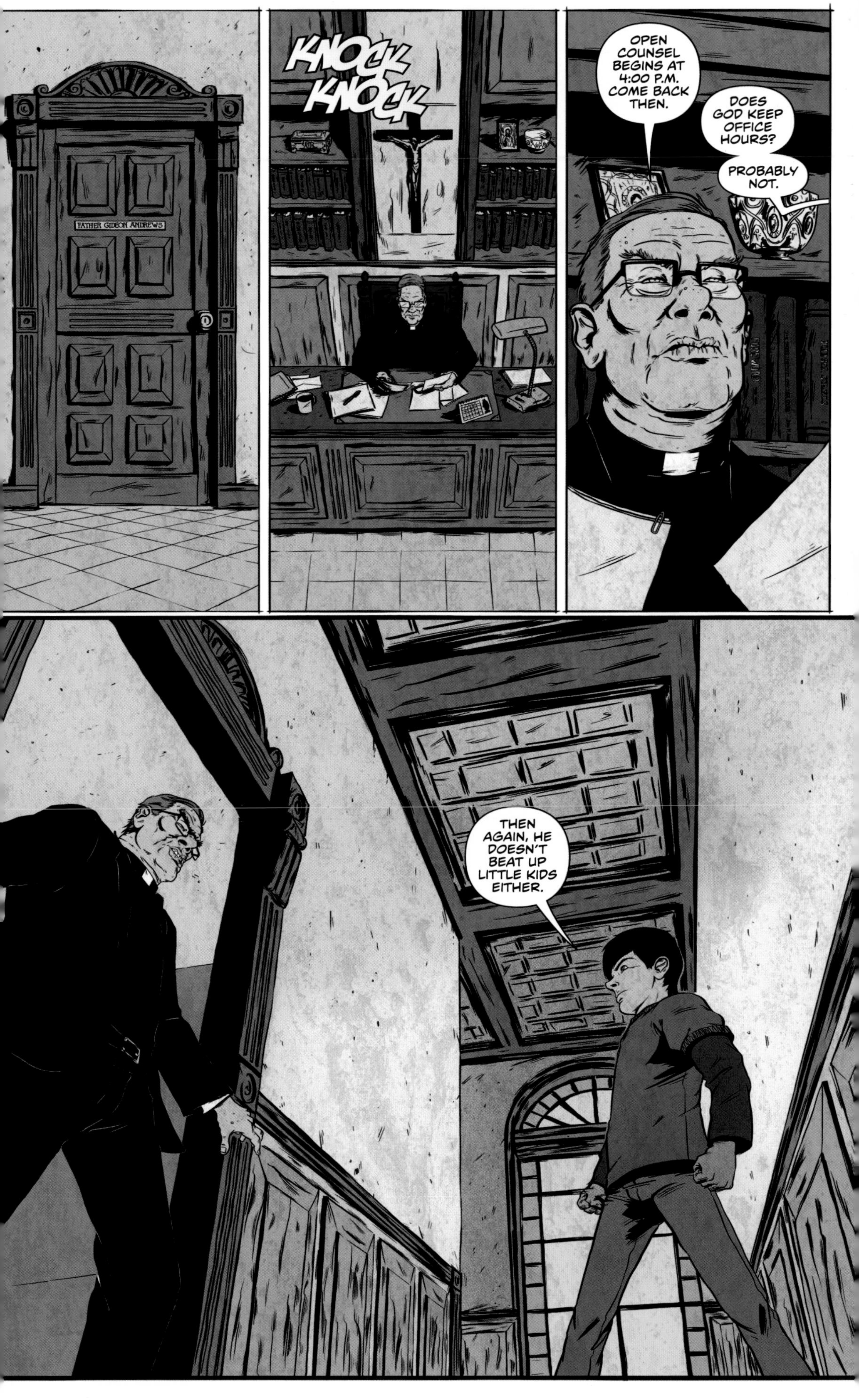
FATHER GIDEON ANDREWS
KNOCK KNOCK
OPEN COUNSEL BEGINS AT 4:00 P.M. COME BACK THEN.
DOES GOD KEEP OFFICE HOURS?
PROBABLY NOT.
THEN AGAIN, HE DOESN'T BEAT UP LITTLE KIDS EITHER.

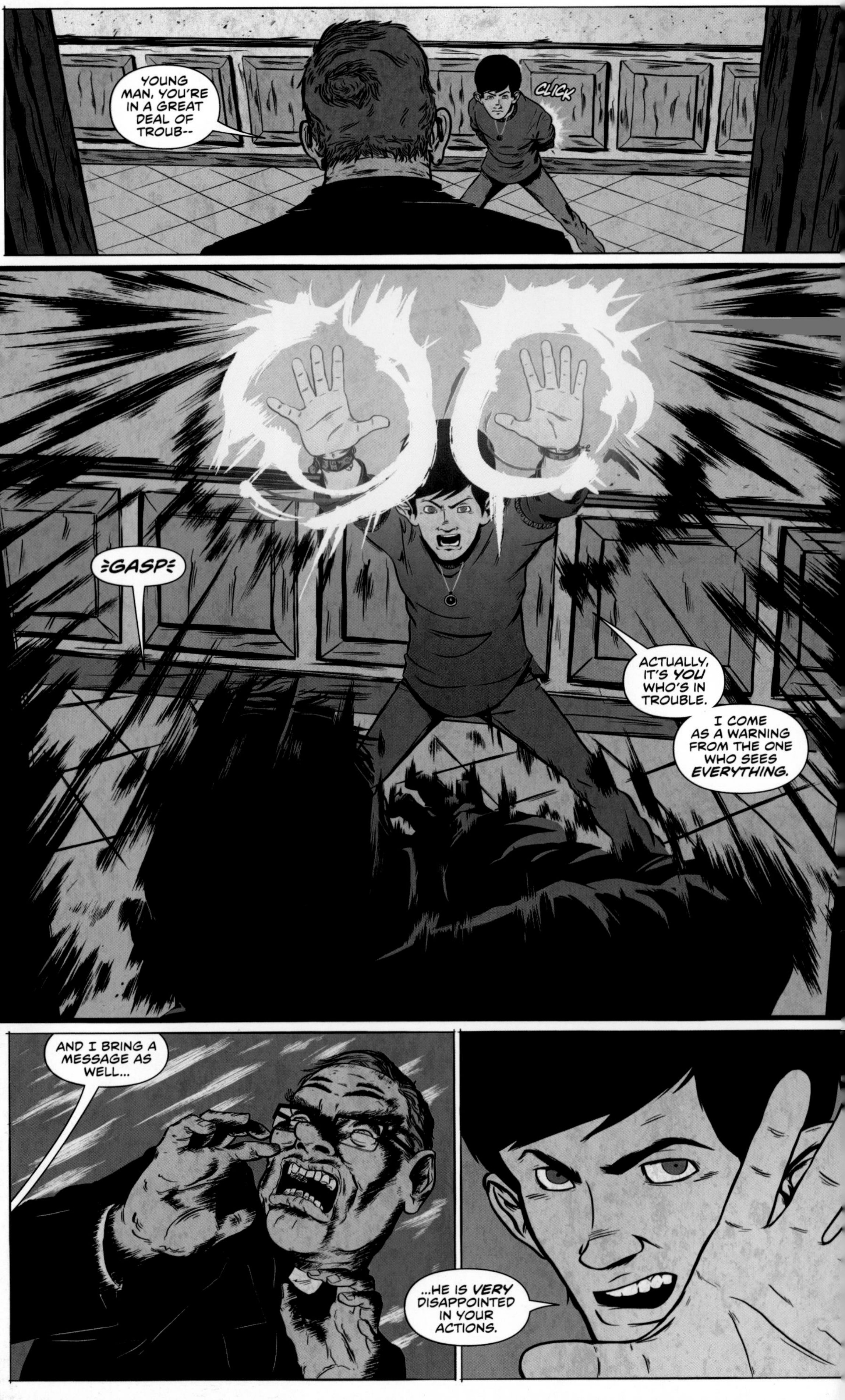
YOUNG MAN, YOU'RE IN A GREAT DEAL OF TROUB--
CLICK
GASP
ACTUALLY, IT'S YOU WHO'S IN TROUBLE.
I COME AS A WARNING FROM THE ONE WHO SEES EVERYTHING.
AND I BRING A MESSAGE AS WELL...
...HE IS VERY DISAPPOINTED IN YOUR ACTIONS.

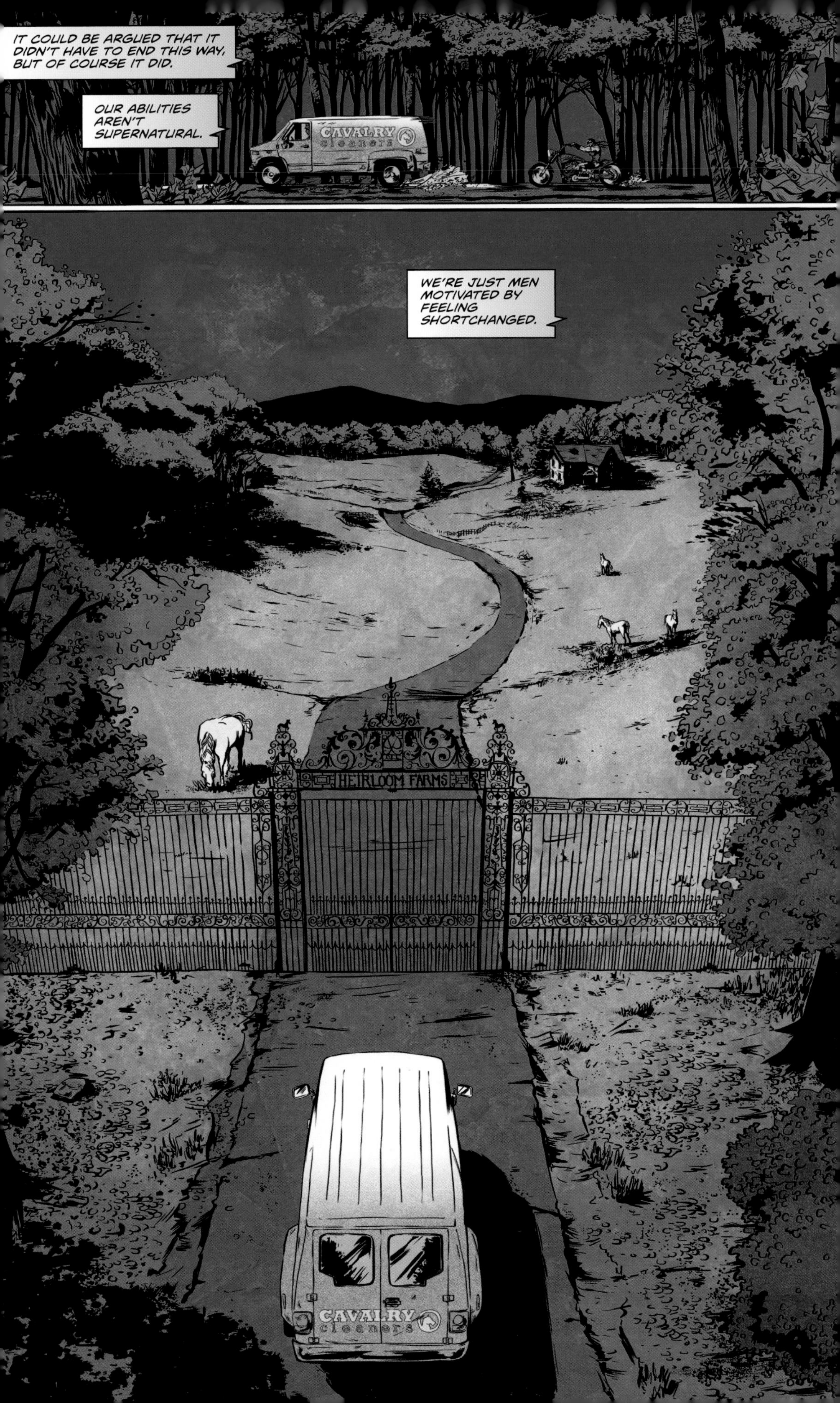
IT COULD BE ARGUED THAT IT DIDN'T HAVE TO END THIS WAY, BUT OF COURSE IT DID.
OUR ABILITIES AREN'T SUPERNATURAL.
CAVALRY cleaners
WE'RE JUST MEN MOTIVATED BY FEELING SHORTCHANGED.
HEIRLOOM FARMS
CAVALRY cleaners

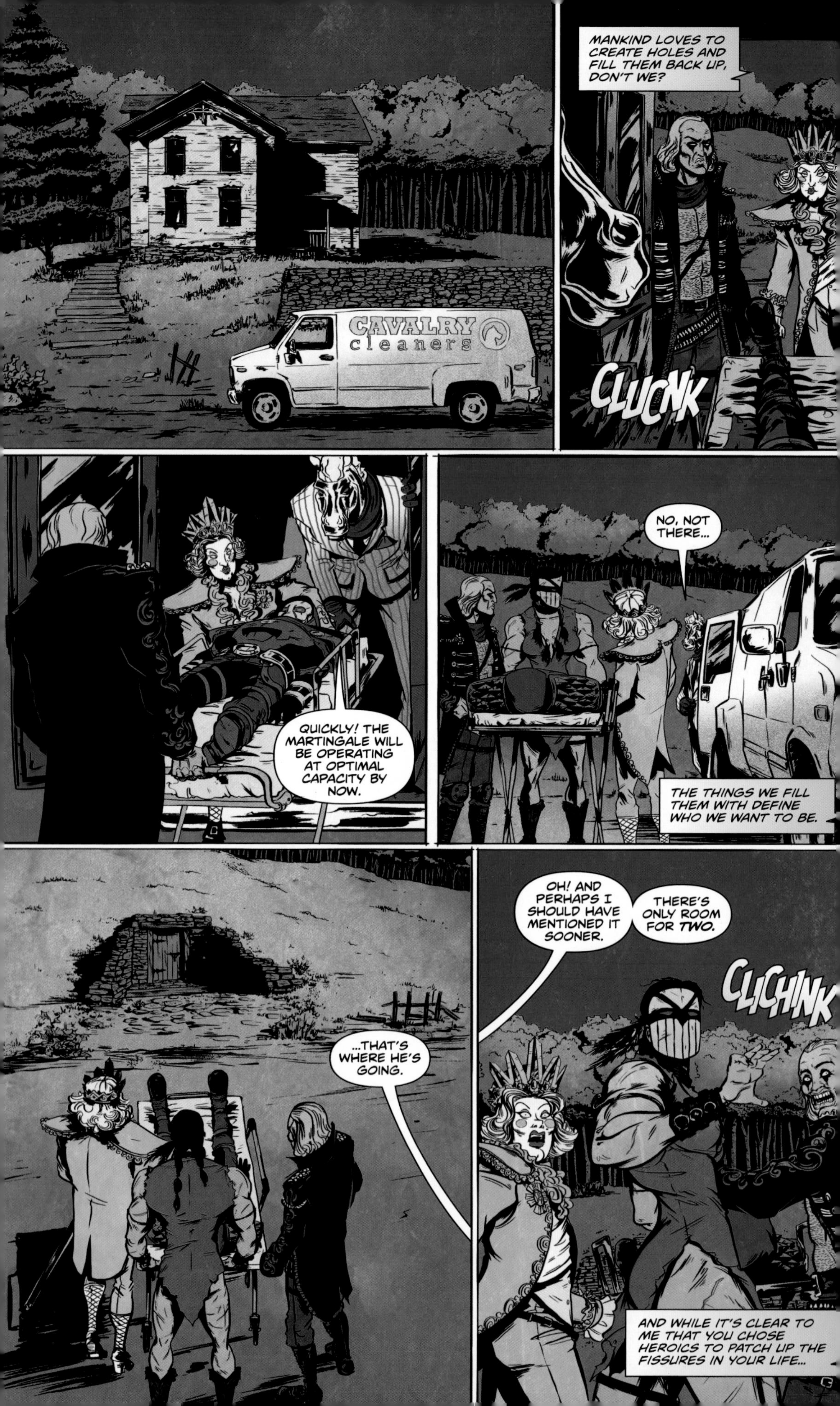
CAVALRY cleaners
MANKIND LOVES TO CREATE HOLES AND FILL THEM BACK UP, DON'T WE?
CLUCNK
QUICKLY! THE MARTINGALE WILL BE OPERATING AT OPTIMAL CAPACITY BY NOW.
NO, NOT THERE...
THE THINGS WE FILL THEM WITH DEFINE WHO WE WANT TO BE.
...THAT'S WHERE HE'S GOING.
OH! AND PERHAPS I SHOULD HAVE MENTIONED IT SOONER.
THERE'S ONLY ROOM FOR TWO.
CLICHINK
AND WHILE IT'S CLEAR TO ME THAT YOU CHOSE HEROICS TO PATCH UP THE FISSURES IN YOUR LIFE...

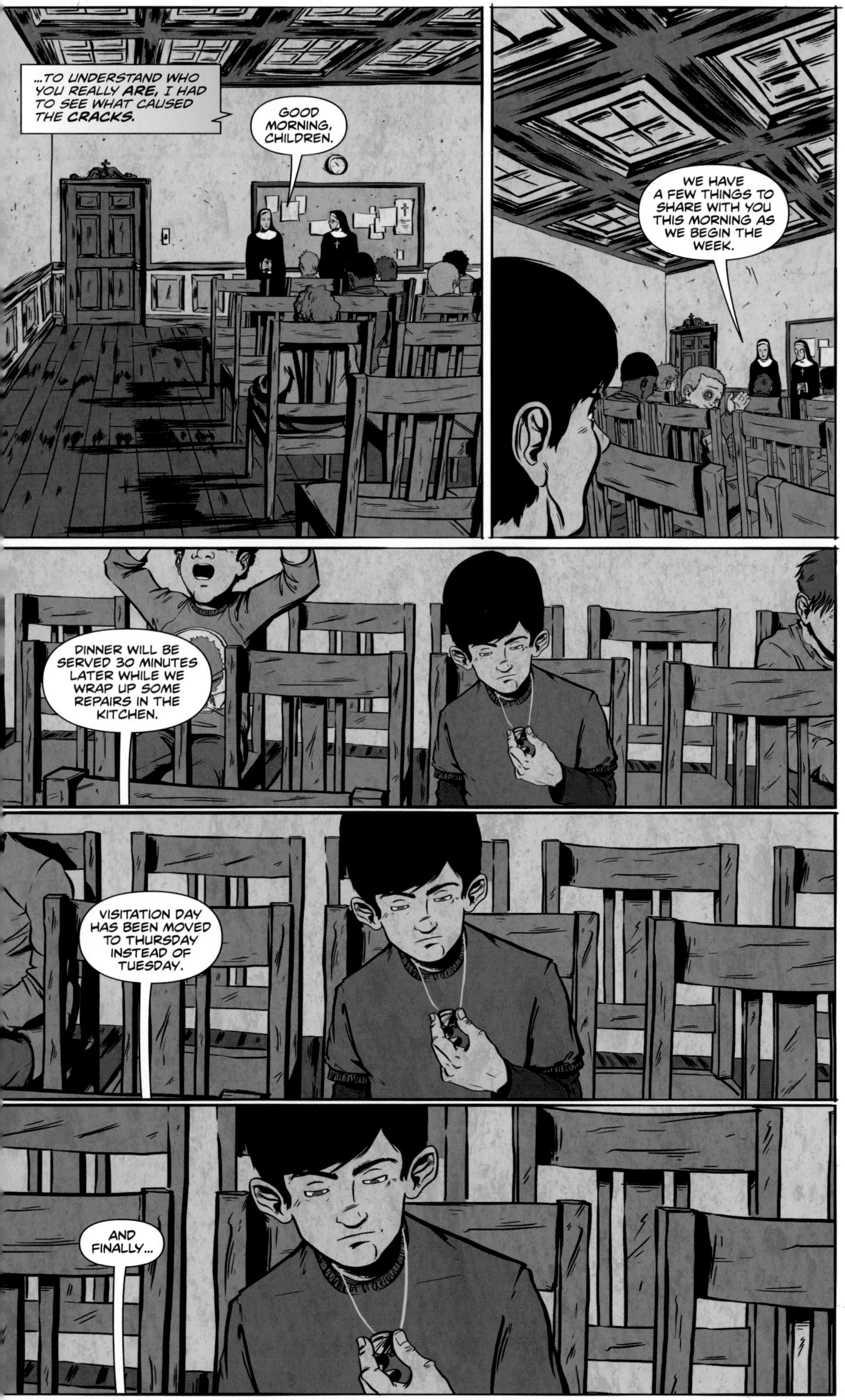
...TO UNDERSTAND WHO YOU REALLY ARE, I HAD TO SEE WHAT CAUSED THE CRACKS.
GOOD MORNING, CHILDREN.
WE HAVE A FEW THINGS TO SHARE WITH YOU THIS MORNING AS WE BEGIN THE WEEK.
DINNER WILL BE SERVED 30 MINUTES LATER WHILE WE WRAP UP SOME REPAIRS IN THE KITCHEN.
VISITATION DAY HAS BEEN MOVED TO THURSDAY INSTEAD OF TUESDAY.
AND FINALLY...

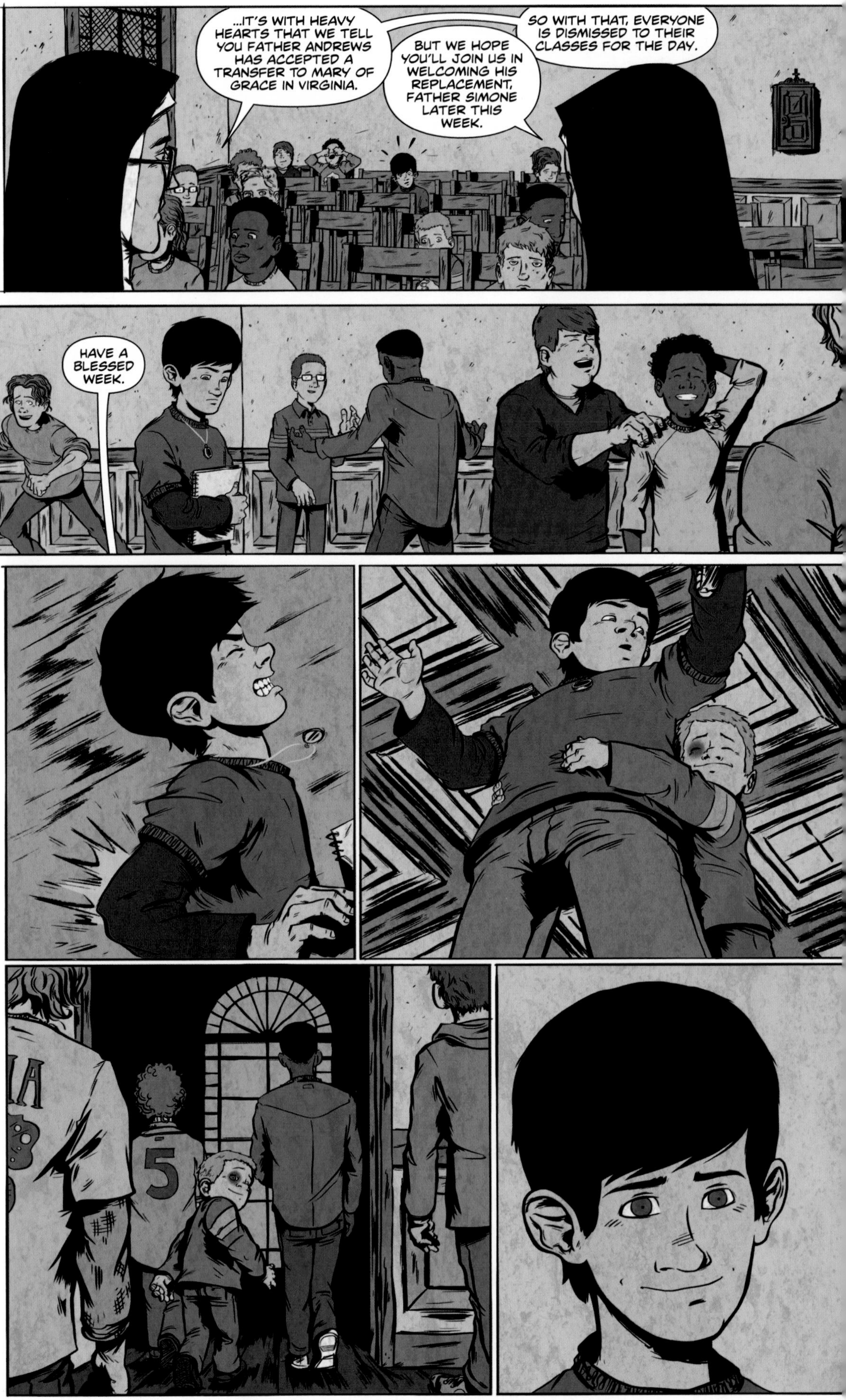
...IT'S WITH HEAVY HEARTS THAT WE TELL YOU FATHER ANDREWS HAS ACCEPTED A TRANSFER TO MARY OF GRACE IN VIRGINIA.
BUT WE HOPE YOU'LL JOIN US IN WELCOMING HIS REPLACEMENT, FATHER SIMONE LATER THIS WEEK.
SO WITH THAT, EVERYONE IS DISMISSED TO THEIR CLASSES FOR THE DAY.
HAVE A BLESSED WEEK.
5

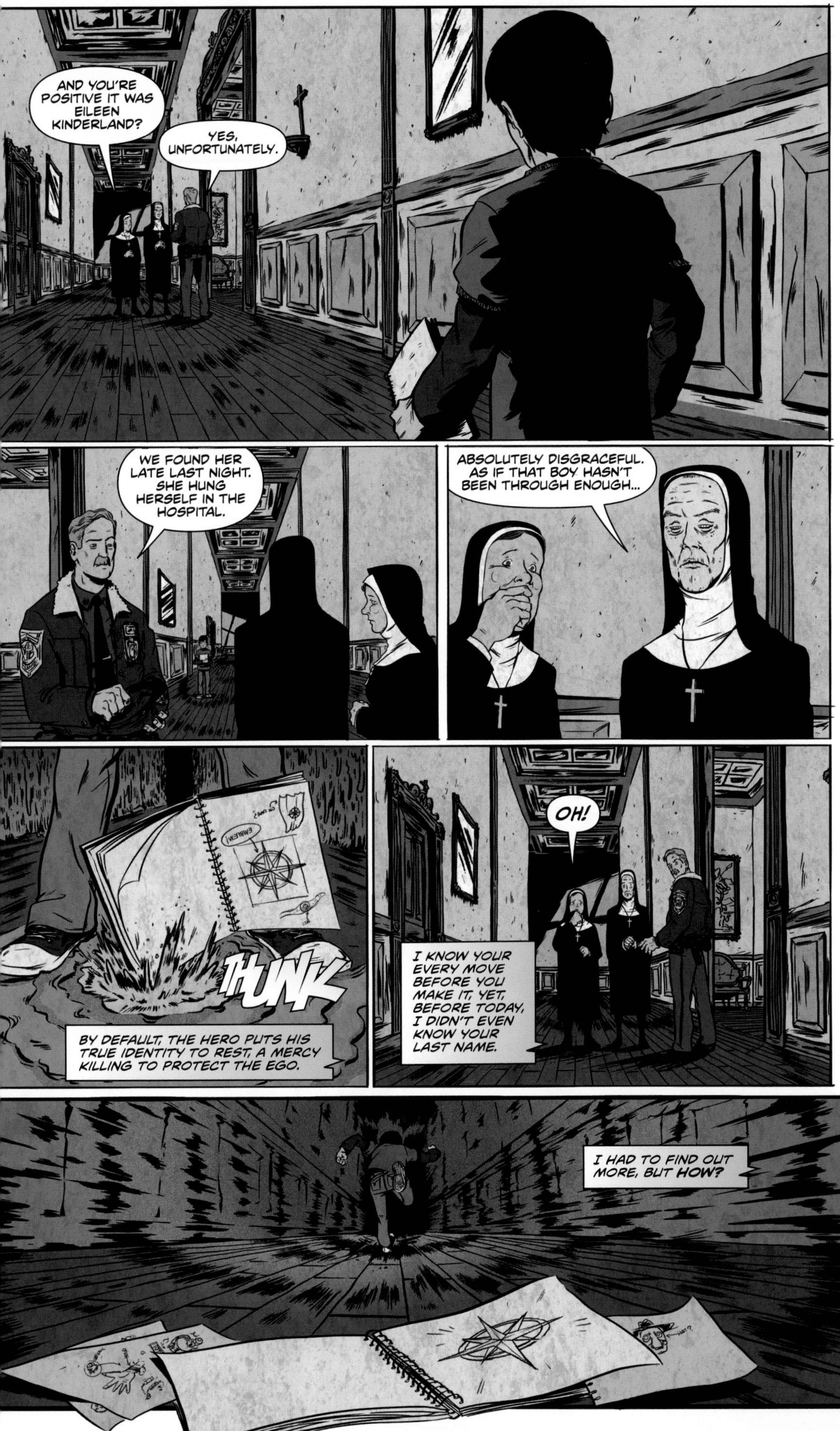

AND YOU'RE POSITIVE IT WAS EILEEN KINDERLAND?
YES, UNFORTUNATELY.
WE FOUND HER LATE LAST NIGHT. SHE HUNG HERSELF IN THE HOSPITAL.
ABSOLUTELY DISGRACEFUL. AS IF THAT BOY HASN'T BEEN THROUGH ENOUGH...
THUNK
BY DEFAULT, THE HERO PUTS HIS TRUE IDENTITY TO REST, A MERCY KILLING TO PROTECT THE EGO.
OH!
I KNOW YOUR EVERY MOVE BEFORE YOU MAKE IT, YET, BEFORE TODAY, I DIDN'T EVEN KNOW YOUR LAST NAME.
I HAD TO FIND OUT MORE, BUT HOW?

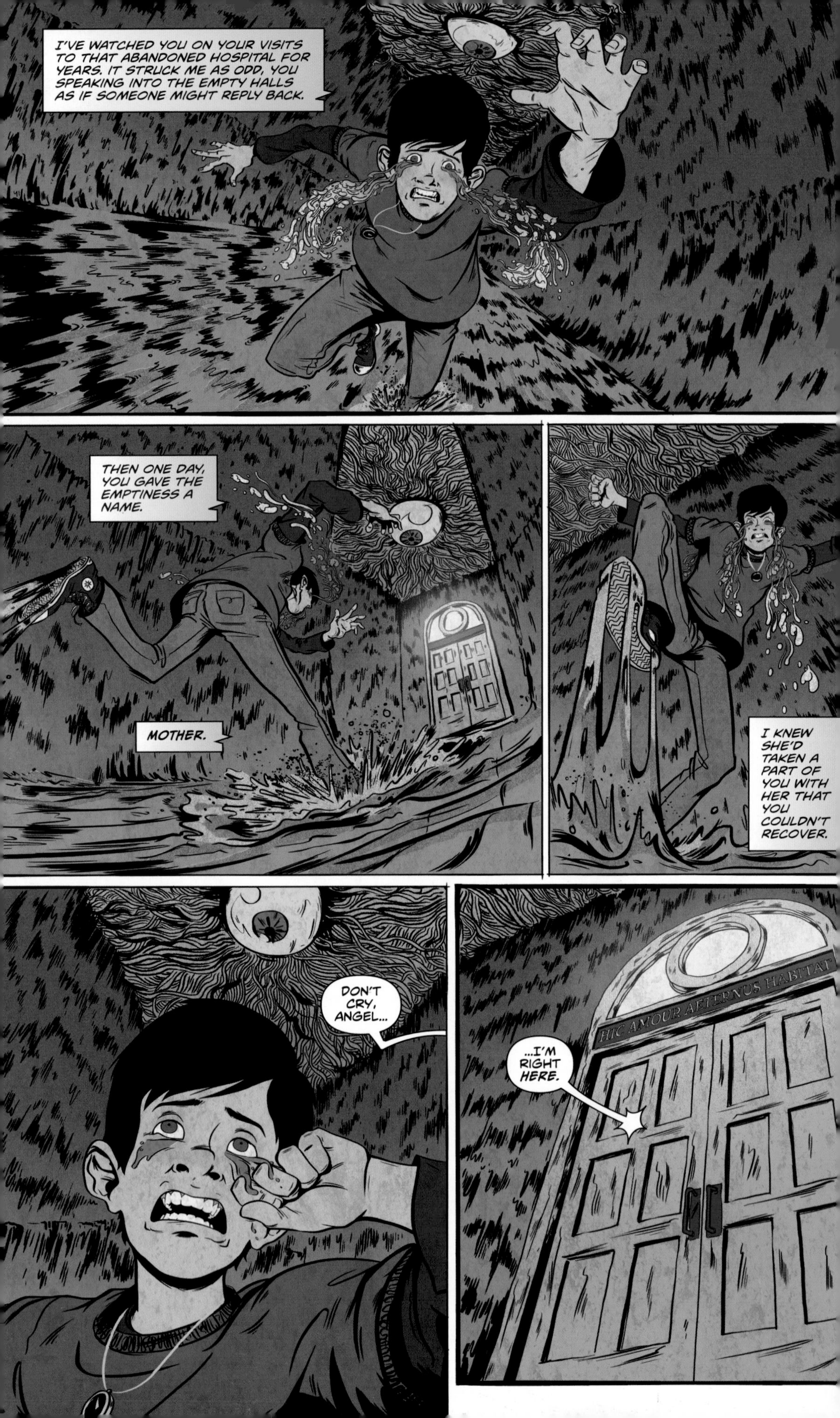
I'VE WATCHED YOU ON YOUR VISITS TO THAT ABANDONED HOSPITAL FOR YEARS. IT STRUCK ME AS ODD, YOU SPEAKING INTO THE EMPTY HALLS AS IF SOMEONE MIGHT REPLY BACK.
THEN ONE DAY, YOU GAVE THE EMPTINESS A NAME.
MOTHER.
I KNEW SHE'D TAKEN A PART OF YOU WITH HER THAT YOU COULDN'T RECOVER.
DON'T CRY, ANGEL...
HIC AMOUR AETERNUS HABITAT
...I'M RIGHT HERE.

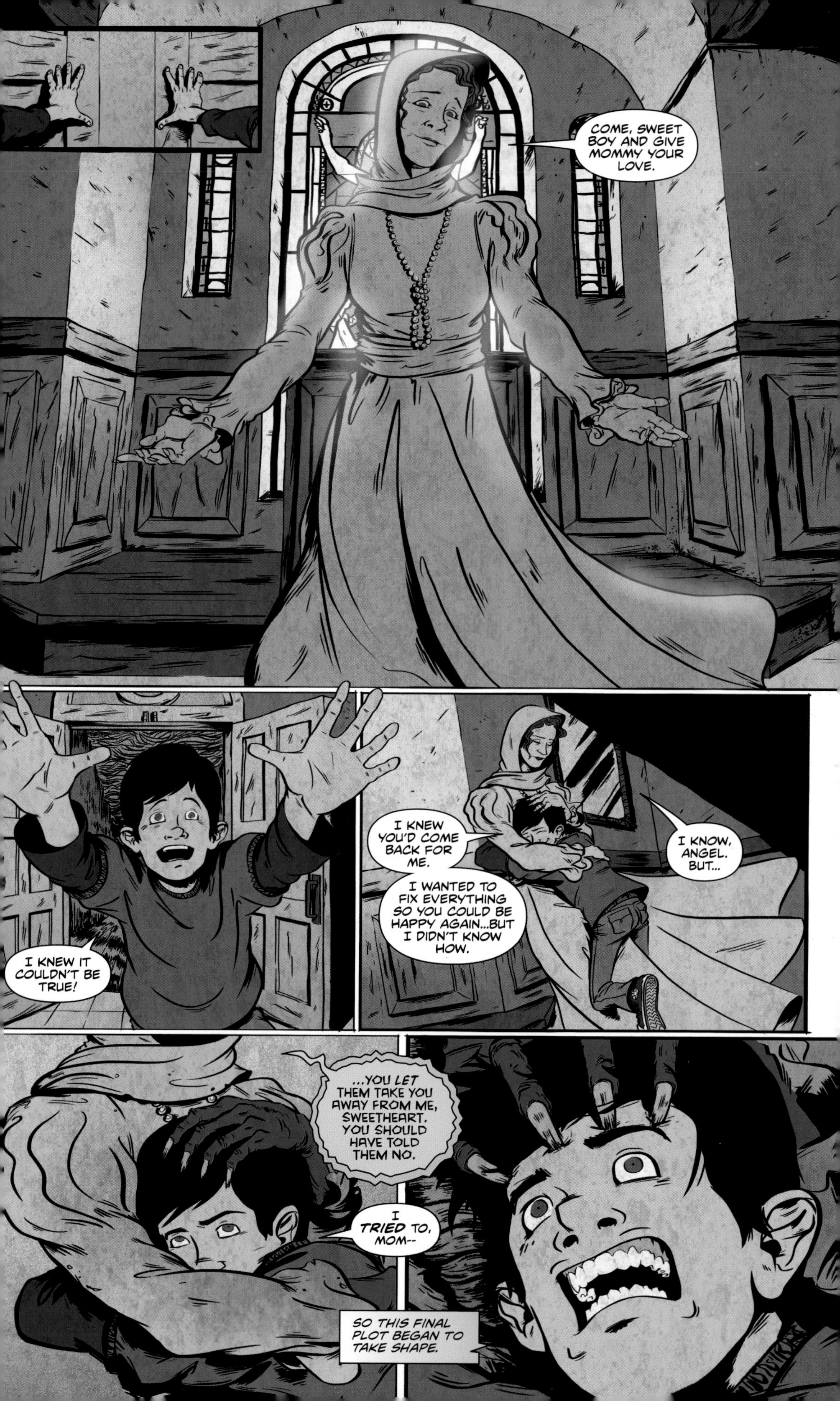
COME, SWEET BOY AND GIVE MOMMY YOUR LOVE.
I KNEW IT COULDN'T BE TRUE!
I KNEW YOU'D COME BACK FOR ME.
I WANTED TO FIX EVERYTHING SO YOU COULD BE HAPPY AGAIN...BUT I DIDN'T KNOW HOW.
I KNOW, ANGEL. BUT...
...YOU LET THEM TAKE YOU AWAY FROM ME, SWEETHEART. YOU SHOULD HAVE TOLD THEM NO.
I TRIED TO, MOM--
SO THIS FINAL PLOT BEGAN TO TAKE SHAPE.

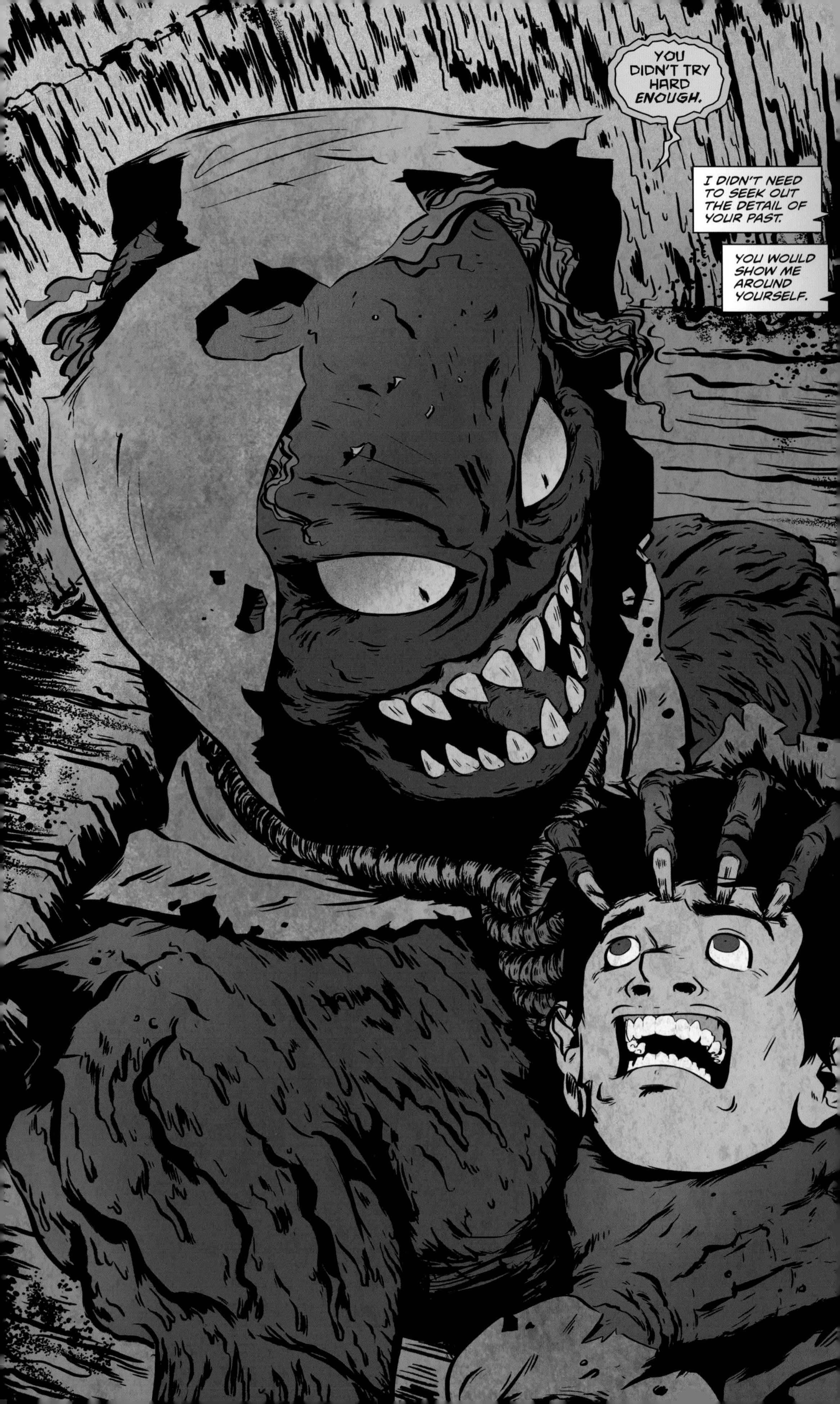
YOU DIDN'T TRY HARD ENOUGH.
I DIDN'T NEED TO SEEK OUT THE DETAIL OF YOUR PAST.
YOU WOULD SHOW ME AROUND YOURSELF.

ISSUE FIVE BOOM! STUDIOS EXCLUSIVE COVER BY **FELIPE SMITH**

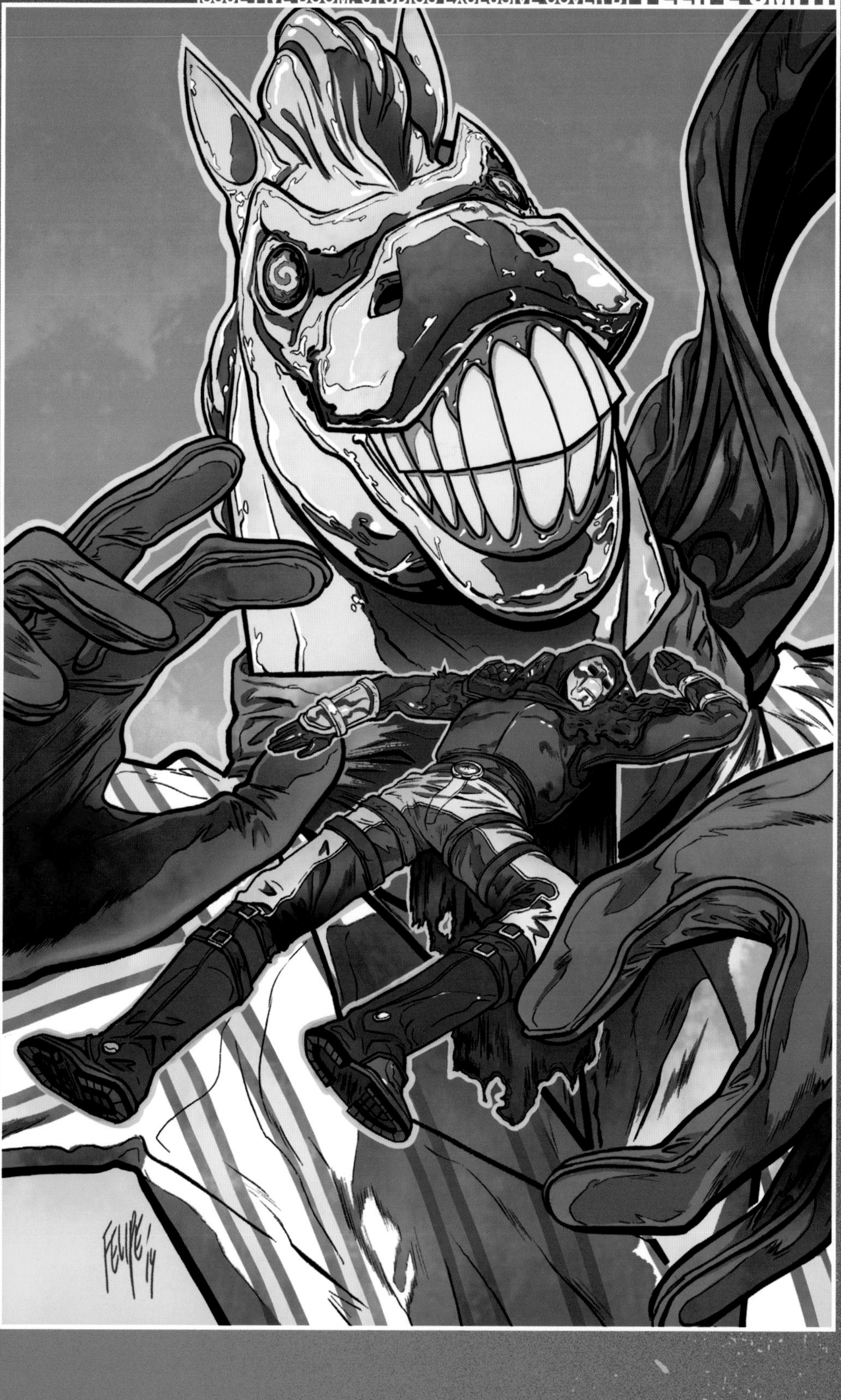
FELIPE '14

ISSUE SIX COVER BY **JEFF STOKELY**

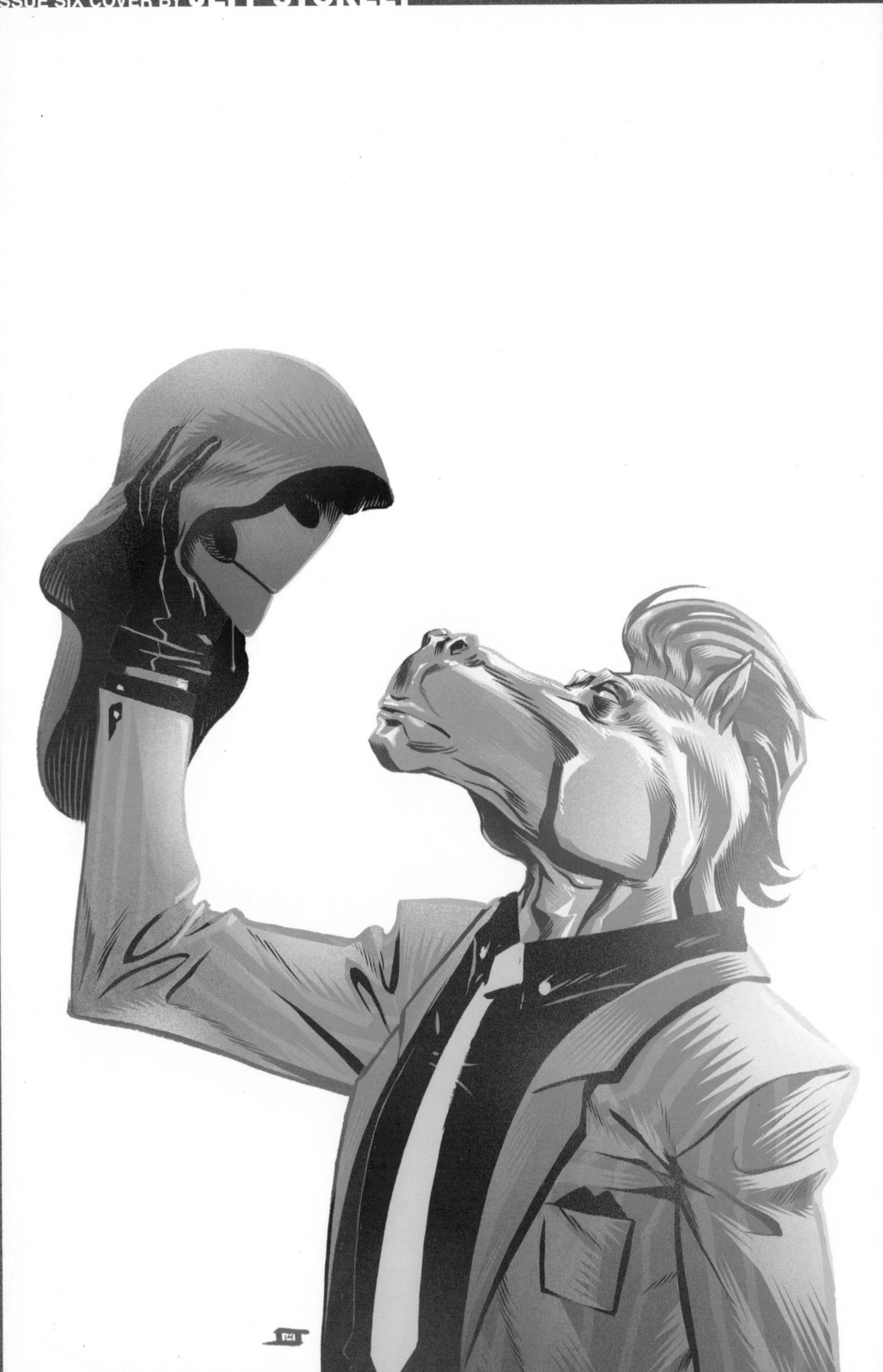

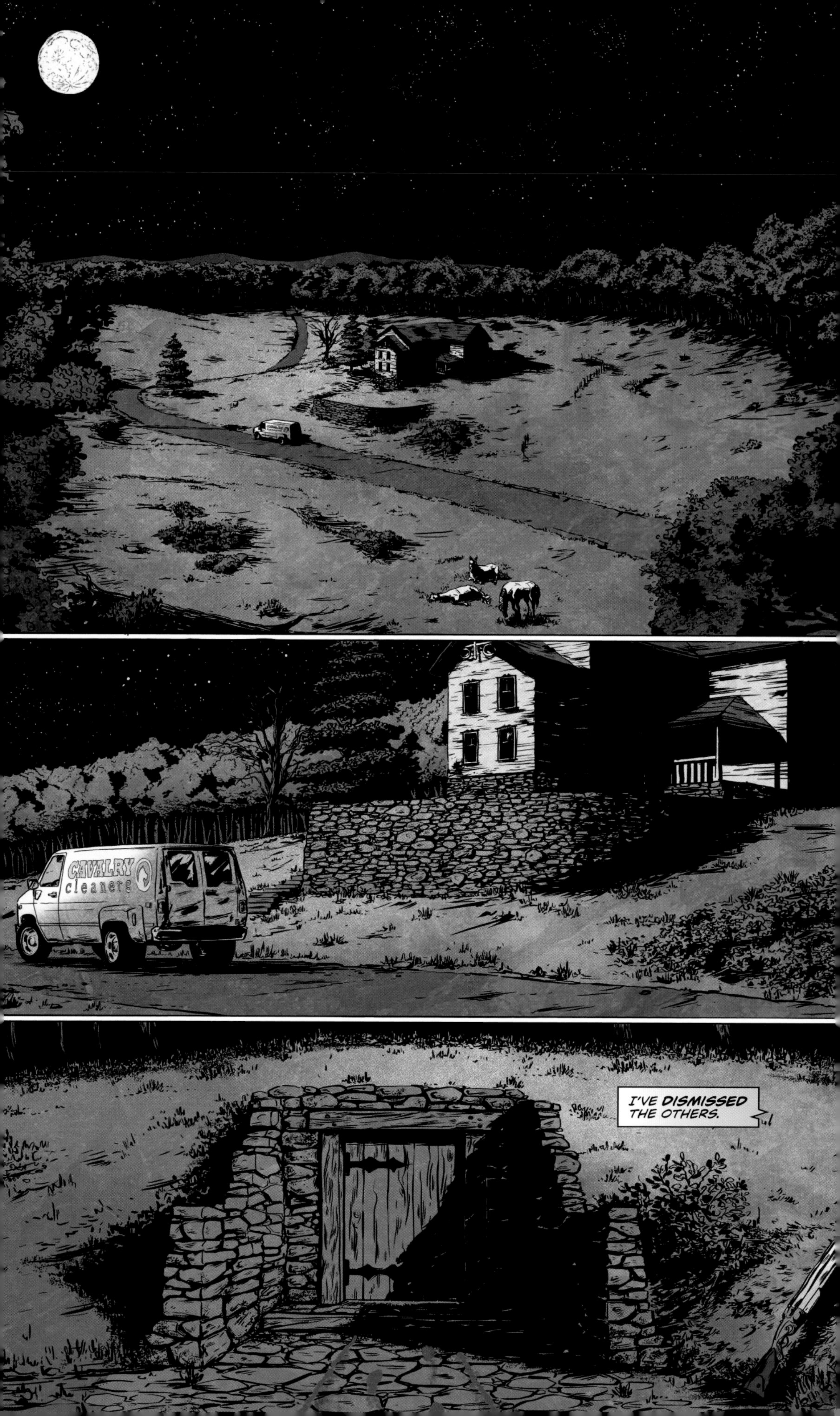
CAVALRY cleaners
I'VE DISMISSED THE OTHERS.

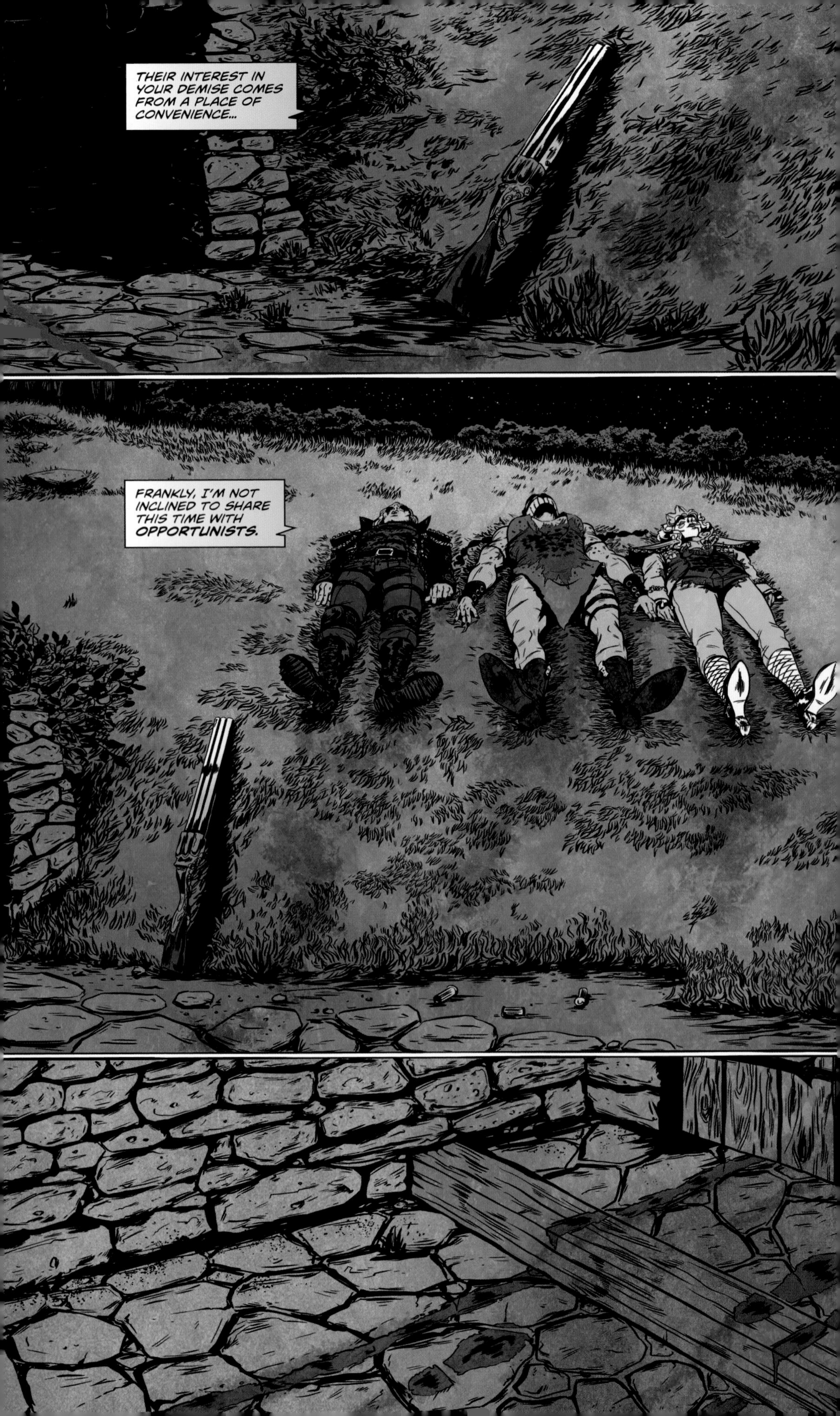
THEIR INTEREST IN YOUR DEMISE COMES FROM A PLACE OF CONVENIENCE...
FRANKLY, I'M NOT INCLINED TO SHARE THIS TIME WITH OPPORTUNISTS.

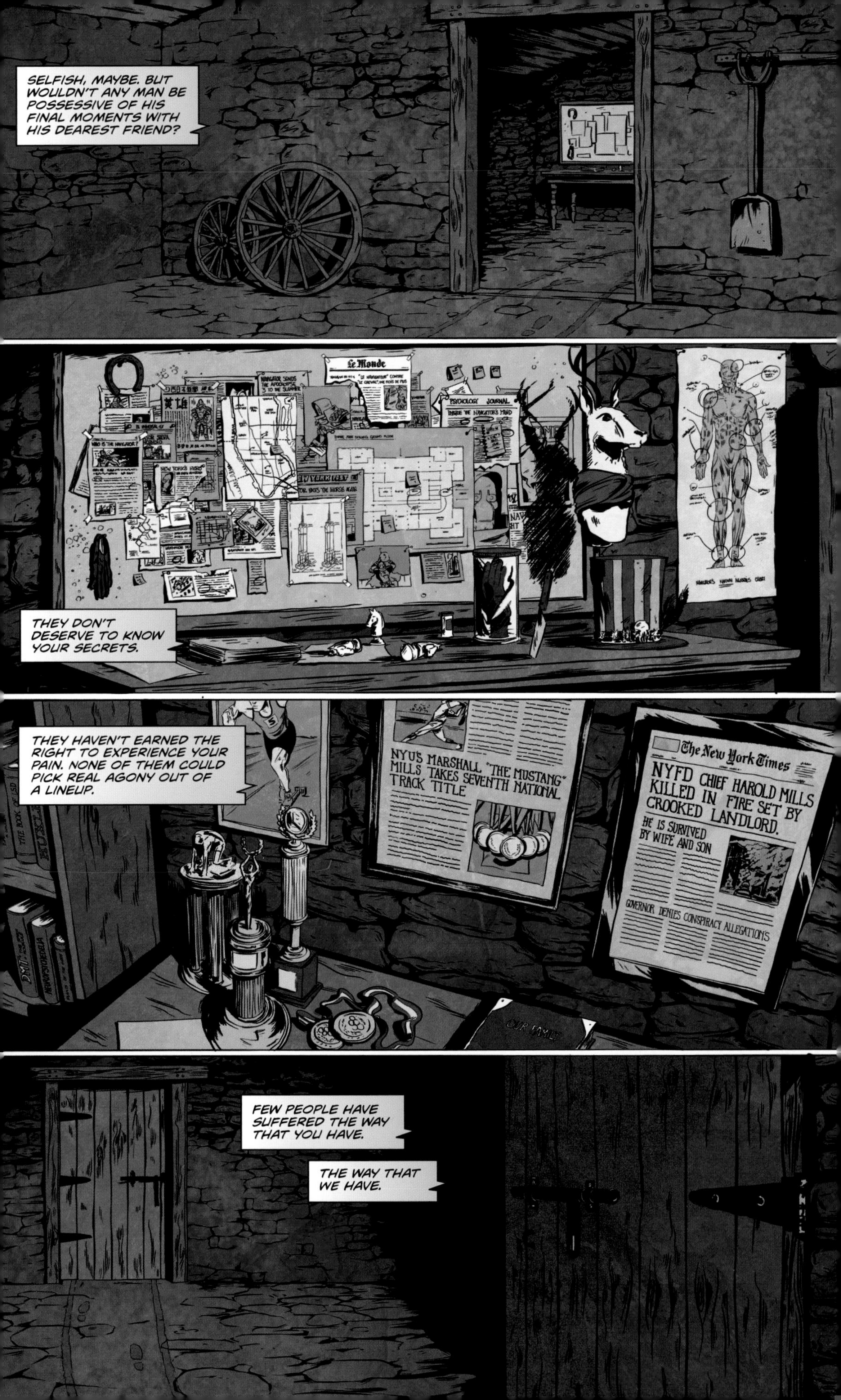
SELFISH, MAYBE. BUT WOULDN'T ANY MAN BE POSSESSIVE OF HIS FINAL MOMENTS WITH HIS DEAREST FRIEND?
THEY DON'T DESERVE TO KNOW YOUR SECRETS.
THEY HAVEN'T EARNED THE RIGHT TO EXPERIENCE YOUR PAIN. NONE OF THEM COULD PICK REAL AGONY OUT OF A LINEUP.
NYU'S MARSHALL "THE MUSTANG" MILLS TAKES SEVENTH NATIONAL TRACK TITLE
The New York Times
NYFD CHIEF HAROLD MILLS KILLED IN FIRE SET BY CROOKED LANDLORD.
HE IS SURVIVED BY WIFE AND SON
GOVERNOR DENIES CONSPIRACY ALLEGATIONS
FEW PEOPLE HAVE SUFFERED THE WAY THAT YOU HAVE.
THE WAY THAT WE HAVE.

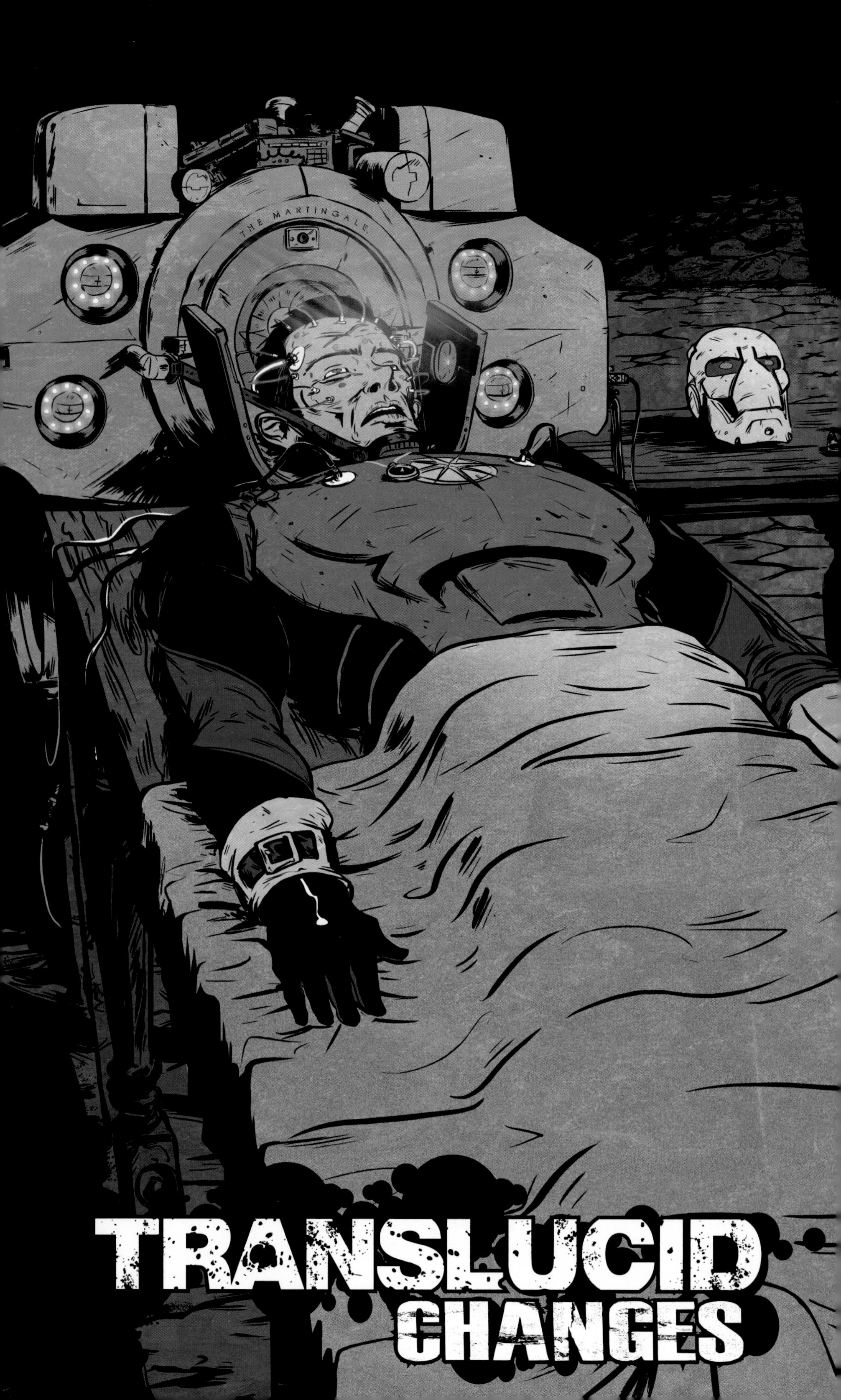
THE MARTINGALE.

TRANSLUCID CHANGES

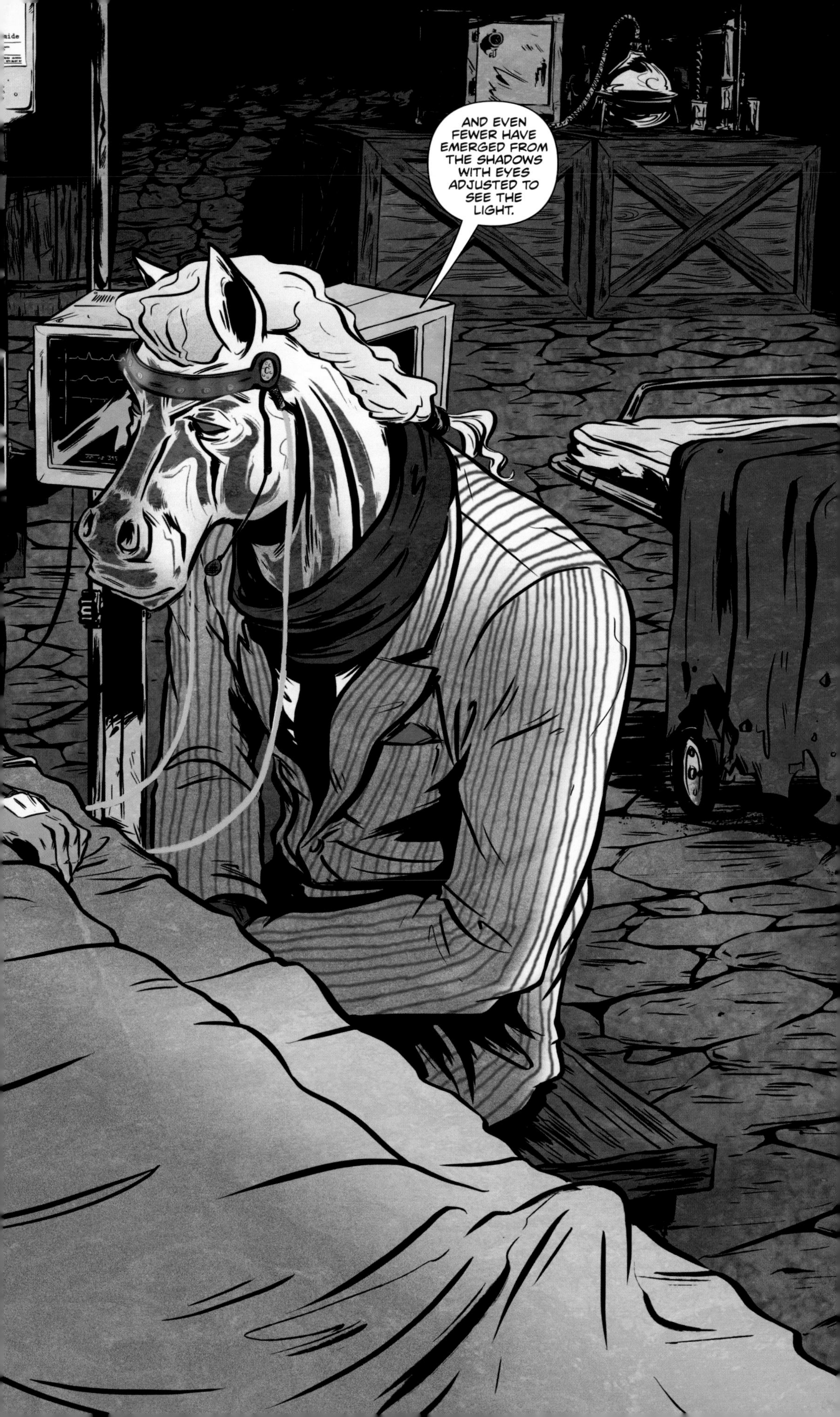
AND EVEN FEWER HAVE EMERGED FROM THE SHADOWS WITH EYES ADJUSTED TO SEE THE LIGHT.

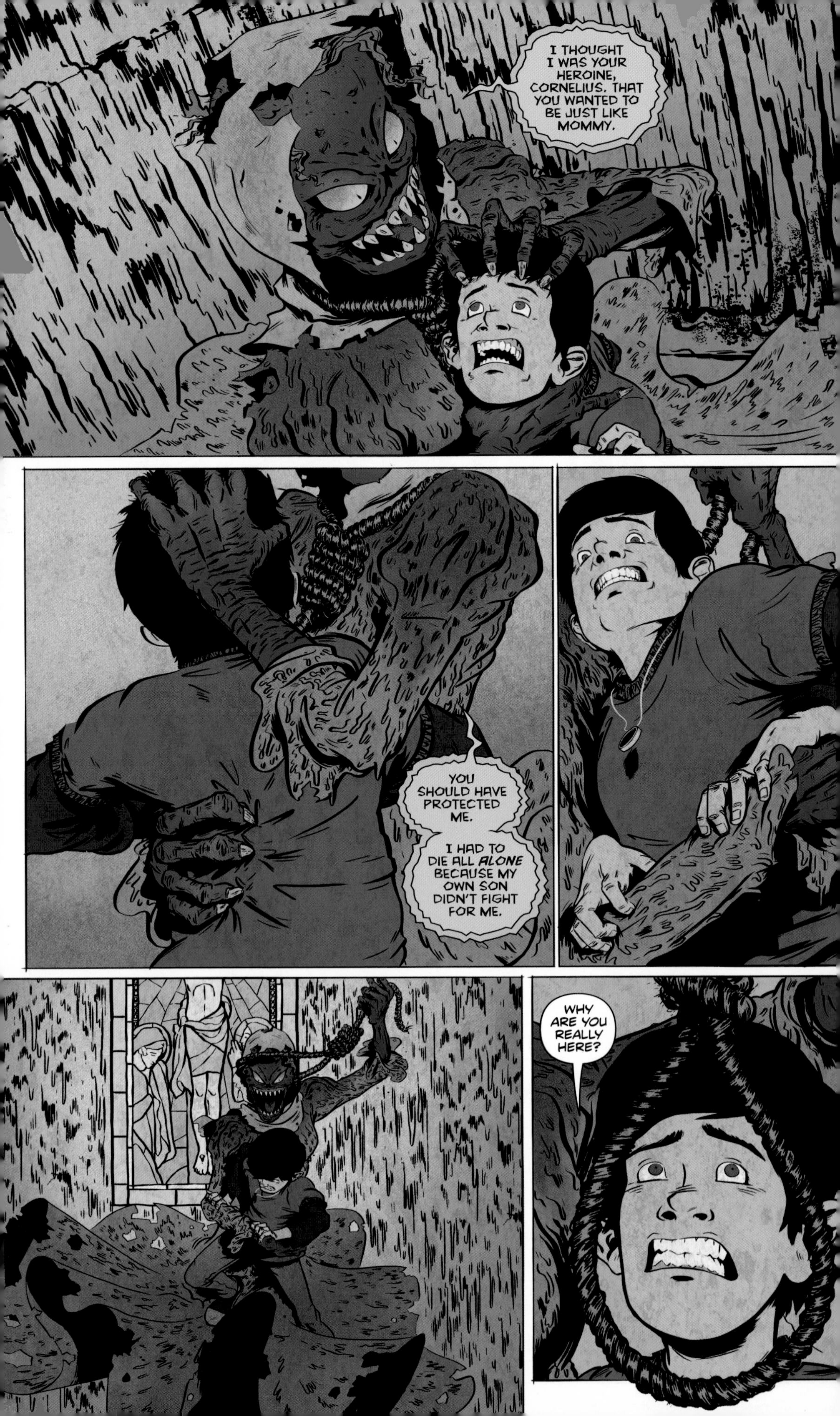
I THOUGHT I WAS YOUR HEROINE, CORNELIUS. THAT YOU WANTED TO BE JUST LIKE MOMMY.
YOU SHOULD HAVE PROTECTED ME.
I HAD TO DIE ALL *ALONE* BECAUSE MY OWN SON DIDN'T FIGHT FOR ME.
WHY ARE YOU REALLY HERE?

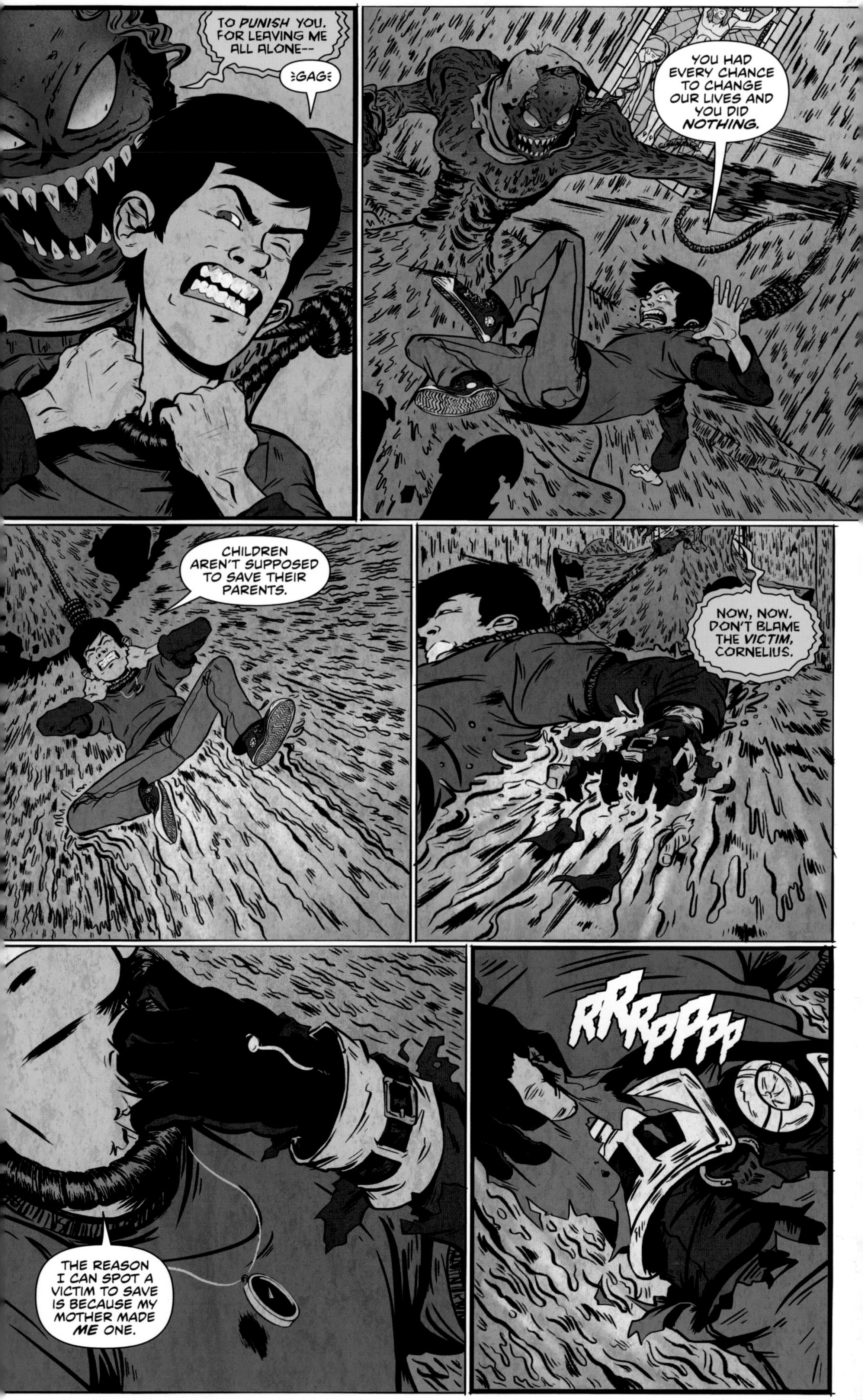
TO PUNISH YOU. FOR LEAVING ME ALL ALONE--
GAG
YOU HAD EVERY CHANCE TO CHANGE OUR LIVES AND YOU DID NOTHING.
CHILDREN AREN'T SUPPOSED TO SAVE THEIR PARENTS.
NOW, NOW. DON'T BLAME THE VICTIM, CORNELIUS.
THE REASON I CAN SPOT A VICTIM TO SAVE IS BECAUSE MY MOTHER MADE ME ONE.
RRRPPPP

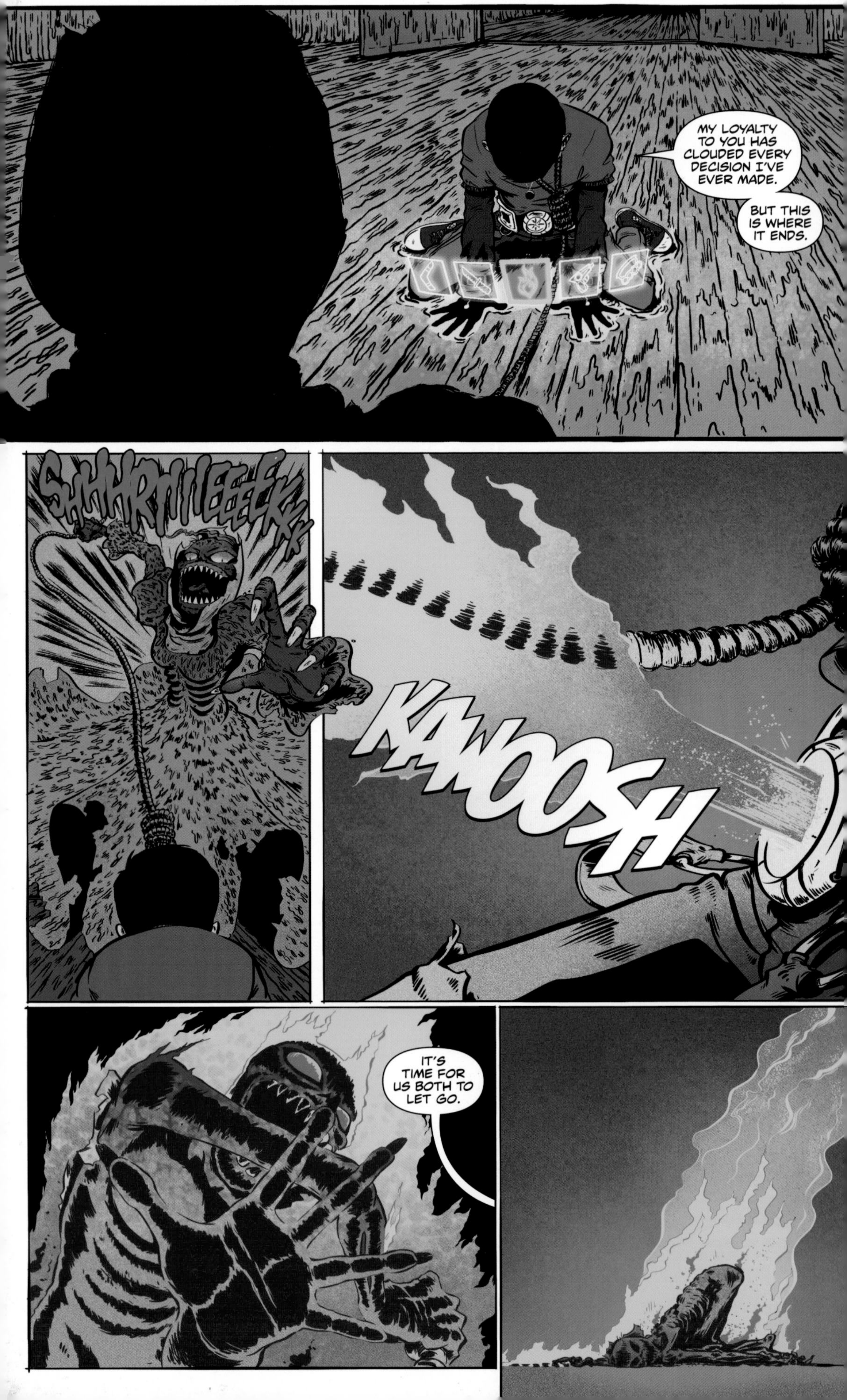
MY LOYALTY TO YOU HAS CLOUDED EVERY DECISION I'VE EVER MADE.
BUT THIS IS WHERE IT ENDS.
SHHHRIIIEEEEKK
KAWOOSH
IT'S TIME FOR US BOTH TO LET GO.

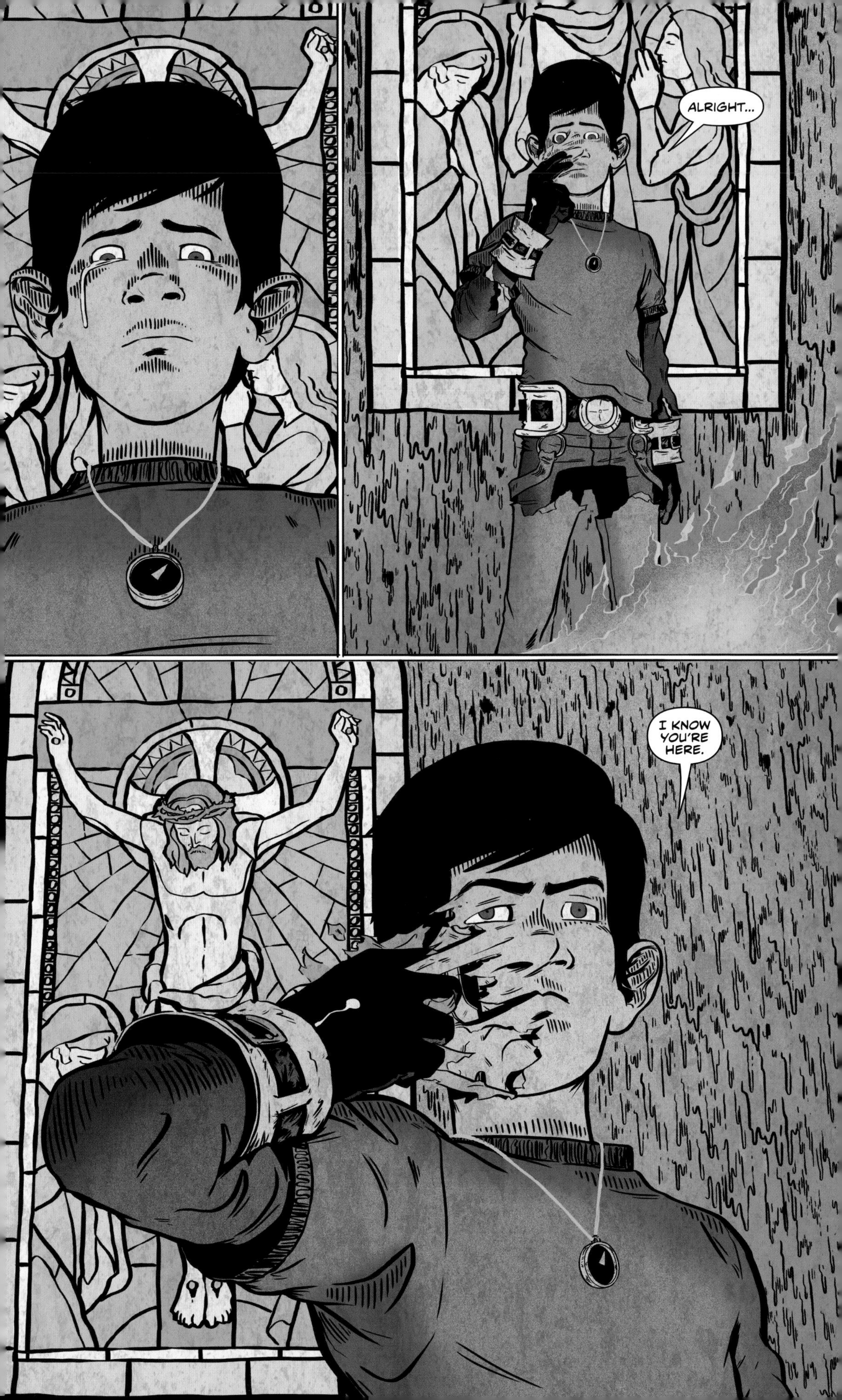

ALRIGHT...
I KNOW YOU'RE HERE.

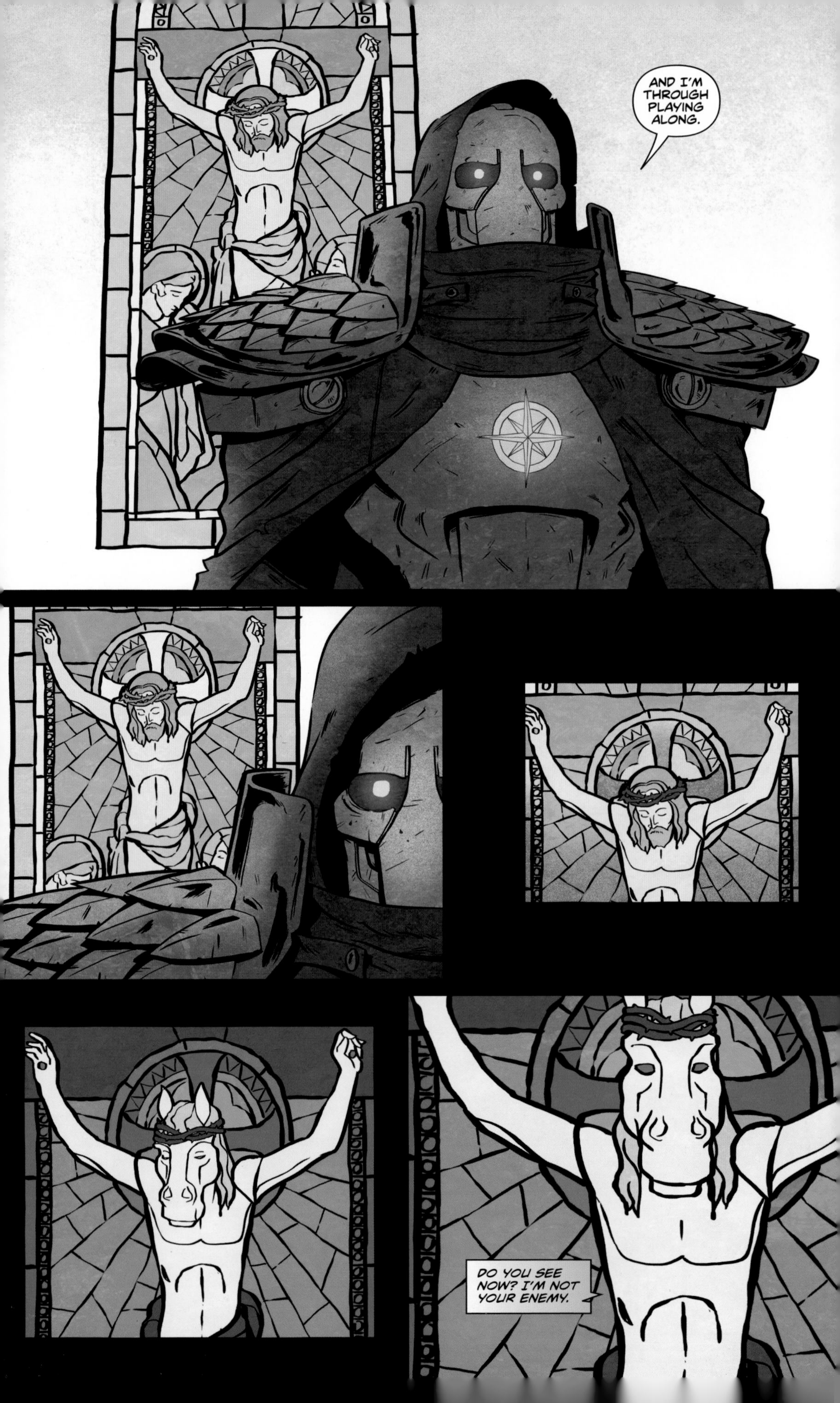

AND I'M THROUGH PLAYING ALONG.
DO YOU SEE NOW? I'M NOT YOUR ENEMY.

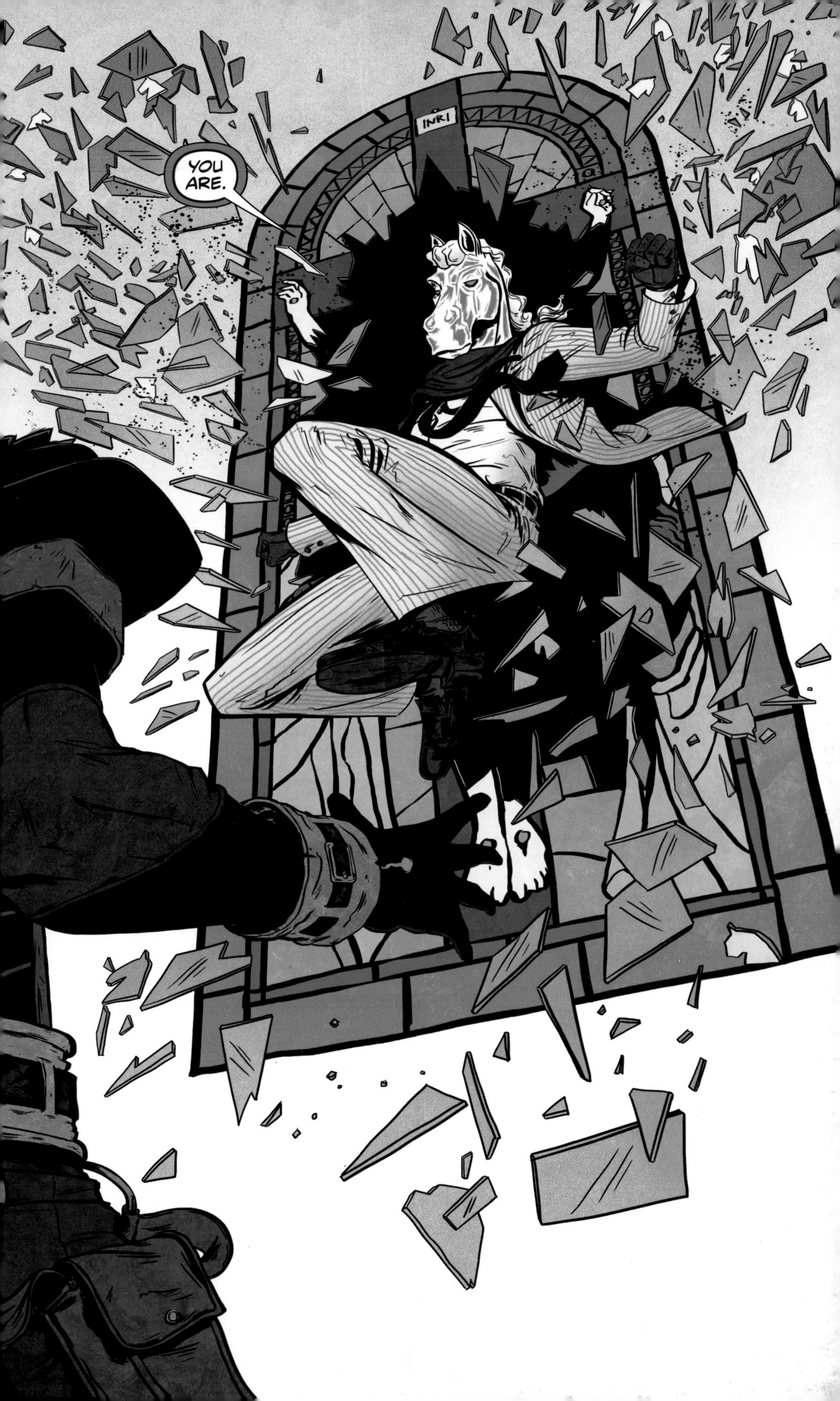
INRI
YOU ARE.

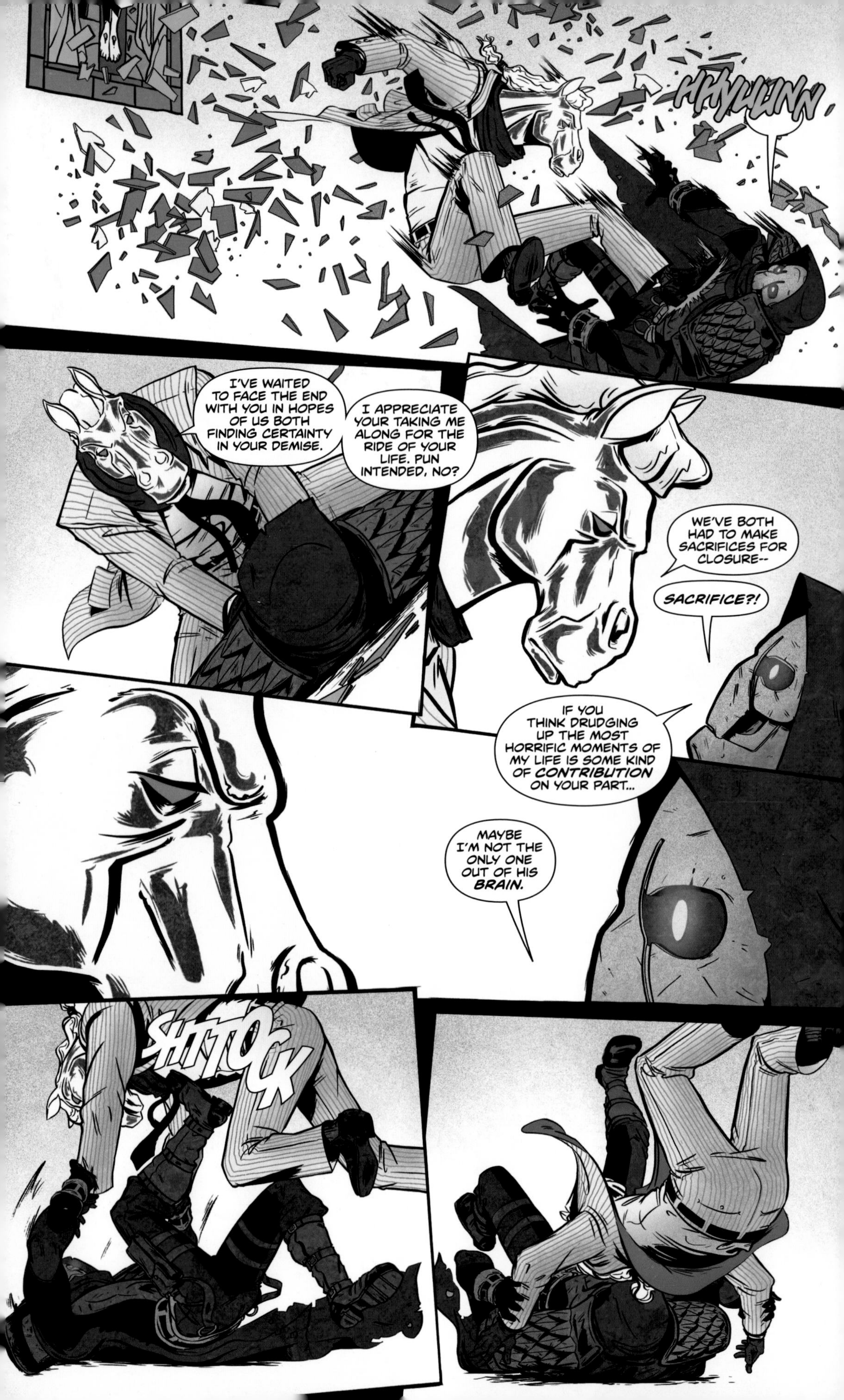
HYYLLINN
I'VE WAITED TO FACE THE END WITH YOU IN HOPES OF US BOTH FINDING CERTAINTY IN YOUR DEMISE.
I APPRECIATE YOUR TAKING ME ALONG FOR THE RIDE OF YOUR LIFE. PUN INTENDED, NO?
WE'VE BOTH HAD TO MAKE SACRIFICES FOR CLOSURE--
SACRIFICE?!
IF YOU THINK DRUDGING UP THE MOST HORRIFIC MOMENTS OF MY LIFE IS SOME KIND OF CONTRIBUTION ON YOUR PART...
MAYBE I'M NOT THE ONLY ONE OUT OF HIS BRAIN.
SHTOCK

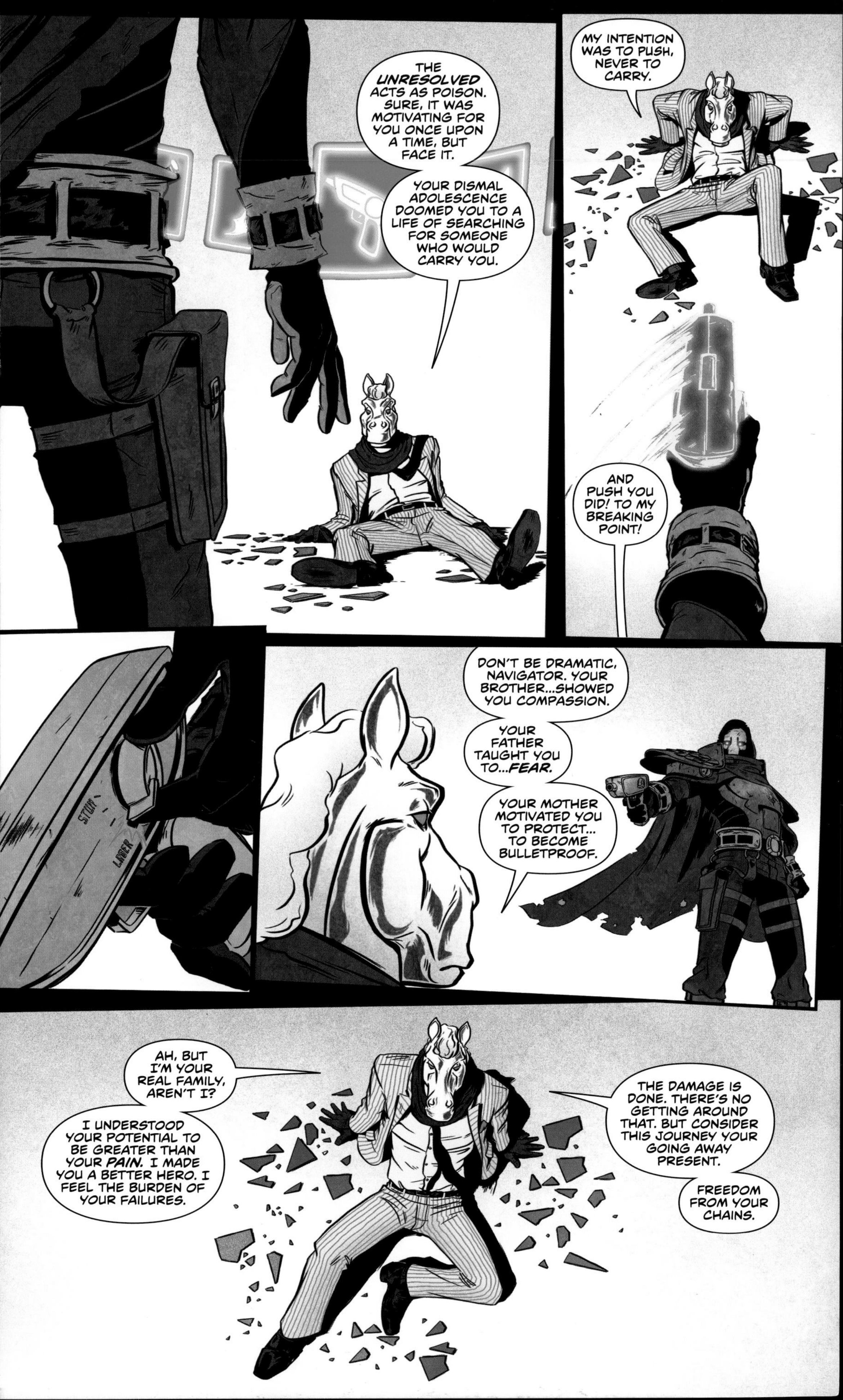
THE UNRESOLVED ACTS AS POISON. SURE, IT WAS MOTIVATING FOR YOU ONCE UPON A TIME, BUT FACE IT.
YOUR DISMAL ADOLESCENCE DOOMED YOU TO A LIFE OF SEARCHING FOR SOMEONE WHO WOULD CARRY YOU.
MY INTENTION WAS TO PUSH, NEVER TO CARRY.
AND PUSH YOU DID! TO MY BREAKING POINT!
STUN
LASER
DON'T BE DRAMATIC, NAVIGATOR. YOUR BROTHER...SHOWED YOU COMPASSION.
YOUR FATHER TAUGHT YOU TO...FEAR.
YOUR MOTHER MOTIVATED YOU TO PROTECT... TO BECOME BULLETPROOF.
AH, BUT I'M YOUR REAL FAMILY, AREN'T I?
I UNDERSTOOD YOUR POTENTIAL TO BE GREATER THAN YOUR PAIN. I MADE YOU A BETTER HERO. I FEEL THE BURDEN OF YOUR FAILURES.
THE DAMAGE IS DONE. THERE'S NO GETTING AROUND THAT. BUT CONSIDER THIS JOURNEY YOUR GOING AWAY PRESENT.
FREEDOM FROM YOUR CHAINS.

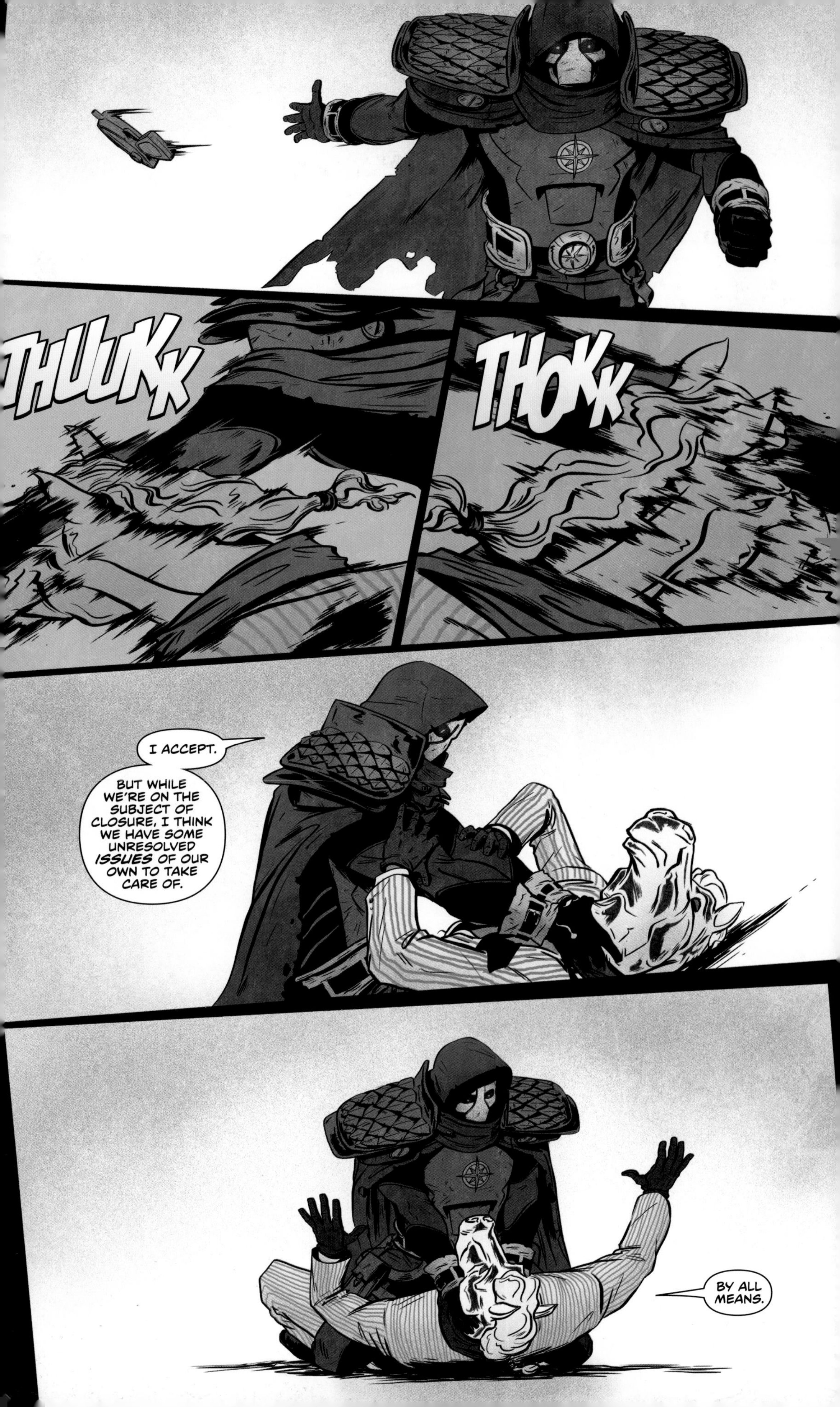
THUUKK
THOKK
I ACCEPT.
BUT WHILE WE'RE ON THE SUBJECT OF CLOSURE, I THINK WE HAVE SOME UNRESOLVED *ISSUES* OF OUR OWN TO TAKE CARE OF.
BY ALL MEANS.

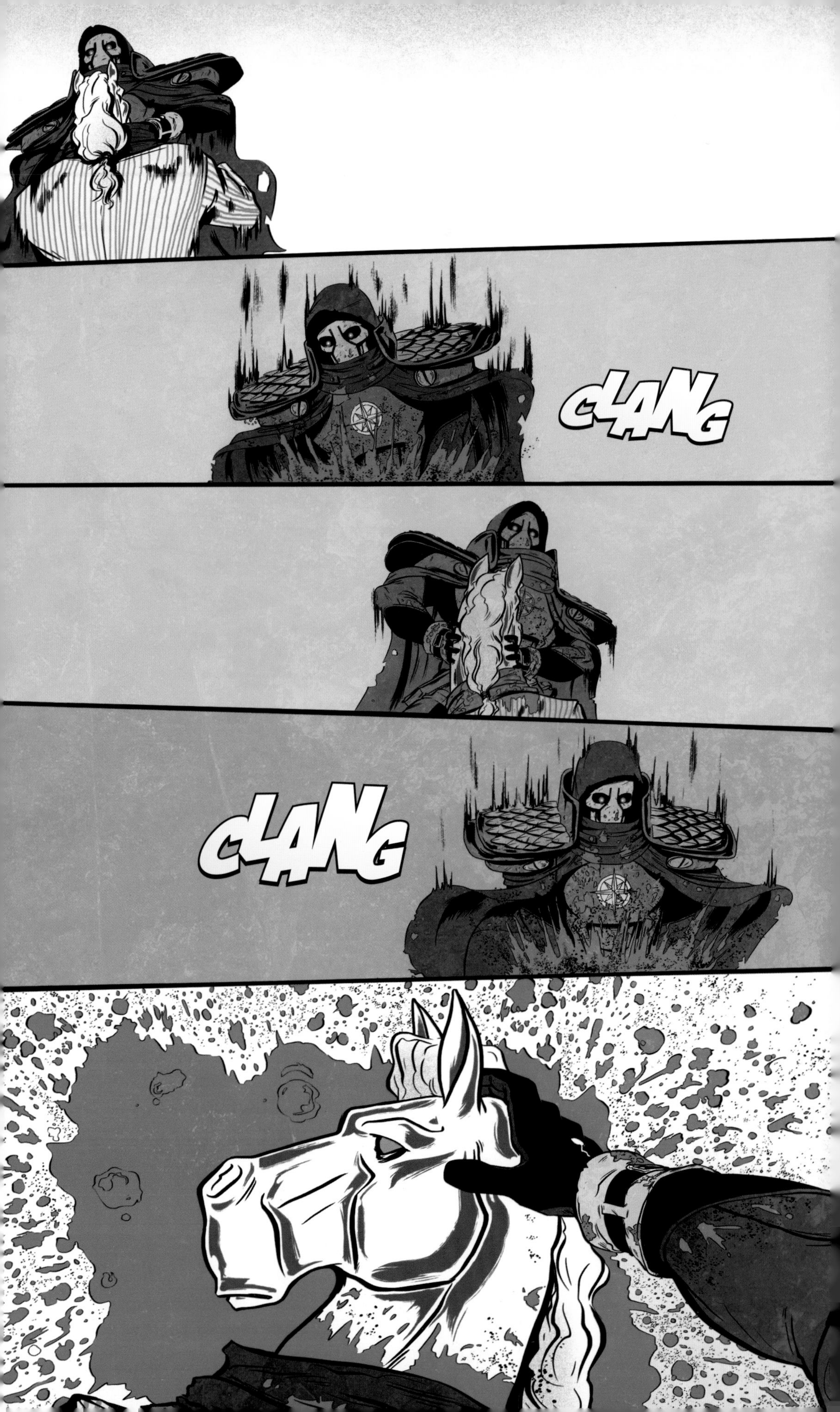
CLANG
CLANG

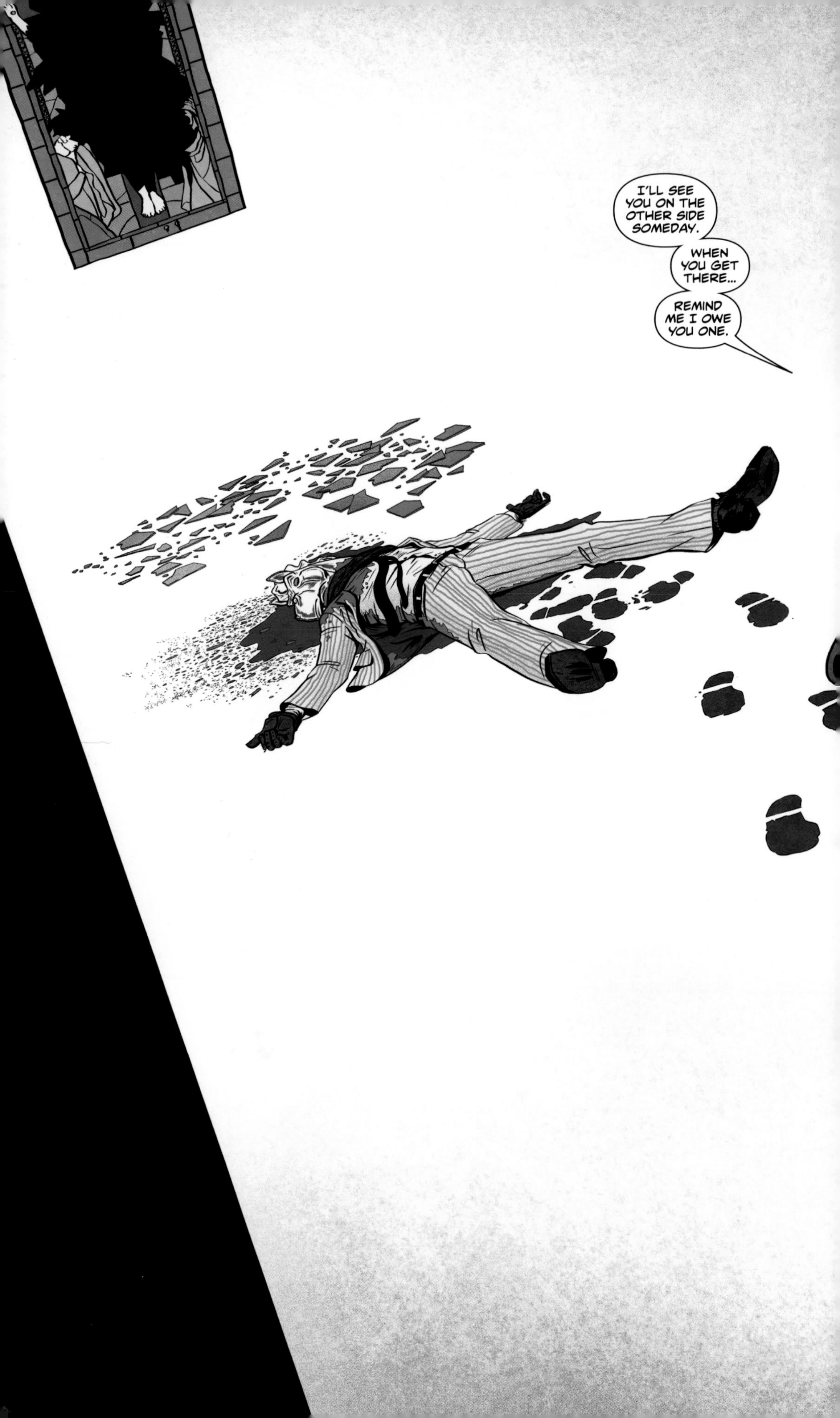
I'LL SEE YOU ON THE OTHER SIDE SOMEDAY.
WHEN YOU GET THERE...
REMIND ME I OWE YOU ONE.

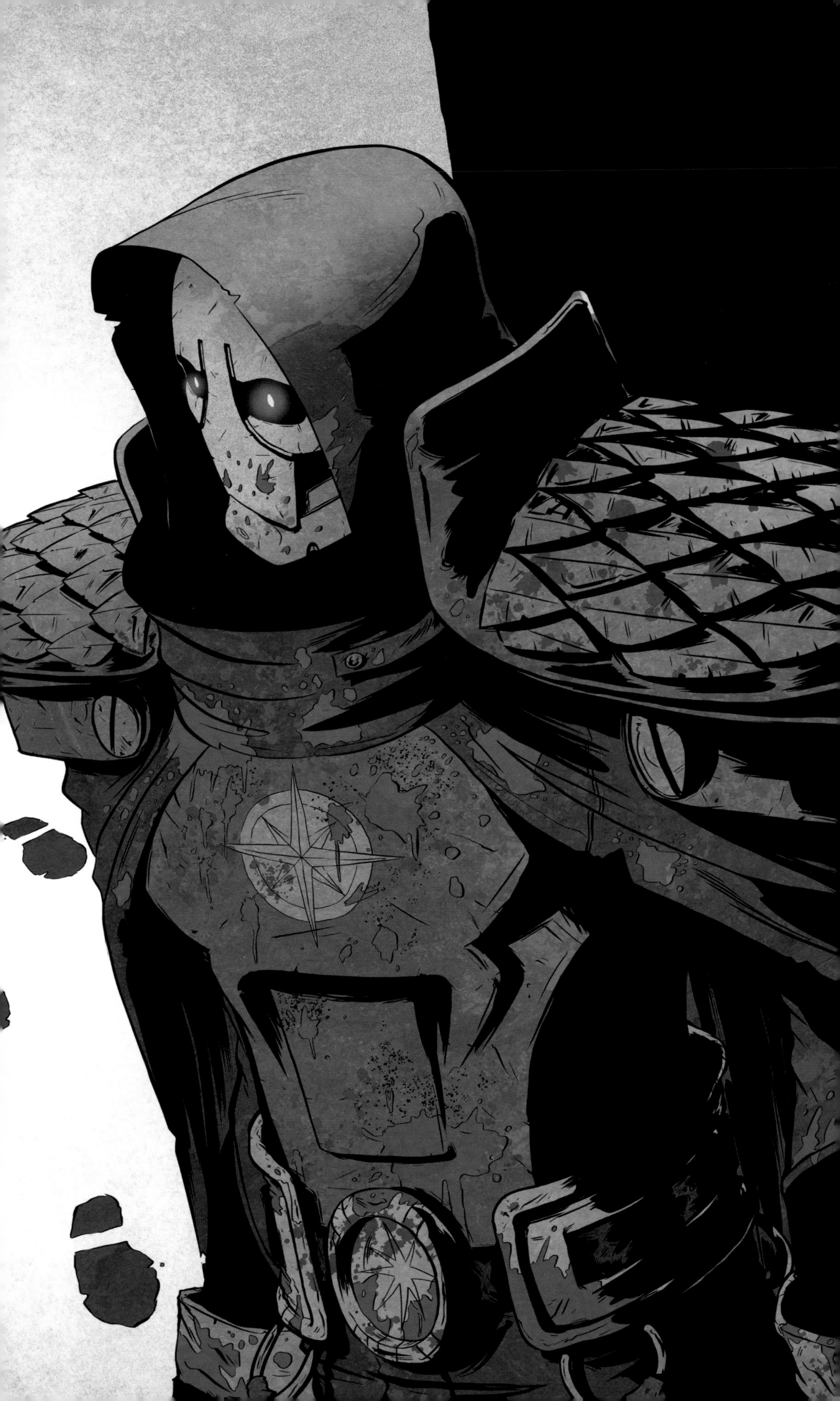

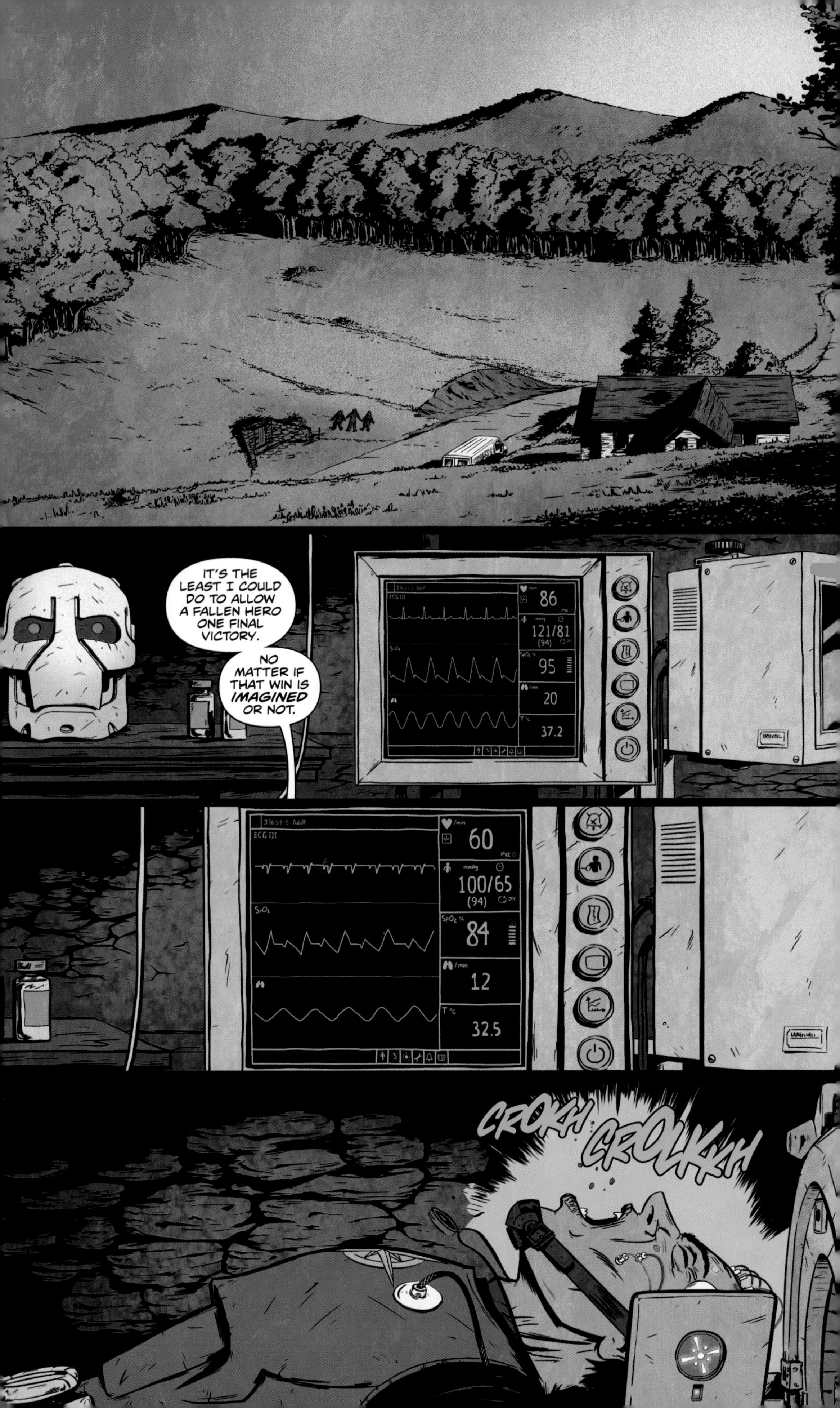
IT'S THE LEAST I COULD DO TO ALLOW A FALLEN HERO ONE FINAL VICTORY.
NO MATTER IF THAT WIN IS *IMAGINED* OR NOT.
CROKH
CROLKKH

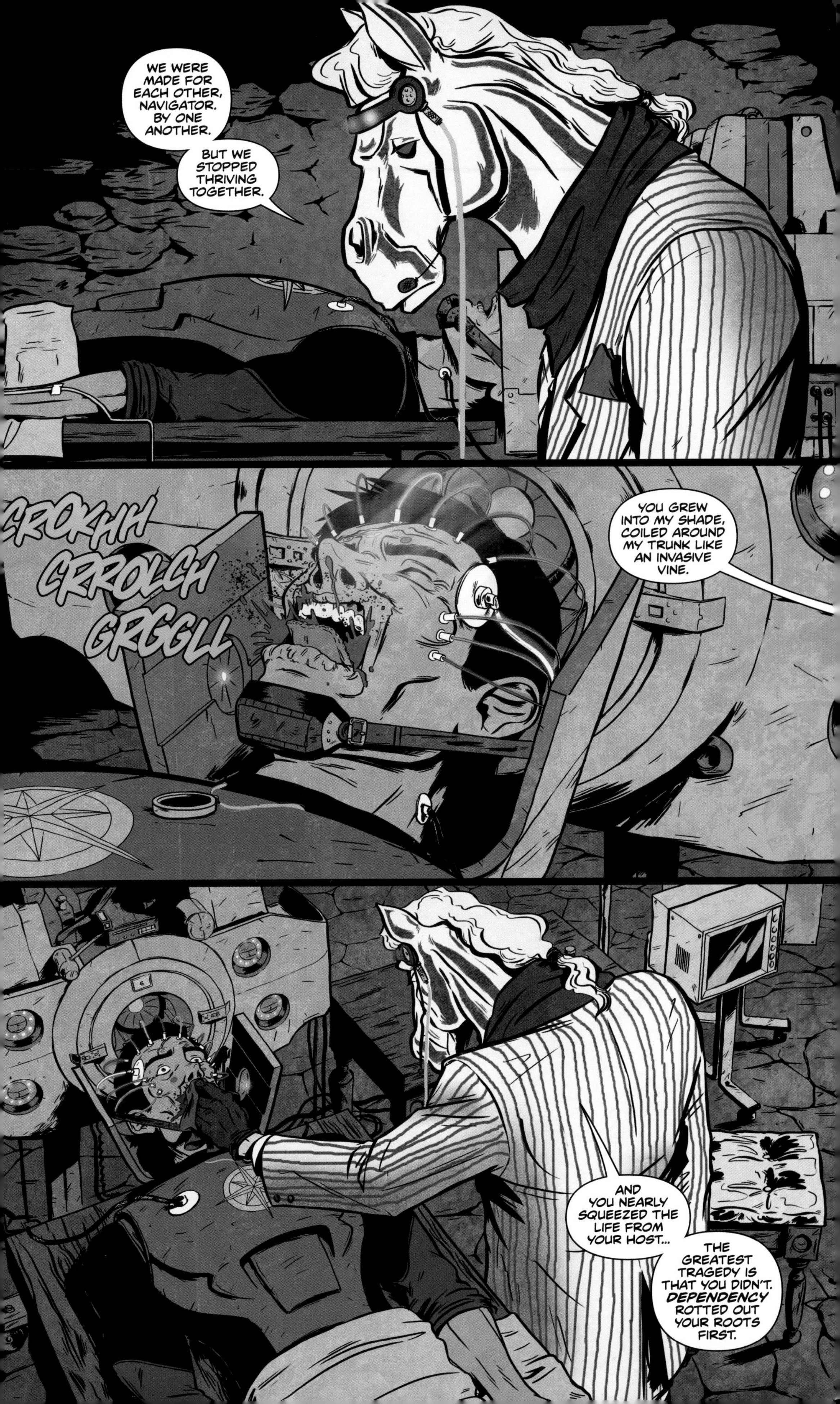
WE WERE MADE FOR EACH OTHER, NAVIGATOR. BY ONE ANOTHER.
BUT WE STOPPED THRIVING TOGETHER.
CROKHH
CRROLCH
GRGGLL
YOU GREW INTO MY SHADE, COILED AROUND MY TRUNK LIKE AN INVASIVE VINE.
AND YOU NEARLY SQUEEZED THE LIFE FROM YOUR HOST...
THE GREATEST TRAGEDY IS THAT YOU DIDN'T. DEPENDENCY ROTTED OUT YOUR ROOTS FIRST.

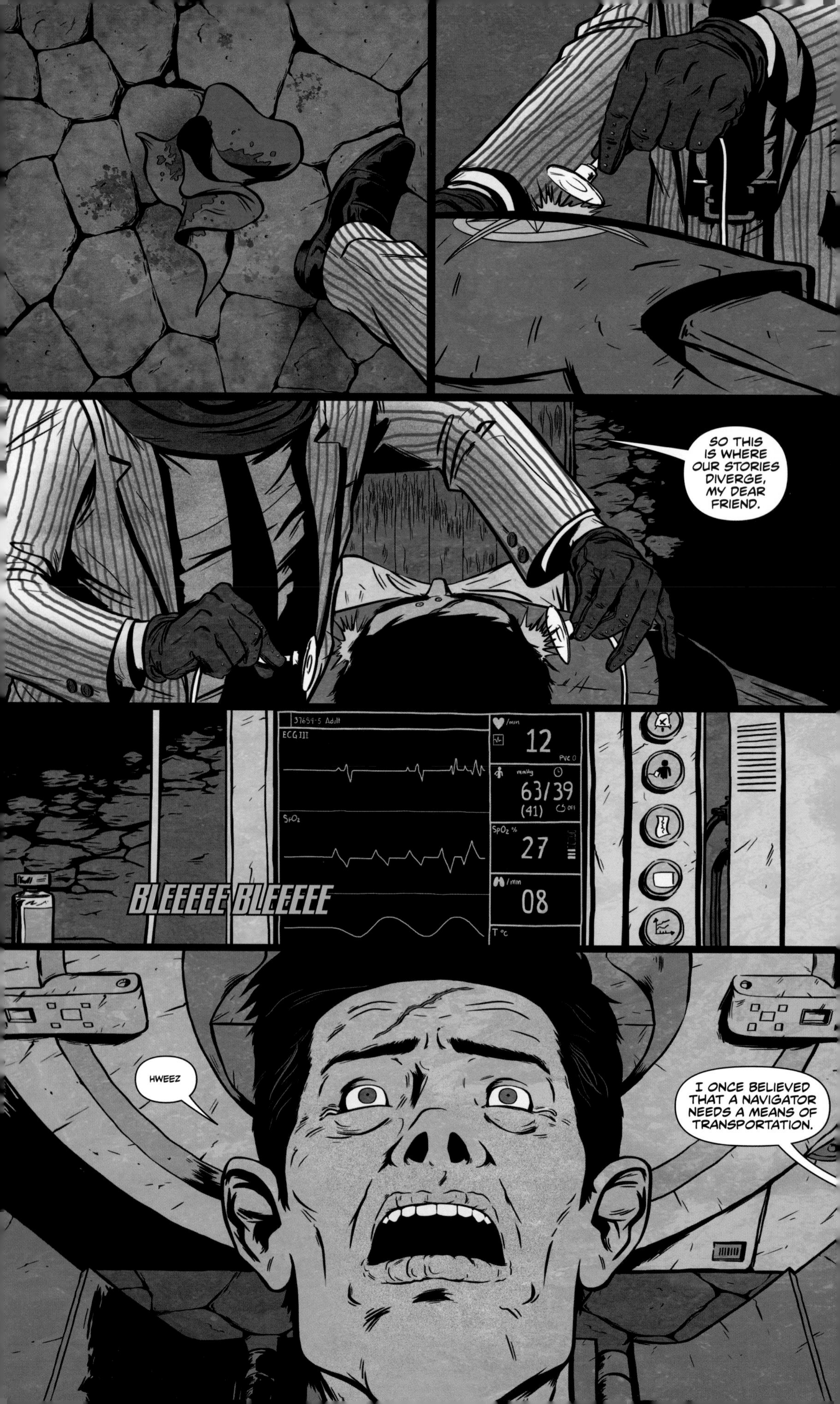
SO THIS IS WHERE OUR STORIES DIVERGE, MY DEAR FRIEND.
37654-5 Adult
ECG III
SpO2
12
PVC 0
mmHg
63/39
(41)
OFF
SpO2 %
27
/min
08
T °C
BLEEEEE BLEEEEE
HWEEZ
I ONCE BELIEVED THAT A NAVIGATOR NEEDS A MEANS OF TRANSPORTATION.

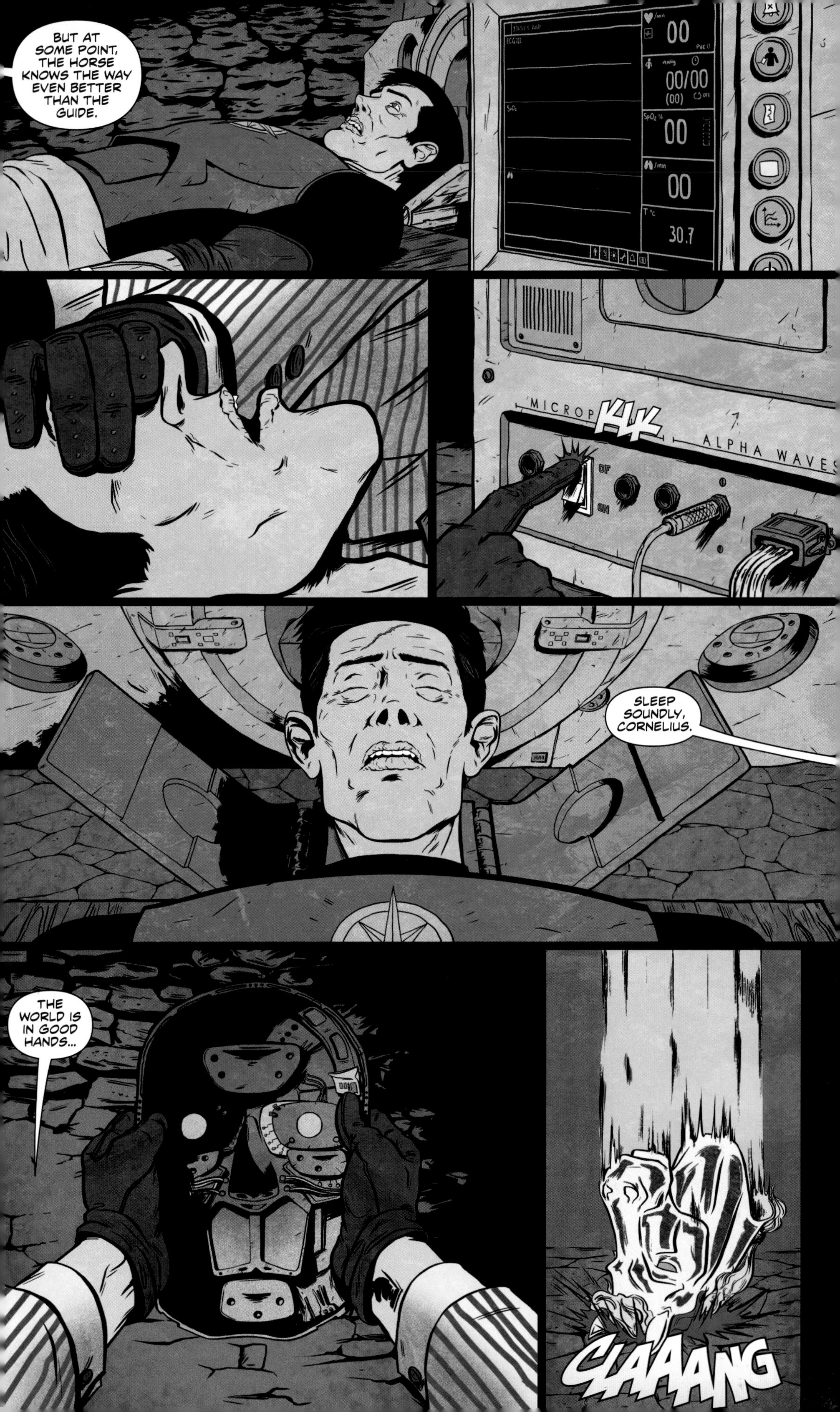
BUT AT SOME POINT, THE HORSE KNOWS THE WAY EVEN BETTER THAN THE GUIDE.
00
00/00
(00)
00
00
30.7
MICROP
KLIK
ALPHA WAVES
ON
SLEEP SOUNDLY, CORNELIUS.
THE WORLD IS IN GOOD HANDS...
CLAAANG

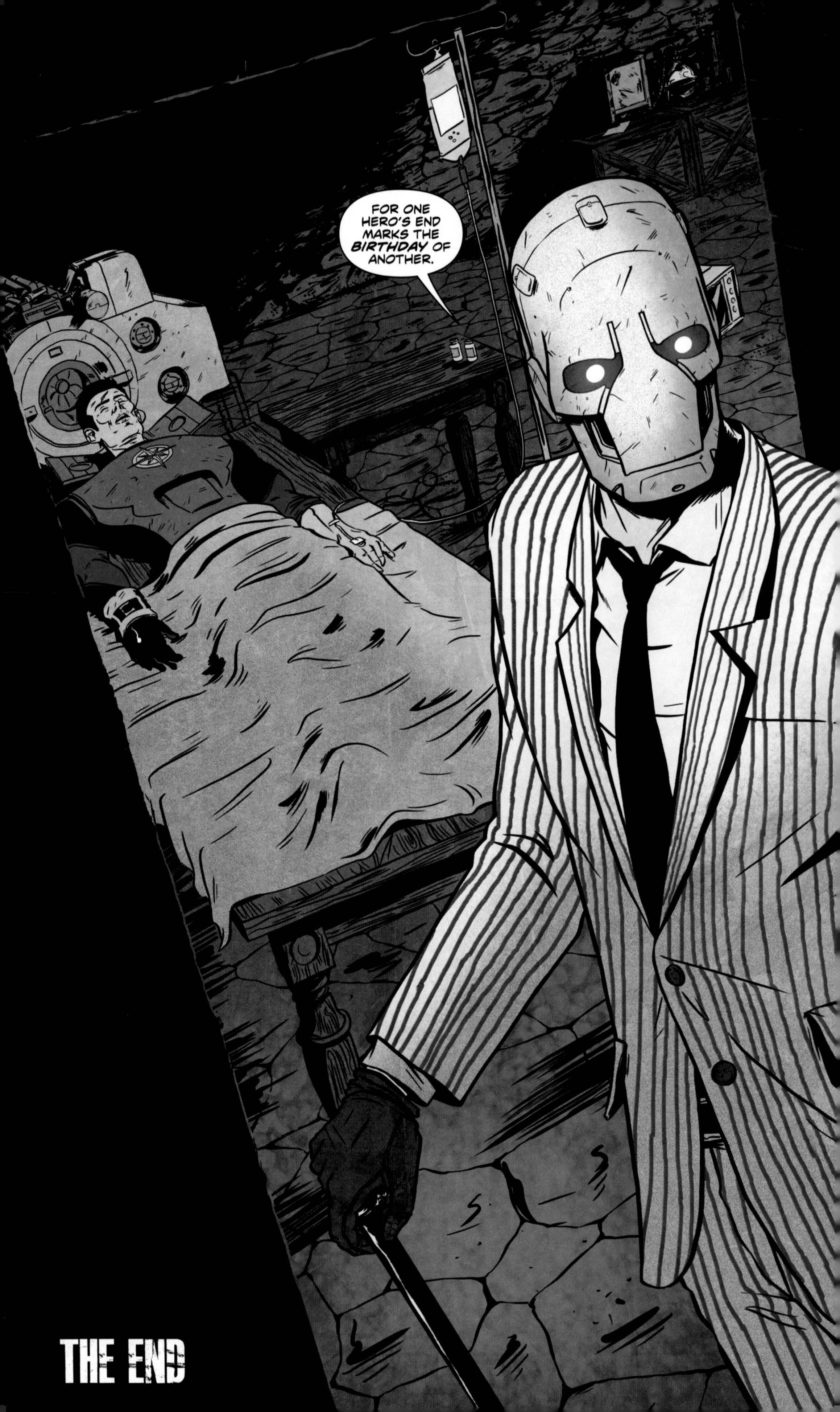
FOR ONE HERO'S END MARKS THE *BIRTHDAY* OF ANOTHER.

THE END

ISSUE SIX BOOM! STUDIOS EXCLUSIVE COVER BY **FELIPE SMITH**

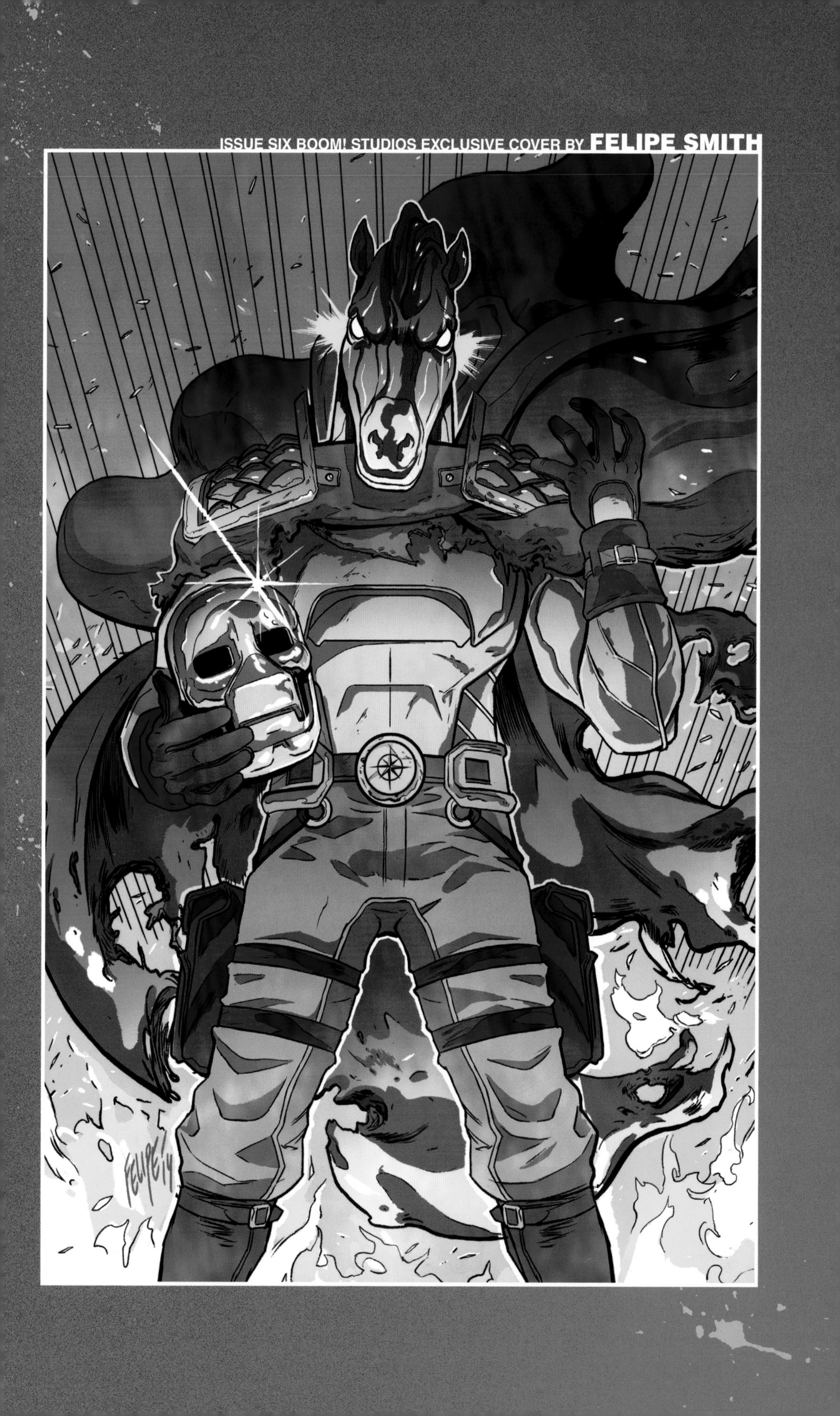
FELIPE '14

TRANSLUCID

COVER GALLERY

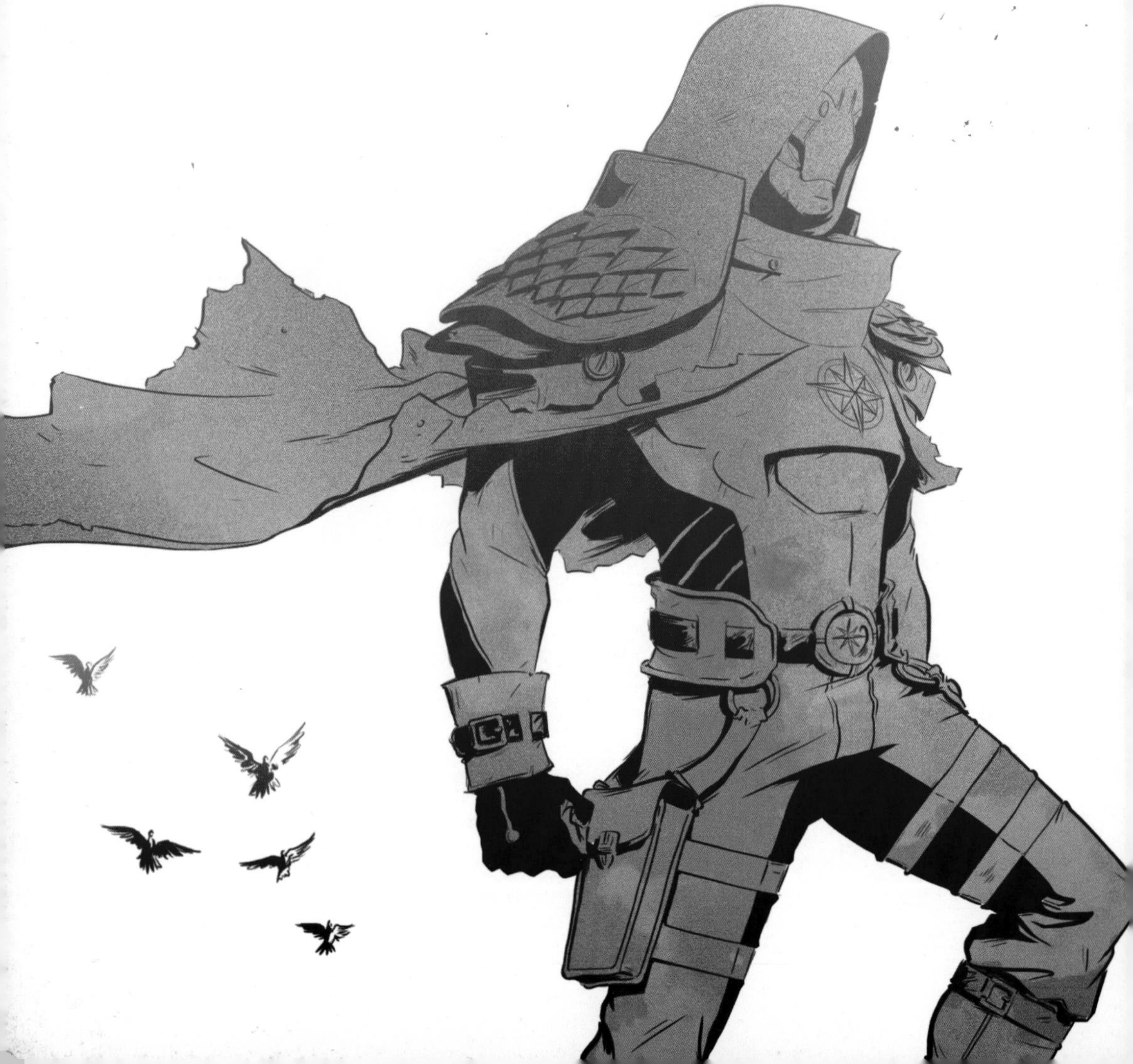

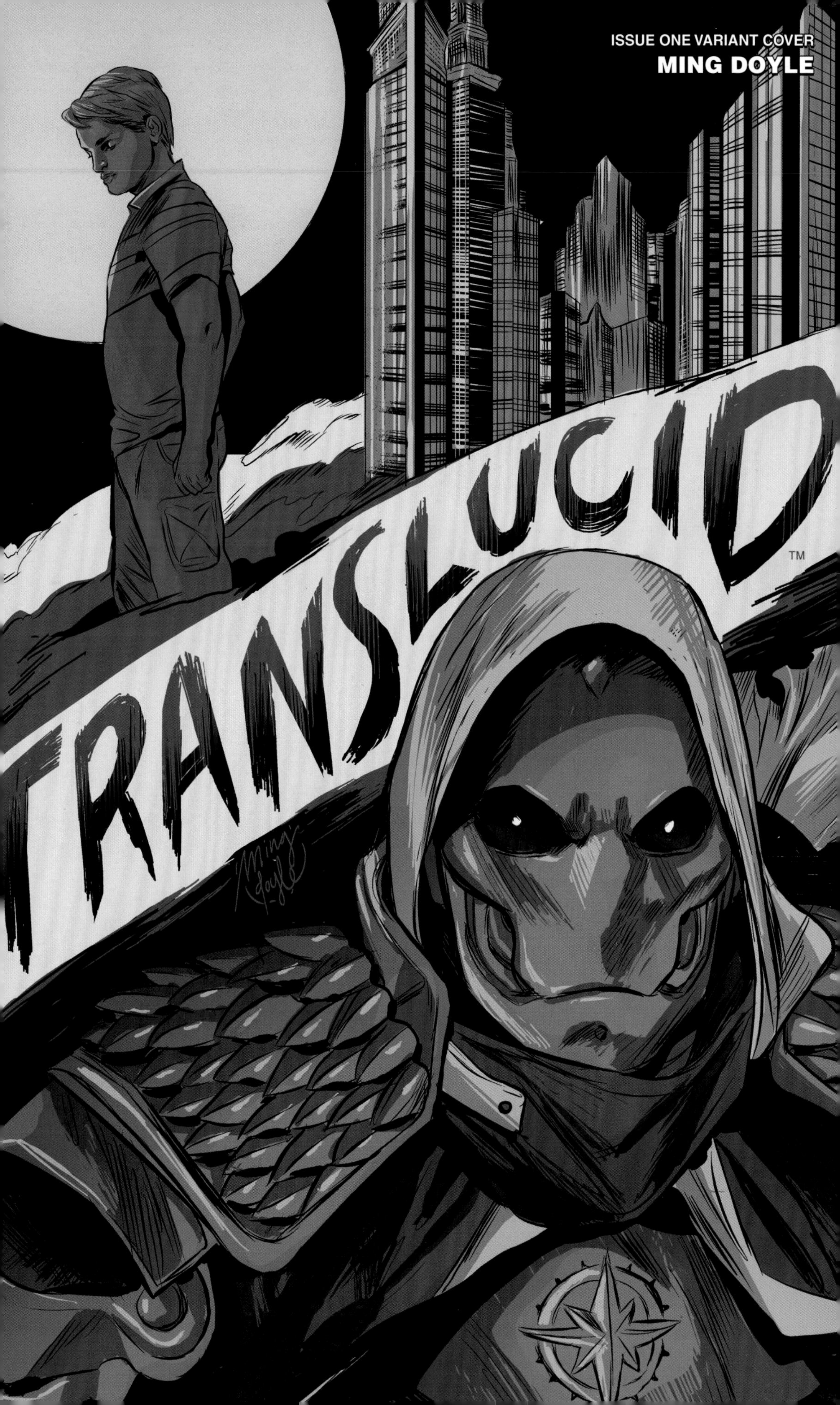
ISSUE ONE VARIANT COVER
MING DOYLE
TRANSLUCID™

ISSUE ONE PHANTOM VARIANT COVER

SCOTT NEWMAN

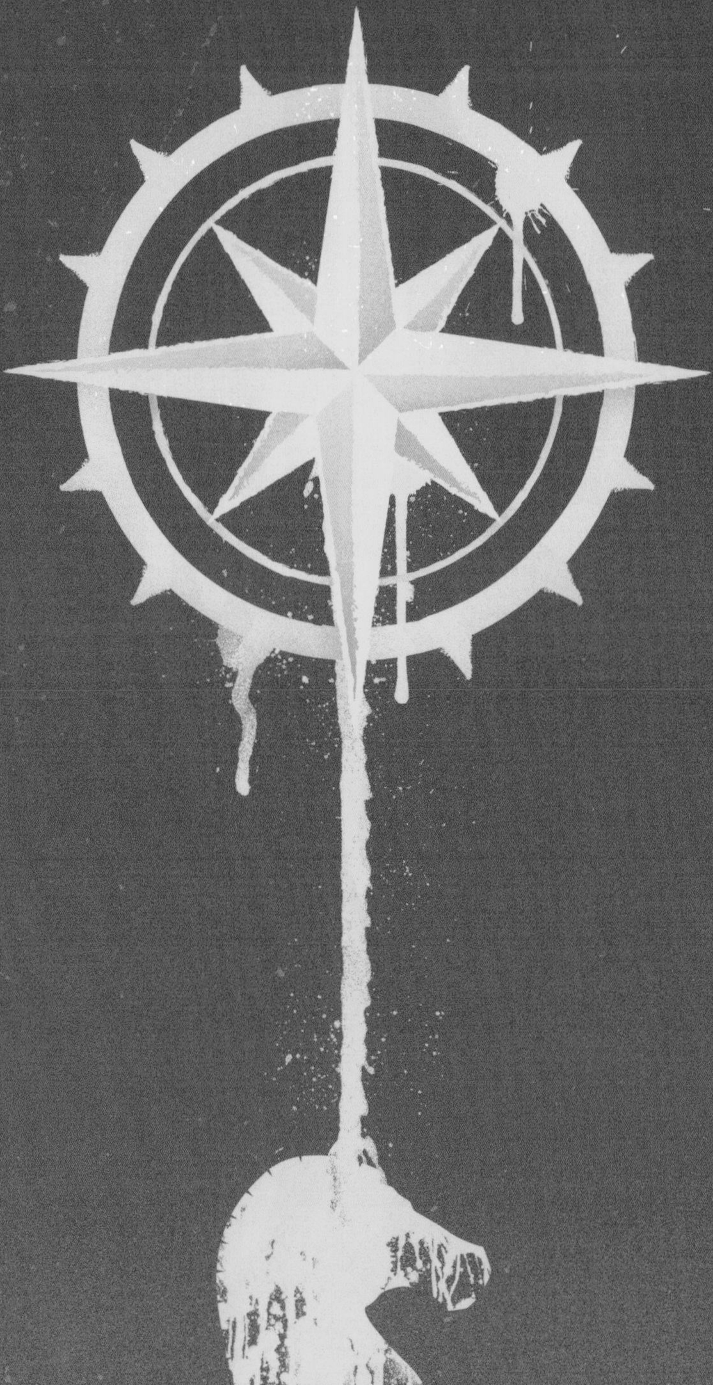

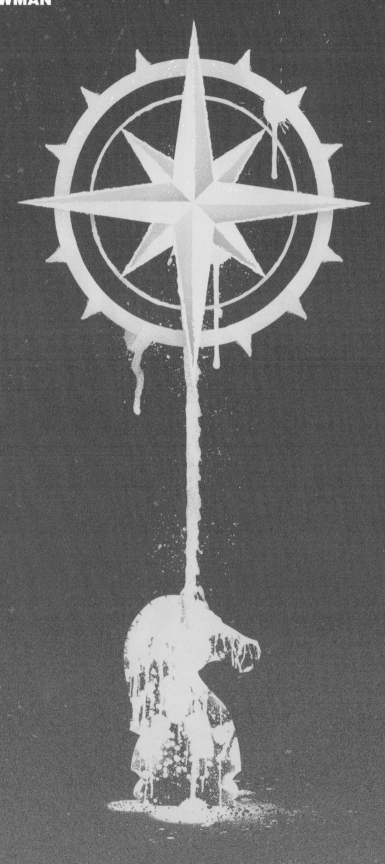

ISSUE ONE WONDERCON EXCLUSIVE COVER
DAN DUNCAN

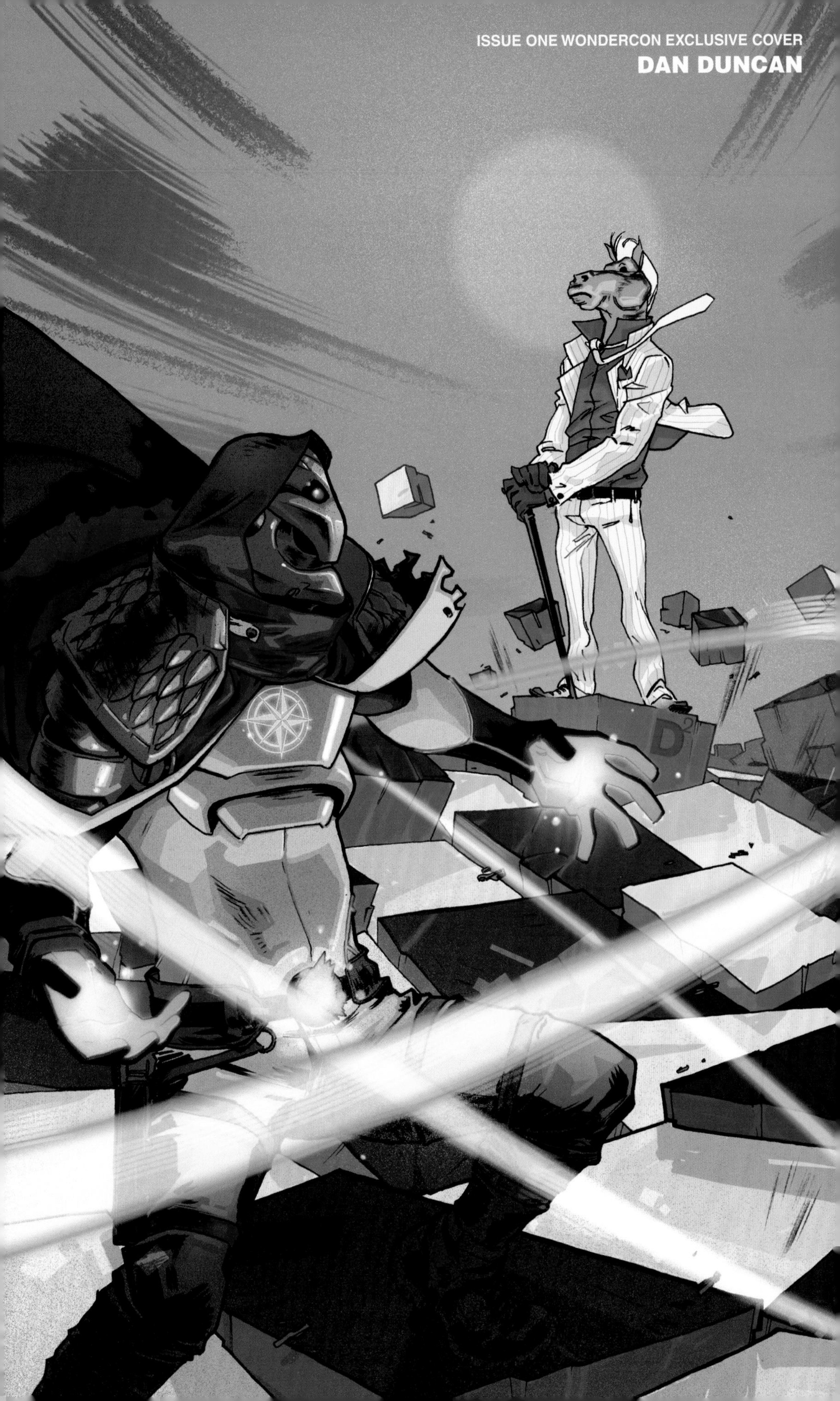
D²

ISSUE ONE C2E2 EXCLUSIVE COVER

KHARY RANDOLPH WITH COLORS BY **MATTHEW WILSON**

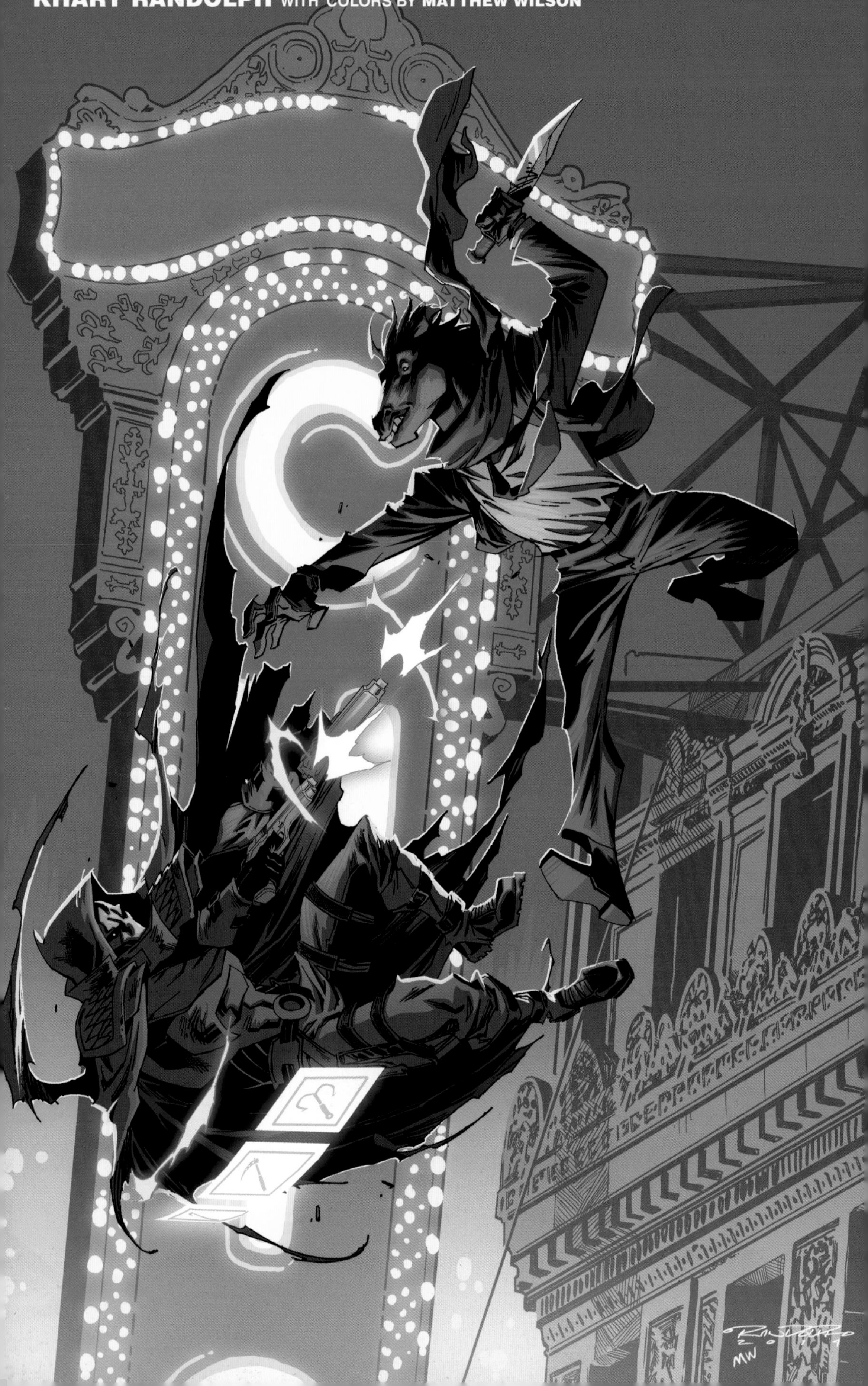

ISSUE FOUR SDCC EXCLUSIVE COVER
ALEXIS ZIRITT

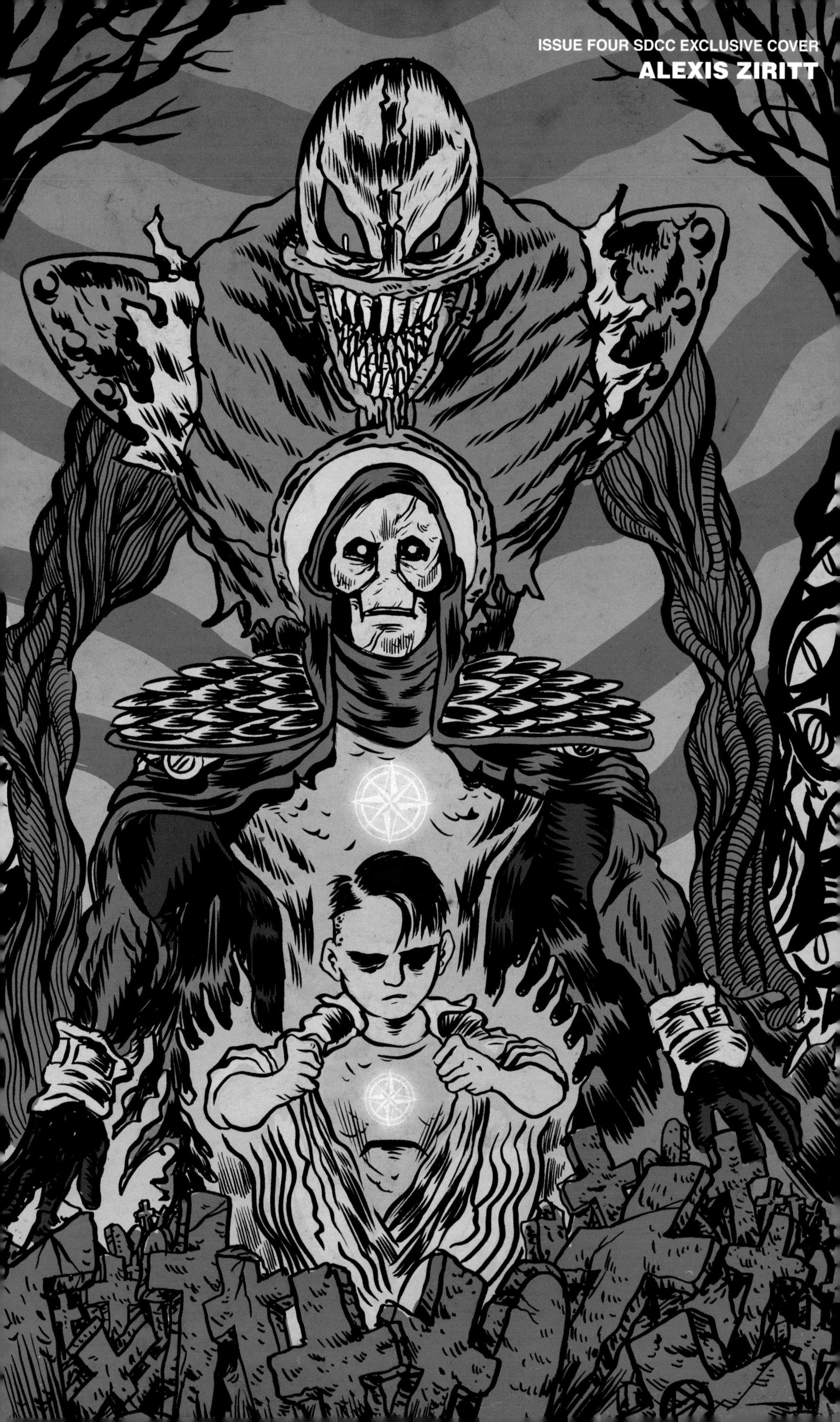

ISSUE SIX NYCC EXCLUSIVE COVER

DANIEL BAYLISS

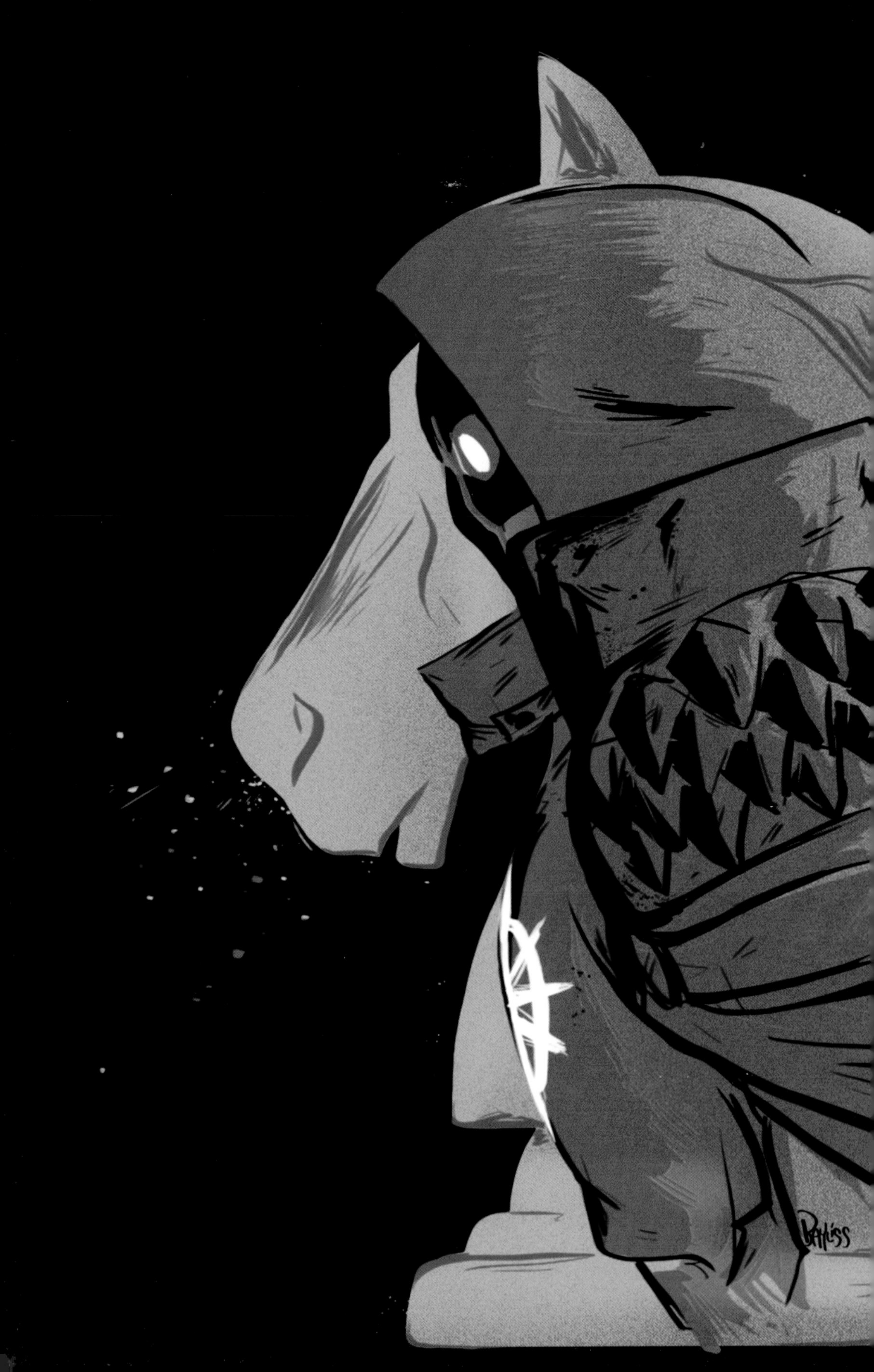
BAYLISS

TRANSLUCID OUTLINE

A look at the complete outline of TRANSLUCID 1-6. As often happens in the creative process, certain elements were changed and shifted around during the scripting process. Enjoy this glimpse behind the scenes! Character designs by Dan Duncan.

ISSUE ONE *2030* - The Horse is getting out of prison and has solicited three other villains--The Apocalypse 3, collectively--to join forces with him. "It's your call, gentlemen." The Horse's captions explain that he believes this will help to re-establish the balance of things, putting The Navigator on the spot to prove himself as a worthy hero.

Cut to a news flash of the disturbance at the Empire State Building, where The Horse has been turned on by The Apocalypse 3. The Navigator shows off his hologram belt and its capabilities to get to the scene of the crime, creating a grappling hook to move up to the top. From there he accesses his digital database to track the villains at the bottom of the building. When he gets there, The Navigator finds The Horse, restrained to a bomb device that gives him the option to save The Horse or the building. Unable to live without the villain that has come to define him, he opts to save The Horse. For The Horse, this move is the final straw in The Navigator's long-growing co-dependency on him. It was The Navigator's ability to navigate the fine lines of right and wrong--his ability to be the hero that the city deserved--which initially inspired The Horse to become a villain. But now, as The Navigator has chosen his own well-being over the needs of the city, The Horse is sure The Navigator can be that hero no longer. "You've made the wrong decision," The Horse says, and clicks the detonator--

September 22, 1998 - A glass bottle shatters on a door as the young Cornelius awakens in his room to a fight between his parents in another room. Scattered around his bed are hologram tools and it's clear that the boy had fallen asleep working on something. Scared, he starts tinkering with a contraption that projects a very crude hologram of something soothing to him--a beam of light splays across the room into the mirrors, reflecting and creating an intricate web of light. Footsteps get closer and his father pounds on his door, screaming for him to unlock it. (Horse head chess piece on the cover of a book on the nightstand).

ISSUE TWO *September 23, 1998 (Morning)* - Cornelius is on a science class field trip. We introduce Cornelius' lack of true friends and the recurring theme of change/loneliness via his teacher talking about the consistency of molecules as the bus pulls up to the museum. Cornelius toys with a hologram he created on the bus and the teacher takes notice of it. Some of the other students are also intrigued by it--except for one bully who remains unimpressed. Cornelius slips away from the group, wandering into a holographic lecture within the "Holo Exhibit by MIT." The technology at the event is extraordinary and we show the potential of the medium in The Navigator's future. (Holographic chess piece).

September 23, 1998 (Evening) - Cornelius holds the hologram device close as he crosses the street to watch his brother Drake at football practice. We demonstrate the surface differences between the two boys, but show the brothers' solid relationship despite their horrible home life. Introduce the compass

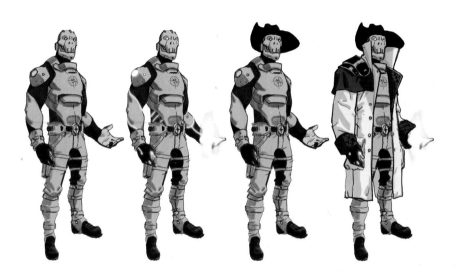

as an item that inspires Drake (and in turn, will become Cornelius' talisman). At the end of the scene, Cornelius focuses in on the chess piece featured on a "chess team meeting" sign hanging on the bleachers, pushing the reader to wonder whether this is something relevant to him...is he the hero or the villain in his imagination?

2007 - Close on a chess piece stuck in a propped open jaw. A dead man is nailed to the wall in an old, abandoned warehouse, with the Horse piece from a chess board. The body is identified as philanthropist John McKelley, a man who'd recently gifted 1 million dollars to a local children's hospital. Unbeknownst to the public, McKelley, is a pedophile. In the Horse's captions he feels justice was served. The media sees it as the work of a serial killer--perhaps the world has a Supervillain on their hands.

November 14, 1998 (Evening) - Cornelius arrives home from school to his mother cooking dinner. His father, drunk, is unhappy with the dinner choice and throws a pot of boiling water on his mother, burning her neck and shoulder. Cornelius picks up a knife to retaliate at his father in a moment of rage--but instead of using it, he picks up the phone to call the police. Drake comes home from practice and convinces Cornelius to put the knife down. The scene plays up the very thin lines between hero and villain. The police take Ron to jail. (A chess game sits on the table).

November 15, 1998 (Morning) - Church. Cornelius, Drake and Eileen are attending church after Saturday's events. Introduce the elaborate hat, which Eileen tells Cornelius she wears "so God can't see me." Eileen tells the boys she is going to get their father from jail the next morning, despite the officers telling her they can get her and the kids to a safe house. We illustrate Eileen's weakness and dependency as she enables a dangerous man to remain in their lives. Drake is irate and leaves church angrily, astonished his mother won't take advantage of the freedom they've been given—this could be a fresh start. In this moment, we show how loyal Cornelius is to his mother, shunning even his brother's example in order to please his mom. Close-up on Eileen's hat. (Usher wears a tie with chess pieces on it).

2011 - Open on The Navigator's helmet. On the Verrazano bridge, where The Horse has put a group of politicians (who've made a recent cut in funding to police and fire programs) in danger to prove a point. This is also the first head-to-head between Hero & Villain. The Horse forces The Navigator to choose between capturing him--or saving the politicians. The Navigator saves the politicians and attempts to apprehend the Horse using his holographic belt to create something extravagant--but the tech is still a bit glitchy. The glitch allows the Horse his getaway. In the choosing of the politicians, The Horse wants to force The Navigator to question his moral compass and he hopes this will show the world that he is more than a villain. In a way, he's a hero as well. But the message falls on deaf ears. The media begins to color the confrontation, has The Navigator met his match?

CLIFFHANGER WITH FATHER FIGURE RE-ENTERING THE HOME.

ISSUE THREE *December 1, 1998 (Afternoon)* - Cornelius and Drake walk the streets of Brooklyn toward the train station, discussing Cornelius's interest in science and Drake's upcoming game that evening. Cornelius has created a very basic hologram dog that projects beside them and is very proud of it. Drake stops to help a homeless person and tells Cornelius "Tonight, the scouts will put their final

picks together." Drake mentions that he's been looking into what he'd need to do to legally adopt his brother when he turns 18 to get him out of the house. Drake leaves to head to his game, telling Cornelius he'll see him there later.

However, on the way home, Cornelius, distracted by the hologram, runs into the bully from school and his posse. The hologram is glitchy and the bully heckles him, breaking the controller. Cornelius is livid and a fight breaks out between him and the kids. End on broken controller. (Chess piece statue at the edge of park).

2012 - 2020 - A montage of newspapers opening on The Navigator's holographic belt and how it works. The Navigator and The Horse are established as yin & yang. Another incident between the two shows the escalating methods on both sides and an escalating interest in the duo by the public. The Horse is increasingly interested in toying with The Navigator's tormented ethical system. The news spins the event as The Horse being an accessory to the country's beloved Navigator. The final headline ends with the Horse behind bars.

December 1, 1998 (Evening) – Parents show up at the police station where Cornelius has been detained with the bully and others. He feels a great deal of guilt for having missed his brother's game and keeping his family from attending with his nonsense. His father is irate that they've missed the game, but Eileen is as doting and concerned as ever as the police chalk it up to a one-time incident. From within the station, they hear the officers discussing an accident on a subway that just happened, a minor having been killed. On the TV in the waiting room, there's footage at the F train, near Midwood high. "Have they been able to notify the family yet?" "Parsons is trying to call them down to the station now." Eileen's phone begins to ring. On the news coverage happening on screen, Cornelius begins to hallucinate, watching as a train comes barreling up out of the subway station into the streets. Its doors open and hundreds of horses flood out, trampling onlookers. (Chess piece on the ring of officer who explains what happened).

December 11, 1998 (Afternoon) - Drake's funeral. Cornelius faces his first confrontation with CATALYST #1. The Navigator is there amongst the bystanders, attempting to alert Cornelius that this isn't real... Cornelius wins the battle.

ISSUE FOUR *December 14-20, 1998* - At the Kinderland home. Drake's college scholarship letters arrive and it's the final straw for Ron. He leaves the home for good. The door slams for the last time. Chess piece school logo on a letter.

2023 - An intimidating query from a villain to The Navigator. In the absence of The Horse, other lesser villains have risen up to antagonize The Navigator. They are not of the caliber The Navigator is used to and he is lonely without The Horse in his life. The media waxes poetic about the loss of the dynamic duo. The Navigator feels completely alone.

December 25, 1998 (Morning) - A solitary Cornelius can be seen through the window of an exterior shot showing all the other homes decorated for Christmas, trees in the windows--save for the Kinderland home. There are no gifts or celebration as Eileen is deeply immersed in her psychosis, leaving Cornelius

to fend for himself. He's spending his holiday sketching superhero costumes, Drake's compass dangling around his neck. The mother of the boy saved by Drake on the subway stops by unexpectedly to bring flowers, but Eileen refuses to see her. Cornelius opens the door for her anyway, wanting a glimpse into his brother's final moments. The little boy with the woman begins to cry and Cornelius creates a hologram to entertain him...but he closes the door as behind him as his mother screams for him. From out of nowhere, taunts about his brother come whispering through the house. Cornelius is unsure where they're coming from as he he walks past a family portrait on the mantel to attend to his mother. Suddenly, the father emerges from the image as a horrific monster, CATALYST #2. (Card in the flowers is from Knight Florist and features the chess piece). This scene leads into Cornelius realizing he must battle CATALYST #2, his father. Cornelius fears his father greatly, but The Navigator appears in the scene, to help him to realize he can defeat him. Cornelius kills the father monster, screaming in victory.

February 1, 1999 (Morning) - A scream from the bathroom at school, as the recurring bully is antagonizing one of Cornelius' classmates. Cornelius retaliates by nearly blinding him with a hologram--until he backs off. (Chess piece t-shirt on bully).

2029 - The Navigator head-to-head with another villain who is mimicking The Horse's vibe. The villain is thrown in jail. The Horse observes the scene, growing jealous. He kills the villain in jail, recognizing that he doesn't want anyone else to have the relationship with the hero that HE helped to create by making him better. He comes to the realization he must put The Navigator's heroics to the test. The scene ends on the bloody guts of the dead villain.

February 4, 1999 (Evening) - Close on sweet and sour chicken as Cornelius returns home to his favorite takeout. His mother is out of bed, wearing a dress for the first time in months. He is surprised at the change but excited that he thinks his mother is getting better. His food tastes strange and his mother brushes it off as she eats quickly. Cornelius takes a bite to appease her but can barely get it down. She becomes upset: "I thought you missed Drake." Cornelius looks toward her and she's wearing the Horse mask, "Don't you want to see your brother in heaven?" She blacks out. Cornelius calls 911, but gets dizzy. Final panel is black. (Chess piece on takeout box logo).

ISSUE FIVE *2030* - Picking up at the Empire State Building where we see it explode. The Horse and The Navigator engage in a full-on fight. Blows are thrown...close, cool shots. The Navigator is stuck with a needle of hallucinogens.

February 5, 1999 (Morning) - Close on an IV in his arm as Cornelius awakens, groggy and confused in a hospital. Social services is there, explaining that his mother gave him poison and he will be removed from her custody for a time. He's loaded against his will into a car that will take him to the foster home. (The doctor has chess piece scrubs on under his lab coat).

2030 - The Navigator in the back of the van driving out of the city toward upstate NY. In the distance, the Empire State building is nothing but flame and smoke.

February 20, 1999 (Evening) – Establishing shot of Angel Guardian Foster Home. Cornelius has been resistant at the home until he discovers some of the younger boys are being abused at the home. Cornelius goes to the counselor who's been abusing them and uses a hologram to terrorize him into retiring from his position. (Chess-themed wall calendar).

February 22, 1999 (Morning) - Outside the foster home on visitation day. Cornelius is drawing chest piece ideas for The Navigator when a nun announces the counselor has quit. It's a victory for Cornelius and he recognizes that he can help people. The day is going well until Cornelius' mother doesn't arrive for visitation and he overhears the counselors whispering amongst each other that she has committed suicide at the institution. He breaks down. (Stained glass window features chess piece).

CLIFFHANGER. Cornelius runs to the chapel and we close the issue on his "mother" appearing from the darkness. "I knew it couldn't be real, mom." And it's not. As Cornelius hugs her, the reader sees her morph into the monstrous villain she will become for our final fight in issue 6.

ISSUE SIX Reopen on Cornelius in his mother's embrace. He's recognizing what's going on. He references the line she made about the hat hiding her mistakes from God. Now Cornelius realizes too late that she was his biggest mistake in life. "My loyalty to you clouded every single decision I made." Cornelius references the catalysts as having been metaphors—"I've already fought those demons in some way. But you, my most significant mistake...you became a part of me...you fueled me to be a hero...but you also made me weak." And he now understands the only person who could expose that weakness and use it against him is The Horse.

2030 - Establishing shot of Heirloom Farms. We watch the three other villains exit the farm. We move through The Horse's workshop and see all the clippings from his life, including those from his firefighter father's death in the fire set by a crooked landlord. Blood has dripped a trail across the floor into the room where we find The Horse standing by the nearly dead The Navigator. The Navigator is hooked up to the Mind-Trap and The Horse is linked into the wiring via his own helmet-like apparatus. Full-blown hallucination and battle with CATALYST #3 the mother monster. Cornelius is now fully The Navigator.

We show The Horse talking to The Navigator over a microphone-like device, the words filtering directly into The Navigator's brain. The Horse, not Cornelius, has been narrating the flashbacks all along. He explains why he's brought him here, that he's been forcing him to relive the moments that made him choose to be a hero--in an effort to unravel him and understand him before his death. "We were made for one another, by one another. But we've stopped growing together. You grew into my shade, coiled tightly around my trunk like poison ivy. Your dependency on our duo has compromised you as an individual. I can't let you compromise me."

The Horse injects himself into the memory scape. They fight and The Navigator is killed. Resolution within the barn. The monitors stop and The Navigator's heart monitor goes flat. The Horse picks up The Navigator's mask and puts it on.

The End.